FACE TO FILE COMMUNICATION
A psychological approach to
information systems

WILEY SERIES IN INFORMATION PROCESSING

Consulting Editor
Mrs. Steve Shirley, O.B.E. *F International Limited, UK*

Managing Systems Development
J. S. Keen

Face to File Communication
Bruce Christie

FACE TO FILE
COMMUNICATION
A psychological approach to information systems

Bruce Christie

JOHN WILEY & SONS
Chichester · New York · Brisbane · Toronto

Copyright © 1981 by John Wiley & Sons Ltd.

British Library Cataloguing in Publication Data:

Christie, Bruce
  Face to file communication.—(Wiley series
  in information processing).
  1. Information storage and retrieval systems—
  Psychological aspects
  I. Title
  029.7   Z699   80-41686

ISBN 0 471 27939 0

Printed in the United States of America

Some new technology, like some science,
is solutions looking for questions.
What is more important than devising
ingenious answers is knowing the right questions.

Crawling on the planet's face,
Some insects, called the Human Race;
Lost in time,
Lost in space—
And lost in meaning?

(The Rocky Horror Show)

'The chances of anything coming from
Mars are a million to one,' he said,
'The chances of anything coming
from Mars are a million to one.'
But still they come.

(Jeff Wayne's 'War of the Worlds')

What is truth?

(Pontius Pilate)

Acknowledgements

A number of people have contributed to this book. The original idea for an analysis of 'face to file' or 'Type B' communication came from Mr Stuart Yerrell, then at the Department of the Environment, through whom the Department commissioned a report. Professor Robert Smith gave his support to this idea, as he had previously encouraged similar work on 'Type A' communication. Mr David Rennie later took responsibility for the 'face to file' report for the Department and gave up a substantial amount of his personal time to discuss it with me and make various constructive inputs. Clare Birks and Julia Johnson helped enormously in relation to the literature searches involved. I appreciate the support given by all these people, especially David Rennie, and am grateful to the Department for giving permission to use material from the original report as one of the bases for this book.

A second substantial input came from work done for the Commission of the European Communities (DG XIII) on videotex, as part of a study called 'Videotex: market and display study'. I am indebted to my colleagues at PACTEL for their help in conducting the research reported, especially Dr Jonathan Stanfield (UK), Paul Thornton (F.R. Germany), André George (France), Dr Martin Thomson (Holland), and others. I appreciate the support given by Dr George Anderla and Mr Carlo Vernimb of the Commission, and I am grateful to the Commission for giving permission to use material from the original report as one of the bases for this book.

A third significant input came from work done for the Commission of the European Communities (DG IX), examining the needs of officials in relation to information services within the Commission. Various colleagues of mine at PACTEL made important contributions to this work. Clare Birks was especially helpful in relation to the collection, analysis and interpretation of data. Martin Thomson played a significant role in arranging for the questionnaires to be distributed and in providing more general support. Richard Oades and Paddy O'Connor also made important contributions. I appreciate the support given by various people in the Commission, especially Mr Bellieni, and Mr Merucci who gave general support and specific assistance in regard to the distribution of questionnaires.

I am grateful to the Commission for giving permission to use material from the study as one of the bases for this book.

A fourth input came from miscellaneous work conducted by my colleagues and me at PACTEL as part of an ongoing programme of work in the area of 'Information management'. The following deserve special mention:

- Dr Jonathan Stanfield
- Dr Martin Thomson
- Mr Richard Oades
- Ms Clare Birks

- Ms Julia Johnson.

Jonathan Stanfield was consistently helpful and supportive, and made many constructive suggestions in relation to the work done for the Department of the Environment. It was Dr Stanfield who was primarily responsible for setting up The Information management group and for recruiting my immediate colleagues and me to the company. Mr Kep Simpson, Mr David Bayliss and Mr John Jarvis have also played an important role in supporting the Information management group and thus making possible the work reported here.

All this took place within an organizational environment created and supported by Mr Derek Maclaren (Chairman of PACTEL), Mr Holman Hunt (Managing Director of PACTEL) and others within the PA organization.

I am grateful to PA for giving permission to use the material presented in this book.

A number of researchers and others outside PACTEL were very cooperative in providing me with copies of unpublished manuscripts or other material, or discussing points with me by telephone. I should particularly like to mention:

- Ms Ann Kauder
  Social Science Research Council
- Dr Emma Bird
  Communications Studies and Planning
- Dr Ederyn Williams
  British Telecom
- Dr Pat Wright
  Applied Psychology Unit at Cambridge
- Dr Phil Barnard
  Applied Psychology Unit at Cambridge
- Professor Ehrenberg
  London Graduate School of Business Studies
- Dr Mike Howe
  Exeter University
- Professor A. M. McCosh
  Manchester Business School
- Dr Derek Rutter
  Kent University
- Dr Tom Stewart
  Loughborough University of Technology
- Professor Ken Eason
  Loughborough University of Technology

The book would not have been produced were it not for the encouragement given by various friends. Mr Keith Phillips was especially encouraging and made many constructive inputs, especially in connection with the sections on the information sphere and on hypnosis. Ms Sheryn Crarer was also very helpful and made an invaluable contribution to the production of the manuscript.

I am grateful to all the people mentioned, and all those others too numerous to mention individually. All weaknesses and errors remain mine.

The views expressed in the book are my own and do not necessarily reflect those of PACTEL, any other part of the PA organization, the Departments of Environment and Transport, the Commission of the European Communities, British Telecom, or any other organization or person.

Contents

xii

PART 6   CONCLUSIONS

PART 1
Introduction

Chapter 1

The scope of the book

We are standing at the threshold of a new era, a new society. We have moved on from a society dependent on an agricultural economy, and have lived through our 'industrial society'. During that stage in our evolution we learned how to handle physical materials, to create physical possibilities: roads, bridges, buildings, machines, and bombs, and all the tools of physical medicine. And we gained an important, basic freedom: the freedom to move at will through the physical world—through the seas that surround our planet, over the land, through the air, through space itself. And our industrial society has provided us with something else: the technology we need to take the next step.

Now we stand at the threshold of our 'information society'. We shall learn how to handle information, to create new kinds of knowledge, new levels of understanding. And we shall gain a new freedom: the freedom to move at will through the world of information.

One of our great teachers once taught us that we do not live by means of the physical alone. One of the other essential ingredients for life on this planet is information. That is why we have such sophisticated information channels ourselves: our eyes to provide visual information, our ears to provide auditory information, our tactile channels to provide information about physical contact, and so on.

These information channels are unmatched by anything our most sophisticated technology has to offer. The most advanced 'computer' on this planet is still the human 'computer'.

In this book we shall look at the technology we shall use to take our first step into the information society. It is primitive compared with what we shall be using by the close of the 1980s. We shall look at what we know about the psychological aspects of this technology—what information systems mean in terms of their impacts on and other relationships to human behaviour, understandings, and feelings. Little is known, and much needs to be learned. We are like babes, taking our first, stumbling steps into our future.

HUMAN COMMUNICATION

We humans are unique in the Animal Kingdom for our powers of communication. We alone among animals on this planet have developed true languages. Many other animals have developed primitive systems of communication based on limited repertoires of signals, but these systems lack the flexibility and richness of human

3

language. A dog, for example, can indicate when it is 'angry' or 'miserable', but it cannot explain why. Bees can communicate information about the location of flowers, but they are not generally believed capable of discussing the implications of motorways or air pollution on the bee population. Animals can communicate within their limits, but their limits are narrow. Humans alone have developed the capability of using complex rules of language to generate an open-ended stream of communications which have relatively precise meanings.

We are unique not just in the complexity of our languages but we far surpass other animals in terms of our ability to communicate through space and time. It is true that some animals, such as some insects, can send olfactory signals for many miles, but humans can use radio signals to send messages over distances measured in light years. Animals also communicate over time, as when they mark the boundaries to their territories for others to note then or at a later time, but humans can bury information in time capsules which will remain usable for hundreds of years. Humans have conquered time in another sense, as well, and that is in the speed of communication. Not only do modern communication networks cover the globe but they also allow for communication to be virtually instant.

Cherry (1978) cites a particularly dramatic example of the power of human communication. President Kennedy was assassinated in the early afternoon of November 22nd, 1963. The sophistication of human language and the power of radio, television and telephone communication meant that two-thirds of the population of the USA knew of the shooting within half an hour of the event. Over 90 per cent learned of it within two hours.

The technology which has allowed for instant global communications, for humans on Earth to talk to humans on the Moon, for machines on Mars to send detailed information about that planet back to scientists here, this technology has been developed largely within the approximate lifespan of the human. As Cherry (1978) has pointed out, a few people who saw the television pictures of the first landing on Mars probably also witnessed the introduction of the telephone during the 1870s.

The development of the telephone was a major landmark in the history of human communication, but we need to go back still further in time to find what was perhaps the greatest innovation of all. This was the invention, by Gutenberg, of the movable-type printing press, in 1455. This event probably more than any other has contributed to the dramatic acceleration in the rate of change of all fields of human endeavour.

The invention of the printing press was not itself sufficient to create change. It was necessary for the concept of publishing to become widely adopted and the market potentials to be realized. In fact, it was not until the end of the eighteenth century that book publishing came into general use. But then the number of books and other publications grew exponentially to countless millions of different titles today.

There were many scientists before Gutenberg's great invention, of course, but they had no way of communicating their findings and theories except by the slow processes of word-of-mouth, personal letters, and similar methods. Once they could rapidly share their researches with the scientific community at large they could avoid unnecessary duplication of effort and, instead, build effectively on each other's work. The result was an unprecedented surge of new discoveries, inventions and theories, leading to modern science and technology.

One has only to compare the 400 years between Gutenberg's invention and the introduction of the telephone with the 100 years between the latter event and the landing on Mars to see that the rate of technological achievement has increased remarkably. It seems to the author that we have adapted somewhat to this rate of development and fail to be excited by innovations which in fact are at least as significant as the invention of the printing press, the introduction of the telephone, or the landing on Mars. In this book we shall consider recent innovations in information systems—systems that during the 1980s and beyond will make more information more widely available more rapidly than ever before in the history of the human species.

There are many factors contributing to a rapid rate of development in electronic information systems. Among the more important are:

- increasing overheads in offices, including office rents, heat, lighting, and so forth;
- increasing direct costs of employing office workers, including salaries, superannuation, and so forth;
- decreasing costs of equipment.

It is the last of these, the rapidly decreasing cost of equipment, which in many ways is the most clear-cut and dramatic. For example, the power available in a personal computer costing about £1,000 today would have cost about £40,000 ten years ago (in 1981 pounds). For the reader who is not computer-minded, one has only to consider that one can buy a small pocket calculator capable of being programmed by the user to calculate a range of statistics or play simple games for as little as £16 to get an inkling of what this means.

SCOPE OF THE BOOK

We can see from the above that the general topic we are addressing is of potential interest to all intelligent people because the developments which have stimulated this book will affect everyone.

There are three groups, however, for whom the book will be of special interest:

- managers;
- psychologists;
- policy-makers, e.g. in government.

Interest to Managers

The successful manager even today needs to be aware of developments in office technology and their human aspects. The importance of this kind of understanding will become progressively greater during the 1980s as the technology becomes more widely used, more sophisticated, and more encompassing. It is difficult to see how managers in the 1980s will be able to function effectively without being competent in the use of the new 'tools of their trade'. Managers need to understand the impacts of the new technology, the factors governing acceptance, and the relationships to human behaviour, understandings, and feelings. These human aspects will determine the success or otherwise of electronic information systems in particular organizations, and whether any given organization manages successfully to cross the threshold into our electronic future or whether it falls by the wayside, trampled by the competition.

Interest to Psychologists

The equation $B = f(E, P)$ will be familiar to psychologists. It indicates that behaviour (B)—the primary subject matter of psychology—is a function of the environment (E) and the person (P). Psychologists need to give proper attention to developments in electronic information systems because these systems herald the most significant change in the human environment since the industrial revolution. Any psychologist who has the slightest concern for 'ecological validity' will realize the need to take account of the new 'electronic environment' in theory development and experimentation. The change is all the more significant because it impacts directly on that uniquely human quality to which we referred above, i.e. our ability to communicate complex concepts with a high level of precision. Applied psychologists will need to understand the psychological aspects of information systems in order to derive implications for their own specialisms in education, clinical settings or organizations. In this book we shall be concerned with basic principles, relating these to the new electronic technology, reviewing what relevant empirical research has been done, and developing a broad framework within which further research can be conducted fruitfully.

Interest to Policy Makers

The original idea for the book came from a report (Christie, 1979) commissioned by The Departments of Environment and Transport. The purpose of that report was to review the psychological aspects of electronic information systems that will influence the impacts of these systems on office location and transportation patterns. It was recognized that technological possibilities by themselves are not sufficient to shape the future. The possibilities have to be accepted and used by people. The particular possibilities adopted, the particular ways in which they are used—the particular roles the new technology is allowed to play—determine the extent and nature of the technology's impact. The Bell System 'Picturephone'—a major technological achievement—was demonstrated in the early 1960s and introduced commercially during the 1970s. It has had little impact—not because the technology is not available (it is), but because it has not yet been accepted. (Psychological aspects of the video telephone and related technology have been reviewed by Short, Williams, and Christie, 1976.) Numerous other examples of this sort will no doubt occur to the reader.

Another input to the book comes from research commissioned by the Commission of the European Communities as part of a study of videotex developments in Europe. It was recognized that understanding the psychological needs of users in relation to videotex is necessary for a proper evaluation of the possibilities for videotex and the extent of its impact. This applies equally to all technological developments in this general area.

Understanding the psychological aspects of electronic information systems is therefore important to policy-makers. This applies not just to the examples cited, but to education, health care, industry, employment, and all other areas of life where government or other bodies have a responsibility to monitor new developments, understand and evaluate their potential impacts, and influence our choice of futures. We can all point to high-rise apartment buildings, automobiles, and other examples where greater understanding and more careful analysis might have helped us to achieve something better. Let us learn from our experiences and make sure we base our plans in the information area on a firm foundation of adequate knowledge and understanding.

Interest to Others

There are many other groups who will be interested in the topics we shall address. Unions, for example, will need to understand the impacts of the new technology and opportunities it creates. Our analysis in subsequent chapters will provide a broad framework of understanding in which specific questions such as skills needed, effects on formal and informal communication, on job satisfaction, on occupational stress, and so forth, can be considered. Suppliers of equipment and services also have a strong interest in this area. The development of systems like viewdata and Ceefax/Oracle heralds the emergence of a new mass market—information consumers in the home. Suppliers will need to know what consumers want, need, and can cope with. Developments in the office are equally important, and the situation there is more complex because of the need to take account of existing infrastructure. Suppliers will need to know how organizations will use the new systems and services and how these will interface with those that exist already.

In addition to the relatively specific interests of groups such as these, we all need to be aware of what is happening because it affects us all—in our work, and as individual human beings.

Topics Addressed

The new electronic technology has implications in many areas, for example:

- location and design of buildings (including offices, schools, clinics, homes, and others);
- the mix of employment opportunities;
- travel patterns (e.g. working from home more of the time);
- improved access to and use of information (e.g. community information services);
- education (e.g. greater emphasis on how to use information, less on learning specific facts);
- health care (e.g. emergency aid, routine self-screening);
- and many others.

We shall not attempt to explore these areas in detail. Each could be a book in its own right, and a proper subject for detailed analysis by the policy bodies concerned. We shall concentrate on the broad principles that are relevant to all of these more specific areas. Our emphasis will be on the fundamental psychology of people working with electronic information systems, especially in the office. The particular topics we shall consider include, amongst others:

- the nature of information;
- the value of information to organizations;
- the nature of information handling in organizations;
- how office workers, especially managers, spend their time, and their need for information;
- how people seek information, both in the office environment and elsewhere;
- attitudes;
- organizational impacts, and factors affecting the acceptance of electronic information systems;
- characteristics and special training the successful manager of tomorrow will need to have.

We shall consider these aspects in relation to information systems generally but we shall give special attention to a range of systems which illustrate the variety available and which seem to be among the more important, as explained below.

Systems Considered

Examples of the systems which seem to warrant special attention and which we shall describe in more detail in Chapter 5 include:

- Videotex: Systems for storing large quantities of information, usually in 'page' form, in computers to be accessed through telephone lines and displayed on television screens. Prestel is an example of such a system.
- Teletext: Systems for transmitting 'pages' of information 'over the air' to be displayed on television screens. Ceefax and Oracle are examples.
- Networked information systems: Networks of computers containing large

quantities of information, especially scientific and technical information, in varying formats to be accessed through telephone lines using standard computer terminals. Euronet is an example. (Special terminals, e.g. videotex, may also be attached in the future.)

- Word processors: Systems for creating 'pages' of electronic information which can be communicated electronically or converted into paper form using high-speed, high-quality printers. A number of manufacturers are marketing systems of this sort.
- Computer conferencing: Computer systems which allow groups of people to join in on-line 'conferences' by typing what they want to say into the computer. The computer stores these messages in an organised form capable of being printed out as a record of what has been said to date, at the convenience of the user. Various special facilities are available such as private messages to selected participants, use of questionnaires, and others.
- Personal computers: Microcomputers in the home or in one's own office that provide 'local intelligence'. For example, Prestel pages can be taken off the public service, stored in one's personal computer and manipulated at will. Personal computers can be used for many other applications, such as being used in networks, to provide computer conferencing.

In all these systems (at least so far as we shall be discussing them) the emphasis is on information in the form of text and related material, e.g. tables, graphs, and so forth, i.e. the kind of material we expect to find in a book, report, letter, memorandum, or similar item. We are not concerned with 'data processing', i.e. high-speed, high-volume, largely numerical information. This reflects our interest in the impact of electronic information systems in the office and in the home. We shall give more attention to the office than the home because this is where most of the research has been done and where the impacts of the technology are being felt first.

COMPLEMENTARY BOOKS

There are many complementary books which the interested reader may wish to consult. Some references are given later at appropriate points in the text, but the following are good examples.

Donington, J. (in preparation)
   The Automated Office, to be published by John Wiley. This book provides a good overview of the office systems currently available, at a more technical level than here and covering a broader range of systems, and presents a scenario for the 'office of the future'.
Lamond, F. (in preparation)
   The Last Rush Hour, to be published by John Wiley. The author argues that within the lifetime of most people under the age of 50 today, the daily commuting rush hour may become a thing of the past, like the great London smogs. He presents a case for this based on the expected impacts of electronic systems.

10

Cherry, C. (1978)

   World Communications: Threat or Promise? A Socio-technical Approach, John Wiley. An interesting overview of the 'communications explosion' seen from an international perspective, and its social implications.

Short, J., Williams, E., and Christie, B. (1976)

   The Social Psychology of Telecommunications, John Wiley. A 'cousin' to the present book, this discusses the psychological aspects of the video telephone, audio conferencing systems, and other telecommunication systems concerned with direct person-to-person or group-to-group (Type A) communication.

Johansen, R., Vallee, J., and Spangler, K. (1979)

   Electronic Meetings: Technical Alternatives and Social Choices, Addison-Wesley. A useful introduction to the work done on computer conferencing and related systems by The Institute of The Future and elsewhere.

Hiltz, S. R., and Turoff, M. (1978)

   The Network Nation: Human Communication via Computer, Addison-Wesley. An interesting and in parts very entertaining portrait of the future, with the emphasis very much on computer conferencing and closely related systems.

Others could be included in this list but these provide a good starting point for those who wish to go into this area in depth.

Chapter 2

Glimpses of tomorrow

There is no single future, but an infinite set of possible futures. Which one shall we choose? We are like an artist with a blank canvas. We can choose the vision we create. We are, however, constrained somewhat by the materials we have available. The use of lasers and photography makes it possible for us today to create visions that were not possible even a few years ago. We are also like a traveller, driving up a motorway. Our destination, or a small set of likely destinations, can be guessed from the direction in which we are travelling, but we can choose to turn off or turn around at any time. Sometimes people do that. The revolution in Iran is a case in point. We always have a choice.

At the moment we are travelling towards an information society. This has been clear for some time, as the graphs in Figure 2.1 show. They show that we have moved on from a society in which agriculture predominated (Stage I), through one in which industry predominated (Stage II), and are entering one dominated by information and the 'service industries', e.g. banking, insurance, consultancy services of various sorts, and other services where the handling of information is the main activity (Stage III). This shift in emphasis will create many visible changes in our everyday lives, reflecting the impacts of the electronic systems which form the basis for this new society.

In assessing the impacts which electronic systems are likely to have, the most appropriate way of viewing the systems is as serving a facilitating function, helping organizations to achieve their goals. It is quite unreasonable to suppose, for example, that electronic systems will *necessarily* result in organizations dispersing their operations, or in people working from home. What, if anything, will happen along these lines will depend upon more basic pressures and incentives.

What exactly the systems could facilitate will depend upon the roles which they are allowed to play within an organization. This will depend directly upon their organizational acceptance, as discussed in Chapter 15, on the way individual people react to them, as discussed in Chapter 13, and on their effectiveness, as discussed in Chapter 5.

Some possibilities which electronic systems could facilitate under favourable circumstances include, for example:

- Working from home or at neighbourhood work centres:

11

12

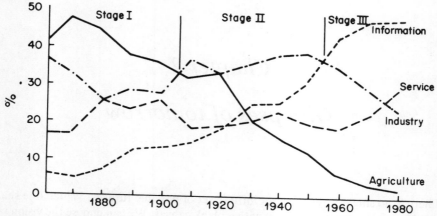

Figure 2.1. Four-section aggregations of US workforce 1860–1980, using median estimates of information workers (per cent) (from Parker, 1976).

This would be particularly attractive for part-timers, where the time and money spent in travelling can be significant. It would also have effects on energy expenditure and environmental pollution.

• Greater use of bureaux:

An organization could send documents electronically from its own word processing system to a bureau (over standard telephone lines, assuming the regulatory environment allowed it), for the bureau to work on and return electronically to be printed out on the organization's own word processor (or simply held in electronic form). The communications to and fro would take only a few minutes and the organization would be paying only for the time the word-processing operators actually spent operating.

This could be a significant improvement over employing permanent or temporary staff who are paid for the number of hours spent in the office, whether or not that time is 100% productive. The bureau system could also mean faster turnaround times. Large, dispersed organizations could set up their own, internal 'bureaux'.

• More direct contact with the public:

The availability of large, up-to-date databases on information systems with terminals in people's homes or in convenient places, e.g., post offices, banks, supermarkets, libraries, could reduce the pressure on government agencies and other 'intermediary' organizations currently attempting to provide information services largely based on face-to-face contact. These organizations could be developed to fill a perhaps more useful role of providing *advice* rather than simply information. Videotex makes such possibilities practicable.

• Dispersal or relocation of offices:

Statistics from the location of offices bureau suggests that many firms are uncertain about whether to relocate or not. Between 1963 and 1977 almost half the firms that considered moving eventually decided against it. It is not clear to what extent the non-movers were influenced by communications factors but even if the new electronic systems were sufficient to persuade only a small proportion of such firms that could still mean a significant number of jobs.

We shall consider some possible impacts of electronic information systems in more detail later, but first we need to examine the ways in which these systems might facilitate change.

THE FACILITATING FUNCTION OF ELECTRONIC SYSTEMS

The process envisaged by which electronic systems play a facilitating function is shown in Figure 2.2. This suggests that the process is cyclical and continuous, though its rate may increase. Not only do new electronic systems influence the evolution of new patterns of working, but these new patterns feed-back to influence further technological developments directly, or to influence the pressures and in-

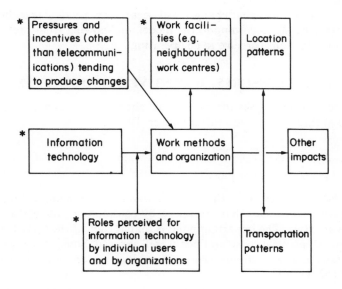

Note: Only the most important influences are shown.
        Feedback loops are not.

*Points where government policy might be expected to impact.

Figure 2.2   The evolution of patterns of working.

centives on organizations to change. They may also lead to requirements for new facilities (e.g. neighbourhood work centres), some of which may be related to information only indirectly (e.g. new designs for homes if people are to spend more of their time at home, especially if they need work space).

The points at which government policy might be expected to impact are asterisked. Two are direct:

- influencing the pressures and incentives on organizations, e.g., through grants or subsidies;
- influencing developments in information technology in similar ways.

Two are less direct and more risky:

- providing new facilities which may be needed and which might be expected then to influence the pressures and incentives on organizations;
- attempting to influence the roles which individual users and organizations give new systems, through training/education, demonstration applications, and increased public awareness.

Our ability to forecast what changes will occur given particular technological developments depends, according to the model, on knowing what pressures and incentives organizations perceive to be operating.

SOME PRESSURES, INCENTIVES, AND EFFECTS

The pressures and incentives for change and the effects of change can be conceptualized at three main levels (after Glover, 1974):

- society
- organizations
- individual people and their jobs.

Glover (1974) illustrates this with reference to working from home. Figure 2.3 illustrates the sorts of issues that are raised by considering this relatively major change in work style. The important point is that at each of the three levels there are physical and financial considerations as well as social. Some of the issues raised are relevant to much less extreme changes in working patterns and, conversely, the table is not exhaustive.

The various pressures and incentives involved must be taken account of to understand the full possibilities of information-communications technology. The following are some of the more important factors involved.

Redefinition of Office Roles

Developments in office technology will result in adjustments being made to the roles people perform. To take word processing as an example, accumulating evidence

Figure 2.3 Some issues raised by working from home (from Glover, 1974)

	Social	*Physical*	*Financial*
The individual job level	Job satisfaction Relationship between work and non-work Substitutability of job Strain of travelling to work Opportunities for the handicapped	Location of home Size of home	Travelling to work Work space at home Equipment at home Pension rights, etc.
The company level	Supervision of employees both home-based and non-home-based Turnover of staff	Number, type, and location of centralised buildings	Rental of central offices, and provision of affiliated services Equipment for staff at home Extra payments for home-based and office-based staff
The societal level	Changing values about styles of life Greater separation of rich and not so rich	Changing Structure of the city Demands for services in different locations changing	Impact on taxation Impact on the rating system Impact on land and property prices

16

based on practical experience with such systems suggests that at least the following functions need to be separately identified:

- activities of a routine 'word processing' kind, e.g., standard letters, reports, and so forth;
- preparation of very brief, one-off items or material which is very urgent or highly confidential;
- personal assistant functions.

There is also evidence that increasingly the management of these functions will need to take account of secretaries' demands for a proper career structure. It may be that office technology will follow a similar path to computer technology. At first, there may be attempts to transfer existing procedures to the new technology but as development continues and people gain more experience more use will be made of the technology to release the human resources in the organization to do higher-level, more rewarding work.

Job Substitutability

Some roles are likely to emerge which are common and standard across different parts of an organization and even across different organizations. The people performing these roles may feel greater allegiance to their professional group than to any particular company. Again, there is a parallel here with computers. Mumford (1965a) has argued persuasively that computer specialists tend to identify with computer technology rather than with the aims of the business. Their reference group is made up of systems analysts and programmers in other firms, not their firm's management group. They are often physically separated from the day-to-day operation of the business. The same may apply to office technology. It is not out of the question that word processing, for example, may evolve to be a sophisticated specialism such that the preparation of semi-routine reports can be almost entirely delegated to the 'reports people', leaving the manager with more time for more productive activities. It may also be that the 'reports people', like the computer specialists, will often be physically separate from the central management functions.

Industrial Democracy

Developments in office technology are unlikely to be exempt from the influence of industrial democracy which is one of the most widely discussed subjects in industry at the present time. It is a complex subject and there is not the space to go into it in detail here, but it is clear that attitudes in this area generally favour greater involvement of employees, especially users and operators, in the design of systems, including information-communications systems.

Attitudes to Work

Related to the question of industrial democracy is the more general question of attitudes to work. Glover et al. (1975) completed a review of the literature on attitudes to work as an input to the long-range planning activity of the Post Office (now British Telecom).
They reached the following conclusions:

- over the next 20 or 30 years there will be more pressure to increase job satisfaction by changing the content of jobs;
- large organizations where jobs are arranged in a pyramidal fashion may come under pressure to change this structure;
- loyalty to individual companies is likely to decrease and more people are likely to change jobs more often;
- there is likely to be greater employee participation in decision-making;
- training policies will have to be reassessed to meet an increasing need to train and retrain people for second and third careers;
- the number of jobs concerned with producing knowledge rather than goods is likely to increase;
- the proportion of women in the work force is likely to increase;
- the work force is likely to have higher expectations of their jobs;
- the so-called 'swing from science' may have been exaggerated;
- there is little evidence that interesting or autonomous work is a substitute for more pay;
- people are likely to spend less time at work, either through shortened work weeks or through absenteeism;
- some 'drop-out' (qualified people doing mundane work or working only part of the year) is occurring but it is not possible to quantify it very accurately.

Glover et al. suggest that the evidence they present could be used in conjunction with traditional manpower planning models and with the opinions of employees to achieve a better understanding of likely organizational developments.

THE OFFICE OF TOMORROW

Broad factors such as those considered above suggest the general direction in which we are moving. One of the first stages on our journey is what has become known as the 'office of tomorrow' or the 'automated office'. These terms mean slightly different things to different people but they usually refer to a 'best guess' at what the office of the mid-1980s is likely to look like. The following seem to be among the key concepts involved.

The Work Station

The simple office desk of today will give way to a work station. At today's prices this is likely to be based on about £1000–5000 worth of electronic equipment, depending on its role. This would be a fairly basic, 'executive' model. More expensive work stations, costing perhaps £5000–20 000 would be used for specialist operations such as full-scale word processing.

A typical version of the executive work station is likely to include:

A telephone. As today, this will allow for simple voice communication with anyone almost anywhere in the world. This will remain one of the most powerful tools the manager has at his or her disposal. Its usefulness will be enhanced by a number of features which today's telephone typically does not have, for example:

- push-button dialling (of the fully electronic, 'touch tone' type);
- a memory to facilitate dialling of frequently used numbers;
- a transferable extension number or 'logical address' (discussed below) so that telephone calls can be routed automatically (probably by the private exchange computer—the PABX) to the person concerned, whichever work station (s)he happens to be using;
- connection to a variety of devices to allow for non-voice communication, such as those described next.

Where work stations as such are not used, the telephone of tomorrow may include a number of other features that would normally be incorporated routinely as part of a work station, for example:

- a cassette attachment for recording voice messages or receiving data, or for sending data;
- a calculations facility using the memory and buttons normally used for dialling;
- the date, and limited other information (e.g. a 'diary' of important dates up to several years into the future).

A personal computer. Personal computers (microcomputers) vary in price and in what they can do. A typical work station computer would cost of the order of £1000–1500 at early 1980 prices, and would include:

- floppy disc or other convenient medium (e.g. bubble memory) for storing personal files;
- sufficient memory and computer power for simple scientific or business data analyses such as correlations, t-tests, chi-square tests, and so forth;
- routines for management of personal files;
- facilities for connection to the telephone and communication with other computers, including computer conferencing;
- facilities for connection to videotex (both public and private videotex);
- other features as required.

A television set. This would be used for displaying the outputs from the personal computer (including items of information received by telephone from elsewhere), and pages of information held on the company's own videotex computers or on other such computers. The set would normally provide a medium-size display of say, 40–50 cm (16–20 in), in colour. Where work stations as such are not used, smaller videotex sets—possibly providing only a monochrome display—may sometimes be used.

Slow-scan video. The television set would also allow slow-scan video to be used. In a system of this sort, a person wishing to send a picture points a small camera at the object (a page of text, his or her face, or some other object) and presses a 'freeze' and 'transmit' button. The picture is then sent over the ordinary telephone system and about thirty seconds later (or later in some systems) the picture appears on the receiving set. This has many potential applications. Used in conjunction with personal computers we can imagine it might provide a way of showing (still) pictures of the people speaking during a multi-way telephone (voice) conference.

A printer. In the early days there will still be a lot of paper used, and many work stations will be equipped with a printer to give 'hard copy'. This will take output from a range of sources, including: the microcomputer (which in turn may take data or text from the telephone), direct from remote word processors, direct from videotex, and possibly other sources (e.g. cassettes).

Facsimile. Facsimile (or 'fax') is a system for scanning text or other material (e.g. graphs or half-tone pictures), coding the fluctuations in the grey scale, transmitting these codes down a telephone line, and recreating the original 'picture' (e.g. a page of text) at the other end. We can think of it almost as 'remote photocopying'. There may be a trend towards integrating facsimile with word processing, so as to be able to handle all aspects of a typical report (e.g. graphs as well as text) in one system.

Word processing. Word processing is described in Chapter 5. It refers primarily to the production of documents using sophisticated electronic text-handling systems, but advanced systems also offer powerful communications facilities. Bulk word processing is likely to remain the responsibility of specialist operators but managers may have the facilities at their work stations (based on the microcomputer) for doing minor editing.

Other features. Advanced work stations of the late 1980s may include various additional features, especially voice input of text. Using this facility, a manager would be able to dictate a letter or other document directly into a word processing system, treating the system as if it were a human secretary taking dictation. In the interim, managers may make more use of 'remote dictation', i.e. dictating down a telephone line into a cassette recorder which can then be used later by a typist or word processing operator to actually type the letter or other item concerned. Various other devices may be found in the 'office of tomorrow', for example:

- optical character readers (OCR) for taking material produced on conventional typewriters and inputting it into an electronic system;
- video telephones for person-to-person conversations requiring a visual channel—probably used within rather than between organizations initially because of the special communications requirements involved;
- audio and audio–video conference rooms for group-to-group electronic meetings, using either private or public studios.

Many of these devices are already available. For example, video telephones have been available since the 1960s. The office of tomorrow will see more use being made of these devices as electronic systems generally become more widespread.

Physical Arrangements

Increasing office rents and the greater flexibility and mobility offered by electronic systems (e.g. logical addressing, mentioned above and discussed further below) are likely to result in offices being smaller and more facilities being shared. Managers are likely to make flexible use of work stations, according to convenience, facilities required at the time, and so forth. Relatively few people (those who are very senior or who need to be at a work station of a particular type all day) will have a work station dedicated to their own use. Open planning, under-floor cabling, and similar arrangements will facilitate a flexible approach to the use of office space and facilities.

Differentiation of Labour

There is likely to be a restructuring of roles within the office environment. The manager will gain greater flexibility and more direct control over some office functions, e.g. limited computing and text editing using the work station microcomputer. Paradoxically, more functions are likely to be delegated. In particular, the routine aspects of report preparation are likely to be delegated more and more to the 'reports people' (information officers, word-processing operators, and so forth). Managers will be able to request routine reports on certain topics, specify the format and chapter headings, and so forth, and then wait for their tailor-made reports to be produced. The complexity of what is involved in this and other aspects of running an electronic office suggests there will be a better career structure for people on the 'operations side'; for example we might imagine:

- conventional typists taking material from dictation cassettes or handwritten copy for rough drafts to be input to a word processing system through optical character readers;
- basic word-processing operators, responsible for the 'typing' aspects of word processing;

- information officers, responsible for collating the information needed, including the research needed for this;
- senior word-processing operators, responsible for security, communications, resource allocation at the operator level, and related aspects of systems management;
- systems managers, responsible for overall resource control in particular areas—ensuring, for example, that the information officers and senior word-processing operators are working in harmony to provide an efficient service, as well as playing a key role in systems development.

THE HOME OF TOMORROW

Developments in the office are likely to be paralleled by developments in the home. In relation to the range of electronic information-communication systems available in the home, these are likely to include:

- a personal computer, probably using a colour television for display and with a significant amount of storage (e.g. floppy discs or bubble memory);
- a videotex colour television set for accessing pages of information from the public Prestel service and from other sources, e.g. the person's company computers;
- video discs for educational and informational purposes as well as entertainment;
- various other devices, e.g. a video taperecorder, a conventional 'music centre', and so forth.

Some of the implications of this electronic enrichment in the home are indicated in what follows.

DISPERSAL OF OFFICE FUNCTIONS

Consideration of factors such as those discussed above has led to speculation that organizational changes are quite likely in the not too distant future which will involve some degree of physical dispersal of office functions. Chief amongst the schemes which have been given some attention are the concepts of:

- working from home, where employees spend all or part of their time at home, communicating with geographically distant companies by means of suitable communications facilities;
- various ways of segmenting an organization so that it can spread its operations over a wide geographic area, using electronic information-communications systems to assist in coordinating activities in the various parts;
- the neighbourhood work centre, where employees of different organizations share sophisticated information-communications facilities which allow them to work for geographically distant companies without having to commute very far;
- the headquarters city, where business requiring personal, face-to-face contact

is conducted either in futuristic office complexes or in more social settings such as restaurants or hotels.

We shall now consider these and related ideas in a little more detail. We shall see that some of them are fairly speculative.

Working From Home

Studies considered in Chapter 7 suggest that 30–40 per cent is a good 'rule of thumb' for the proportion of time managers spend on paper-oriented activities, but there is wide variability between different organizations. The proportion may be much higher for some other office workers, including secretaries. If we assume that all paper-oriented activities could be done at home, given suitable electronic information systems for communication between home and office, then this suggests managers could spend up to about two days a week working from home. To this we may wish to add that proportion of face-to-face communication that could be conducted electronically. If we assume that managers spend about 50 per cent of their time in face-to-face communication of one sort or another (the proportion varies considerably—see Chapter 7) and that about 40 per cent of it could in principle be handled satisfactorily by audio communication systems using the ordinary telephone network (see Short, Williams and Christie, 1976), then we can add an extra day to the amount of time a manager could spend working at home. This makes up to three days a week. This assumes that all the necessary face-to-face contacts could be scheduled in the remaining two days. This seems rather unlikely to be the case in practice, so three days a week is probably a generous estimate.

Whether the telecommunication costs of working at home for up to three days a week could be justified in terms of commuting costs saved and reduced wear-and-tear on the managers concerned would be for individual managers and their organizations to decide. A lot would depend on the capital costs of the equipment involved, the amount of telecommunication required in particular cases, and related factors. Some negotiation might be involved. For example, the manager concerned might feel the arrangement was worth him or her paying the heating and lighting that would be needed. The organization might feel that the telecommunications costs could be offset to some extent by the extra productivity coming from the manager working during the time that (s)he would otherwise be travelling to and from the office. This extra time might amount to six hours a week (assuming an hour each way for three days). The reduction in stress on the manager could also be quantified in principle in terms of various measures such as days off sick, probability of cardiovascular disease, quality of performance, and other measures (see Chapter 16).

Electronic information systems may facilitate working from home but we see from the above that the impact is likely to be rather small—certainly much less than 100 per cent, and probably considerably less than 60 per cent in the foreseeable future.

Neighbourhood Work Centres

The alternative to working from home need not be having to commute into the centre of the city. We can envisage a situation where an organization disperses its operations, establishing a series of small units outside the central city. Lamond (in preparation) has pointed out that the number of units would have to be quite large—say, of the order of 20–50 in the case of an organization around London—for this to offer any commuting advantage. With a small number, say four or five, most people would still be living an appreciable distance from their work units. This could make commuting even more arduous because it would mean travelling across instead of into and out of the city, which is easier to do using public transport.

Lamond also suggests that each unit should have all the major office facilities, including the systems needed to communicate with other units and other organizations. This could be expensive and result in facilities being under-used if a unit serves a relatively small number of people, and they work at home some of the time. One possibility would be for units from different organizations to share some facilities.

It is from these general notions that the idea of neighbourhood work centres has emerged. Different variants of the basic idea have been proposed. One possibility is that different organizations 'club together' somehow. Another is that the centres are operated as independent businesses, offering their services to whichever companies wish to use them. The centres would then have a degree of similarity with both 'temp' agencies and with hotels (offering conference rooms and similar facilities). They would also be similar to those companies today that offer a business address, an answering service, offices to rent on an hourly or daily basis, and various secretarial services. The neighbourhood work centre would be larger, with a wider range of facilities, and with greater emphasis on electronic information and communications systems.

Logical Addresses

Office information-communication systems have been proposed in which the physical terminals and their identification numbers are distinguished from 'logical addresses'. The basic idea really is very simple. If I leave my usual telephone extension, say to work in the library, I can ask for my calls to be routed to the library. In the systems proposed, this would be done for items of information such as memoranda being sent electronically, and it would be done automatically by the computer responsible for the routing. The computer would route the items according to their 'logical addresses' (i.e. where I actually am at the time) rather than to physical terminals (i.e. my usual extension number). This automatic re-routing of items will become much easier when switching on the public telephone network is done by computer (System X in the UK). It will make it much easier for a person to stay in contact with the 'office' whilst moving freely from one location to another, including neighbourhood work centres and home.

The Community Communications Centre

The community communications centre could emerge as an extension of the sharing of facilities represented by the neighbourhood work centres. One can imagine several independent work centres paying for and sharing the use of especially expensive facilities, such as a visual conferencing studio. Such a studio would be used relatively infrequently by any given organization but the ability of a neighbourhood work centre to offer such a service when needed would be an attractive feature. One might also imagine a suite of video telephone booths being shared in the same way, with the cost of the booths and the necessary 1-megahertz communications lines being shared among several neighbourhood work centres (and therefore many organizations).

The concept of a community communications centre orginally emerged as part of Goldmark's 'New Rural Society' proposals for the dispersal of population and economic revitalization of small towns in the USA (e.g. Goldmark, 1973). It was conceived of as the electronic and cultural heart of the small community. It would be the switching centre for electronic services such as remote shopping, it would contain the studios for locally produced cable television programmes, and it would contain a large-screen auditorium for presentation of major cultural events such as operas, sports events and theatre transmitted electronically from the cities using special broadband communications links (using twice the bandwidth of standard broadcast television).

We can imagine that the 'post-Goldmark' community communications centre might look something like one of the large, enclosed 'shopping centres' that are common in the USA and of which there are a few examples in the UK, e.g. at Brent Cross in London. Instead of shops, however, we might expect to see the following:

- *neighbourhood work centres*, as described above, offering a range of services to business people, including shared facilities such as
- *video telephone booths*, for instances where audio communication is not considered sufficient, and
- *a video conferencing studio*, for group-to-group visual communication when a meeting needs to be held but time does not permit travel or travel is considered unnecessarily inconvenient—some of these studios might be provided as part of the public 'Confravision' service;
- *creche facilities* for people who need to have their children cared for whilst they are at work;
- *restaurants*, wine bars, coffee bars and similar facilities for relaxing and meeting people;
- *remote shopping* collection points, where goods ordered electronically from home or the office can be collected after work;
- *a 'social support centre'* where the unemployed and others needing support can go for:

— benefits to be paid in cash if needed (they would normally be transferred directly to the person's bank account)
— personal counselling
— access to electronic services they may not be able to afford in their own home, with the emphasis on
— information about job vacancies
— information and advice about benefits and financial management;

* *conventional cinemas* for entertainment;
* *a large-screen auditorium* of the type envisaged by Goldmark for the presentation of opera, theatre, sports events, and so on—both 'live' and recorded;
* *studios* for locally originated cable television and radio programmes.

Flexibility in Time Spent Working

The greater flexibility offered by electronic systems, and the close proximity of the work centres to the entertainment facilities in the community communications centre, and to the individual's home, paves the way for a less rigid approach to the working day. There may be greater emphasis on working to deadlines with less emphasis on working '9 to 5'. Some people may choose, for example, to work early and late with a break of several hours in the middle of the day. Such a staggering of activities could result in more efficient use being made of facilities.

Flexibility in the time spent working, and the place of work, has implications in other directions as well, as follows.

Implications of electronic information technology for the so-called 'homebound' have been discussed by several researchers. Usually these discussions have focused on well-defined groups, e.g. mothers (Gordon, undated) and the physically disabled (Smith, E. I., 1973). Actually much of what has been said applies equally well to anyone who is capable of doing useful work but, for whatever reason, cannot or does not wish to commit themselves to working in an office remote from home for a 'full working day', five days a week. If part-time employment becomes a more normal style of working, some of the theoretical possibilities which have been discussed may become of more practical importance.

Gordon outlines some of the incentives toward working at home or at neighbourhood work centres. They revolve around an ability to change the structure of the work day from a basically rigid routine to what Gordon refers to as 'an individualized partitioning of time'. For anyone choosing to, or being required to, work part-time, there could be significant improvements over working part-time under present conditions.

For anyone working, say, 25 hours a week, even a half-hour journey to work means spending 20 per cent of working hours just travelling. Apart from the time involved, this is likely to be very costly as a proportion of earnings. Proximal working, either in the home itself or at nearby centres, would make a more practical and profitable arrangement.

Such arrangements could extend the possibilities regarding 'flexi-time'. In particular, evening work and weekend work would be more feasible and more appealing. There would be advantages both for the employee, in terms of reduced costs and greater flexibility, and for the employer in, for example:

- having some staff available a greater part of the day, possibly improving turn-around times on urgent materials by having work done in the evening ready for the following morning;
- reducing costs by reducing the amount of office space required;
- possibly reducing costs by being able to pay somewhat lower salaries (given the attractiveness to employees of the increased flexibility).

There might also be some possibilities in regard to reducing the number of people unemployed. Apart from part-time working being more practicable, the possibility of two people sharing a job would be much more feasible given flexible and efficient information-communications links between the people concerned.

Finally, there could be significantly less stress on dual-career families. The difficulties involved in finding a place to live which is not too far from either place of work would be greatly reduced if one or both partners did not have to travel to a remote office as often as is usual at present; and difficulties caused by both partners being out of the house at the same time (e.g. shopping, receiving meter readers, and so forth) would be greatly reduced by flexible hours or part-time working (although some of the difficulties will be reduced anyway as electronic systems become more widely used, e.g. for shopping and remote meter reading).

A question posed by these possibilities concerns how the necessary information-communications facilities would be paid for. Would it be the individual employees or the organizations for whom they work? Or could we conceive of centres which are regarded as belonging to and being paid for by the local community in much the same way that libraries, schools and other special facilities are supported? To the extent that employers contribute, in what ways if at all would it be appropriate for the government to provide incentives, perhaps in the form of tax relief or special grants? Would it be necessary or desirable for the costs of communications to be subsidized?

The Headquarters City

The central city is unlikely to disappear as a result of electronic systems, but it will change and we can imagine that it might evolve towards something that Goldmark called the 'headquarters city' (e.g. Goldmark, 1973). This is very much like the kind of community described by Mead (1965).

Mead described the city as 'a point of confrontation'. She is referring not to actual cities, described in their totalities, but to the essential city, the ideal city. The city, she suggests, is a place where strangers can meet. Strangers are accepted, they 'belong' in a city. The concept of the inn, and of the restaurant, is characteristic of the city. Strangers can come and meet others engaged in a wide variety of activities. Groups separated by ethnic lines, and the lines dividing the arts and sciences, and groups separated by class or politics, can 'confront' each other in the city. It is the place where poets, philosophers, scientists, botanists, architects and statesmen and women can come and meet. The ideal city is not 'miles and miles of factories or people working in factories which have no relationship to the city or to any of its benefits, except, possibly—as in the United States—public relief' (Mead, 1965, p. 19).

The kind of 'confrontation' Mead described would form a part of the life of the headquarters city. The products of the 'confrontations', in the form of cultural, educational, and political activities, would be equally important. These would be made available to the nation by the communications systems connecting the cities to the smaller communities outside. Top level management would also use the headquarters cities as the places where high-level negotiation and decision-making activities would take place. Such cities could stimulate, and might require, 'new and imaginative architecture, a 20th Century administration and mass transportation'. (Goldmark, 1973, p. 25.)

OTHER IMPACTS

Impacts of the new technology on office functions have already begun and the potential impacts are wide-ranging, as illustrated by the concepts discussed above. There are other kinds of impacts as well, on the democratic process, on education, on health care, and in other areas.

Impacts On Democracy

Opinion polls, and television and radio 'phone-in' programmes are examples of relatively recent developments facilitating greater involvement of the general populace in the processes of government. Opinion-polling experiments using cable television, and locally originated cable television programmes dealing with political issues are further examples. Much more could be done.

Etzioni and his colleagues (e.g. Etzioni, 1972) have proposed a concept called MINERVA (Multiple Input Network for Evaluating Reaction, Votes and Attitudes) based on the idea of using a hierarchy of technologies starting with telephone conference calls to give everyone the opportunity to participate more in the political process. They point out that people could use telephone conference-call facilities, computer conferencing, or other similar systems to discuss political issues in the comfort of their own homes. If small groups chose representatives for higher-level groups, and those higher groups chose representatives for still higher ones, then a hierarchy of about seven levels could serve a whole country.

Some of the systems we shall be considering in later chapters make this general notion much more feasible now than when Etzioni proposed it originally. Videotex, for example, offers a simple system with expected mass penetration, whereby up-to-the-minute news, reactions, results of votes, conclusions of discussions, and other information can be provided at local, regional, national, and even international levels. Votes can also be taken as and when desired, quickly and easily using the 'response frames'.

Impacts On Education

The new electronic systems can be used to improve the administrative aspects of education in the same general way as for any organization, as discussed in later chapters. They will also have impacts of a more fundamental nature, for example:

- more educational materials used in the home, in the form of:
  — floppy discs and cassettes for personal computers
  — video discs for playing lectures, documentaries, etc. on the television screen when convenient
  — videotex as a source of information for educational projects
  — programmed learning through videotex and personal computers
  — and in other ways;
- more interest in continuing education throughout adulthood as the materials available become more interesting and varied, and the methods of learning more flexible.

The most significant impact, however, is likely to be on what is learned. There will be less emphasis on teaching facts that can be ascertained easily at the touch of a button, and more emphasis on general problem-solving skills and the ability to evaluate information that is available. The latter point is especially important as basically the same information will be available from several different suppliers and we shall have to choose carefully if we are to get good value for money.

Impacts On Health Care

Improved information handling in the health service could improve patient management and relieve medical staff, especially general practitioners, of some of the administrative burden on them. To take just one example: no family doctor can be expected to carry around in his or her head information about all the many new drugs that are constantly appearing on the market. (S)he has to rely on whatever information (s)he happens to have received from the drug companies—received and filed. Videotex is just one of several electronic systems that could provide family doctors with up-to-date information on drugs in a form designed to guide the doctor through to a suitable choice.

Electronic systems could also provide information support to medical ancillary workers, ensuring for example that ambulance staff and other people called upon to deal effectively with emergency situations would have more than their own memories to rely on in crisis situations. Such people could be guided to the correct actions to take by an electronic system capable of asking and answering questions. Videotex could do much along these lines.

Improved medical information available in an easy-to-use form in the home could help people take suitable preventive measures for themselves, their children and old people in their care. Some limited self-diagnosis or preliminary screening might also be possible—either at home or in the doctor's waiting room—to free the doctor of the most routine aspects of the job, allowing him or her to use the time with the patient more productively.

International Communication

Videotex and other electronic systems also pave the way for the improved sharing of information between nations. In agriculture, for example, there are some kinds of information—e.g. on pest control—of potential value to farmers everywhere. Recognizing this, the Commission of The European Communities (DG XIII) held a workshop in Luxembourg in February 1980 to discuss the potential contribution of videotex to the dissemination of agricultural information to farmers and agricultural advisory workers throughout Europe. Videotex could provide up-to-date information relevant to:

- local problems, e.g. local weather conditions;
- national problems, e.g. national industrial disputes, general market conditions, an outbreak of a disease, and other matters of concern to all farmers in a country;
- very general problems, e.g. climatic conditions, and general economic factors which affect all farmers or all farmers of a particular type (e.g. handling a particular crop).

Some areas where there is a very general need for agricultural information throughout the European Agricultural Community include, for example:

- pest control;
- technological advances;
- climatic conditions;
- general market prices;
- crop-growing techniques;
- community regulations;
- and so on.

In the USA also there is interest in using electronic systems. At the time of writing there is an experimental information system called 'green thumb' providing various 'magazines' of information to US farmers, including information on such topics as:

- weather;
- agricultural recommendations;
- market prices; and
- home economics.

We can imagine that the new systems might make valuable contributions to international communication in other areas as well as agriculture—for example, energy conservation.

Other Areas

The areas above are among the more interesting but the need for information is so pervasive that the new electronic systems will have a role to play almost everywhere we care to look.

CONCLUSIONS AND CAUTIONS

We have a choice, collectively, about our future. At the moment, we are moving towards an 'information society'. We do not know exactly what to expect, but we can see indications of some likely impacts. We must decide what we want. As Sarre and Blowers (1974) put it:

"Even the most rigorous approach to the future differs in two ways from the scientific method as commonly conceived. First, since the future does not exist, it cannot be the object of observation but only of conjecture and, second, the main reason for studying the future is the desire to influence it rather than understand it." (Sarre and Blowers, 1974, p. 2.)

We have not attempted in this chapter to describe the future—something that does not exist. We have instead reviewed a number of possible elements: working from home, neighbourhood work centres, headquarters cities, impacts on democracy, on education, on international communication and cooperation, and so forth. Electronic systems can facilitate changes in all of these areas, according to the roles we allow them to play.

We can all point to high-rise apartment buildings, cars, and other examples where greater understanding and more careful analysis might have helped us to achieve something better. What must we be careful of in relation to information systems? Will they result in more and more time being spent at home where more of our needs can be met electronically? Will the deserted streets become just violent playgrounds after dark? Will personal privacy be threatened? What other risks might arise? Let us learn from our previous experiences and make sure we base our plans in the information area on a firm foundation of adequate knowledge and understanding.

PART 2
Basic Concepts

Chapter 3

Types of information

The psychologist often uses the term 'information' when referring to a reduction in uncertainty following communication, often without feeling any need to describe the type of information—the context of the communication—involved. This follows the Shannon–Weiner concept of information discussed in the next chapter. The emphasis is on the amount of information, not the variety. A similar use is made of the term when the psychologist talks of the amount of information 'contained in' an object of judgement. Used in this way, the concept has formed a cornerstone of the theory of pattern recognition (e.g. Corcoran, 1971). It has also been applied to the question of human preferences for certain kinds of patterns (e.g. Dorfman and McKenna, 1966), and could be used to describe consistencies in some kinds of psychophysiological data (e.g. Gale, Christie, and Penfold, 1971). These are just a few of the ways in which the 'amount' aspect of information has proved useful to psychologists.

There are some areas where considering only the amount of information is not sufficient. In designing instrument panels and other types of information display, it is necessary to take account of the sensory modality, e.g. whether the information is visual or auditory, and other parameters, as well as the amount (e.g. Chapanis, 1976). There is some evidence that the type of information is also important in such fundamental areas as psychophysiological responses to stimuli (e.g. Christie et al., 1972; Gale et al., 1972). It is also certainly important in the present context, in considering information at the 'macro' level: information in the form of memoranda, reports, abstracts, news items, books, letters, notes, and so forth. In this chapter we shall see how far we can go towards a taxonomy of information which has general applicability at this level of conceptualization.

What we are looking for is a set of meaningful categories related to one another by an explicit, sensible logic. Some areas of science have benefited from such a scheme for many years. In biology, for example, all living things are allocated to categories called species. All the beings in a particular species share certain characteristics and have some features in common with other species in the same genus (the next level up in the hierarchical classification scheme). All beings in a particular genus share some characteristics with those in other genera belonging to the same class. And so on up to the level of kingdoms, of which there are only two on this planet: animal and plant. By being told or by deducing the category to which a being belongs, a biologist can tell a great deal about it and its 'relatives' in the animal or plant kingdom. The chemist similarly has the benefit of the periodic table of the elements, and other examples could be cited for other areas of science.

Such a useful scheme has not been agreed for the current area of inquiry.

DEFINITIONS

One difficulty concerns definition. To understand this, we need to consider the two most relevant concepts: 'information' and 'communication'. These two are intimately connected. For example, Ference (1970) suggests that 'The term "information" includes any input to a person in the communications system.' Variety of information is connected with variety of communication. For neither concept, however, has a definition been agreed by all, or even the majority, of scientists.

An indication of the variety of definitions which have been proposed is provided by Dance (1970). Dance drew a wide range of definitions of communication from published sources and subjected them to an analysis of their content. The substantive terms of each definition were listed and collated into a master list. Out of approximately 4560 words or tokens, fifteen terms were identified which were considered to be distinct conceptual components. The variety of definitions seemed to be explicable largely in terms of these components, which were:

- symbols/verbal/speech;
- understanding;
- interaction/relation/social process;
- reduction of uncertainty;
- process;
- transfer/transmission/interchange;
- linking/binding;
- commonality;
- channel/carrier/means/route;
- replicating memories;
- discriminative response/behaviour modifying/response/change;
- stimuli;
- intentional;
- time/situation;
- power.

As an example, the definition of communication as 'the verbal interchange of thought or idea' (from Hoben, 1954, p. 77) largely reflects the first of Dance's components, symbols/verbal/speech. Defined as 'a process that makes common to two or several what was the monopoly of one or some' (from Gode, 1959), it largely reflects Dance's 'commonality' component. Clearly, a very wide variety of definitions is possible by combining the fifteen components above in various ways, which is exactly what Dance found.

In a similar vein, Barnlund (1968) has suggested that communication can be conceptualized:

- structurally (sender–message–receiver);
- functionally (encoding–decoding);
- in terms of intent (expressive–instrumental);
- with reference to source (production of messages);
- with reference to channel (signal transmission);
- with reference to receiver (attribution of meaning);
- with reference to code (symbolizing);
- with reference to effect (evoking of response);
- as the process of transmitting stimuli (e.g. Schramm);
- as the establishment of a commonage (e.g. Morris);
- as conveying meaning (e.g. Newcomb);
- as all the procedures by which one mind affects another (e.g. Weaver);
- as interaction by means of signs and symbols (e.g. Lundberg);
- as the sharing of activity, excitement, information (e.g. Hefferline);
- as the signals that individuals make to each other and which may be conscious or unconscious (e.g. Cameron).

This will give some idea of the range of concepts that have been discussed in the literature. The lists above are meant only to be illustrative; they are by no means comprehensive.

TYPES

A second difficulty concerns an overabundance of terms that have been proposed to describe different types of information. Information has variously been described as or as relating to:

- various types of uncertainty, e.g. structural or relational uncertainty (Whittemore and Yovits, 1973);
- innovative compared with unequivocal (e.g. Weick, 1969);
- quantitative, time-phased, short, or as relating to a wide range of other characteristics (e.g. McCormick, 1976);
- input or output (Baird, 1977);
- internal resources or external (Stamper, 1973);
- environmental, motivational or instrumental (Farrace, Marge, and Russell, 1977).

These are just a few of the distinctions which have been considered particularly important by the authors concerned. The list could easily be lengthened manyfold by adding new terms or expanding on those already mentioned as in many cases the authors use the terms to cover a range of even more specific examples.

It seems that types of information have been identified according to all sorts of different criteria. To return briefly to the biological analogy, it is as though the following types of animals and plants had been identified: tall ones; short ones; beings that live a long time; beings that have four legs; beings that are green; beings that can change their colour to merge with their background; beings that eat fish; and so on. Clearly, such a 'typology' would only lead to confusion.

It could be argued that the situation is akin to another area of psychology: the description of personality. Here, at first glance, one might be dismayed at the apparently open-ended way in which personality can be described: good-humoured; unsociable; thinking; feeling; warm; pleasant; erratic; introverted; and so forth. However, much progress has been made in sorting out this confusion by Cattell (e.g. Cattell, 1965), Eysenck (e.g. Eysenck, 1970) and others by the use of factor-analytic and related methods. Many questions remain to be answered, it is true, but at least there is now a reasonable degree of agreement amongst the major theorists as to what the main dimensions of personality are. It is possible that an analogous approach applied to the areas of information and communication would yield equally fruitful results.

Some progress in this direction has been made in the area of person-to-person communications in business and government. Short, Williams, and Christie (1976), report a series of studies conducted by the Communications Studies Group of University College London in which factor-analytic and related techniques were applied to the problem of describing and classifying meetings. The resulting classification scheme was helpful in integrating the experimental and field research done on the effectiveness and acceptability of telecommunications with the survey work aimed at assessing the impact of these media on the amount of travelling likely to be done in the future. It may be instructive to review briefly what was involved in this research.

The first stage was a round of 65 open-ended interviews designed to elicit words and phrases used by managers to describe their meetings, especially in relation to: the purpose of the meeting; what went on during the meeting; and the atmosphere created. The respondents were drawn from general management, personnel, marketing and planning, and other departments, of organizations in Greater London.

The second stage was a round of self-report questionnaires, completed by 311 personnel in a wide range of business organizations. The questionnaire was based on the material elicited in the interviews, and included 104 descriptors of meetings, in the form of words or short phrases. Respondents were asked to give each descriptor a score from 0 to 6 to indicate its relevance to their most recent meeting. The items were grouped into three sections dealing with: 'functions of the meeting'; 'what went on at the meeting'; and 'atmosphere of the meeting'.

The three sections of the questionnaire were submitted separately to factor analysis. Several factor analyses were conducted, starting with different numbers of factors and performing different rotations. The following orthogonal (varimax) factors were finally adopted as providing the best solutions. In each case the factors are indicated by the highest loading questionnaire item; further details are given by Short, Williams, and Christie (1976).

Functions:

- task allocation;
- information giving;
- dismissal of an employee;
- presentation of a report;
- problem discussion;
- appraisal (of another department's or organization's services);
- review of subordinate's work;
- tactical decision making;
- advice giving.

Activities:

- conflict;
- gathering background information;
- problem solving;
- bargaining;
- work-related gossip;
- generating ideas.

Atmosphere:

- angry;
- constructive;
- cautious;
- informal.

These factor solutions are relevant to some of the research described later. Here, the important point is that a systematic, empirical approach to description and classification paid dividends in relation to person-to-person communications. Short, Williams, and Christie show how later research built upon the foundations provided by the factor analyses to estimate the likely extent to which new telecommunications media would impact business and government meetings.

Very little parallel work has been done in the area of information. The only comparable study appears to be one by Arms and Arms (1978) who have attempted to use cluster analysis applied to journal citations to determine broad categories of information. Their basic reasoning was that two different journals cover similar areas to the extent that they are cited by other journals with similar frequencies. The researchers were disappointed with their results when they applied the method to a sample of 52 000 social-science citations—only about 100 journals could be clustered confidently—and concluded that 'cluster analysis is not a practical method of designing secondary services in the social sciences'.

The disappointment expressed by Arms and Arms should not be taken as a reason for rejecting an empirical approach to the problem of describing and classifying information or information-related communications. Their study was very limited in its objectives, dealing as it did with journal citations, and there are many other possibilities for research. Even given the limited scope of their enquiry, it is possible that more fruitful results might have been obtained by: using judgements of similarity rather than citation patterns; and by using factor analysis instead of cluster analysis.

The systematic, empirical analysis of the variety of information items generated and used by people in offices and at home is an area where much research is needed.

A PRAGMATIC APPROACH

In the absence of a satisfactory, agreed taxonomy, we find ourselves forced to take a pragmatic approach to the problem of describing and classifying the types of information and communications which are the subject of this book. Two main principles have guided the approach adopted: The needs to

- be relevant to technological trends;
- encompass as many as possible of the types of information discussed in the literature.

Type A And Type B Communication

It is important at the outset to recognize that information and communication are closely related. An item of information such as a memorandum or a research report is normally produced with the intention of communicating something to someone. The 'something' may be the content of the item, such as a research finding, or it may be something else—perhaps the fact that some research has been done or even simply that the author is capable of having reports published (which may be important to the author in terms of career advancement, for example). The 'someone' may be a known person (usually the case with memoranda) or an unknown set of people (often the case with research reports). At any rate, the production and use of items of information such as memoranda, letters, reports, and similar items, seems to be associated with one type of communication. We shall call this Type B communication.

Type B communication is to be distinguished from Type A, which is direct person-to-person communication in dyads or groups. Telephone conversations, teleconferences (e.g. two-way television), and face-to-face meetings are examples of Type A communication. The role of electronic systems in relation to Type A communication was the subject of the book by Short, Williams, and Christie (1976). In this book we shall concentrate on Type B.

A defining difference between the two types of communication is that Type B always involves a functionally significant store of some kind, whether it be a paper-based file or an electronic store, whereas Type A never does. The reader who wishes to be pedantic might argue that transatlantic telephone calls (Type A communication) and some other examples of Type A communication involve delays due to the transmission and switching of signals which takes finite time. Such delays, however, should not be considered functionally significant. Examples of functionally significant stores include:

- letters, notes, floppy discs (a form of electronic store), and all other instances where the information can be retrieved repeatedly; and
- all stores where the delay between commitment of the information to store and retrieval from store is so long as to preclude any possibility of a free-flowing conversation with rapid exchanges, e.g. one person interrupting another in mid-sentence.

The second category can include instances where retrieval of the information from store automatically erases it, thus making repeated retrieval of the same information impossible.

This approach to the definition of Type B communication is preferable to adopting a tighter definition as such a definition would be likely to be either too abstract to be helpful or so narrow that it could easily be rendered irrelevant by technological advances.

A Multidimensional Model

Within the domain encompassed by Type B communication any item of information, I, can be described in terms of its values on a set of dimensions, D_1-D_n, as follows:

$$I = D_1 + D_2 + D_3 + \ldots + D_n.$$

The complete set of relevant dimensions is very large, probably infinite. This is reflected in the wide range of terms used to define and describe types of information, as discussed above. Nevertheless, in any given context, some dimensions will be more important than others. This sub-set may be called the set of salient dimensions. Although the dimensions which are salient will vary from one context to another, there are four broad dimensions which are likely to be important in most contexts. These are:

- relation to behaviour;
- organizational penetration;
- item content;
- technological fit.

These reflect the fact that information is:

(a) produced and used by individual people;
(b) produced and used by people in groups of varying sizes;
(c) produced according to some kind of logical structure; and

(d) produced and used using some kind of technology (from quill pen to electronic word processor).

These four key dimensions will now be considered in turn.

Relation To Behaviour

The relation of an item of information to the behaviour of individuals needs to be considered at two main levels:

- general (relating to 'purpose');
- specific (relating to the psychological mechanisms involved).

At the general level, it is useful to relate information to Thorngren's distinction (discussed by Short, Williams, and Christie, 1976, and by Christie and Elton, 1979) between the orientation, planning, and programmed activities of organizations. Very briefly, 'orientation' activities enable an organization to adjust to changes in the environment. They are often novel, unstructured, complex, and involve information about, for example: new markets, new products, new competitors, changes in legislation. By contrast, 'programmed' activities are routine, repetitive and standardized. The information involved is more likely to take the form of routine reports done to a consistent format, standard letters, and so forth. 'Planning' activities come in between and often involve defining programmed procedures.

The differences between information relating to these types of activities in terms of their predictability of structure have implications for the suitability of some electronic systems such as word processing and viewdata, discussed later. Word processing in particular—especially in its simpler forms—offers greatest productivity increases and therefore is most likely to be implemented when used for highly programmed activities. Standard letters are particularly suitable, and it is surprising how many letters can be composed by specifying which paragraphs from a standard set are to be included, which numbers are to be entered into standard places, and so forth. They can be personalized by making minor changes here and there as the person writing them feels appropriate. Contracts and other documents where the contents are used over and over again with only minor changes are also good examples.

Thorngren's classification overlaps with several other theorists'. For example, Vickery's (1973) 'innovative information' overlaps considerably with the concept of 'orientation' activity, and his 'line communications' and 'operational feedback' provide many examples of 'programmed' activity.

The distinction between orientation, planning and programmed activities thus provide a useful way of relating information to behaviour at a general level.

At the specific level, many different psychological models have been proposed to describe the mechanisms by which people make the choices and arrive at the decisions which guide their behaviour. Many of these have been reviewed by Fishbein and Ajzen (1975). For present purposes we shall adopt Fishbein's own model, as it is similar to many others and additionally includes some unique elements.

According to Fishbein's model, actual behaviour (B) is closely related to behavioural intention (BI), although many factors may on occasion intervene to frustrate a person's intentions. Behavioural intention is itself determined chiefly by two main variables: attitude toward the act (A_{act}); and normative belief (NB). These are approximately: how positively or negatively the person feels about the act (behaviour) in question, in terms of salient 'costs' and 'benefits'; and, what the person thinks other key people would expect him or her to do. The central equation is:

$$BI = A_{act} \cdot W_1 + NB \cdot W_2,$$

where W_1 and W_2 are weights that vary according to the type of behaviour involved.

Attitude toward the act can be broken down further into: the strength of salient beliefs (B_i); and, corresponding evaluations (e_i). Thus:

$$A_{act} = B_i e_i.$$

The following example will help to clarify the model. John Smith may have a behavioural intention to stay at home and watch television tonight. This is determined by two main factors. First, he feels the benefits outweigh the costs (A_{act}). Secondly, he feels his wife and his boss would expect him to. His wife would because she has expressed an interest in seeing him stay in more often; his boss would because he mentioned that he would be a member of a panel taking part in a documentary being shown that night. The salient beliefs relating to A_{act} turn out to be as follows:

- money: it costs less to stay at home and John Smith is short of money;
- weather: it is raining heavily;
- convenience: the car is being repaired so he would have to depend on public transport;
- interest: John Smith happens to be interested in seeing the documentary anyway, quite apart from the fact his boss is involved in it.

Fishbein has not discussed his model explicitly in relation to the classification of information, but one can see that it is obviously relevant and indeed provides a very useful scheme. Consider the example of John Smith. Different sorts of information could cause him to change his mind, in particular information relating to:

- A_{act}: John Smith receives a letter from his solicitor informing him he has received some money from a deceased relative, the weather forecast says it will be a fine evening, the garage telephones to say the car is ready, and there is an announcement early in the day that the documentary will have to be postponed due to industrial action;
- NB: John Smith's wife suggests it would be nice for them to go out to dinner together for a change and maybe take in the theatre as well.

There is also a third kind of information suggested by the model: That relating to evaluations (e_i). In the John Smith example, he may evaluate the possibility of spending money very negatively but the possibility of getting wet only marginally negatively. He may receive information that could change these evaluations. For example, if he were to learn that an epidemic of influenza had just broken out, he might then evaluate the possibility of getting wet by going out in the rain more negatively than before.

Even if John Smith's intention to stay at home and watch television remains high, this might not be reflected in his actual behaviour. For example, the television might break down, or friends could turn up unexpectedly for a visit, or an emergency might arise to demand his attention in other directions. Of course, all of these eventualities could be described in terms of information relating to them and the impacts on salient beliefs (including shifts in which items are salient).

Fishbein's model—a variant of expectancy-value theory—therefore provides a useful way of relating information to behaviour at a specific level.

Returning to the general formula above for our multidimensional model for the classification of items of information, and considering only the first of our key dimensions, we can now write the following as examples of possible types of information:

$$I = O; NB + D_2 + D_3,$$

which means an item relating to orientation activity (O) and influencing normative belief (NB) about that activity.

$$I = P; A_{act} + D_2 + D_3,$$

which means an item relating to programmed activity (P) and influencing salient beliefs about that activity, or the evaluations associated with those beliefs (A_{act}), and so on.

Organizational Penetration

Perhaps the fundamental distinction in terms of organizational penetration is between information which crosses the organizational boundary being considered and information which does not. If information crosses the boundary it must either be entering or leaving, and three fundamental types of information can be recognized:

- 'material' or 'input' information;
- 'system' or 'intra-unit' information;
- 'product' or 'output' information.

Product information is the information which an organizational unit produces for outside consumption. It might include, for example: books, newspapers, market research reports, journals, magazines, viewdata pages (discussed later), and so forth.

Material information is the same sort of information on the input side. It is information required by an organizational unit to produce its outputs. It might include, for example: research reports, surveys, statistical abstracts, books, journals, and so forth.

System information is all the information which is produced within an organizational unit and stays within it. It does not enter as material information, and it does not leave as product.

These three kinds of information apply wherever one chooses to draw the boundaries which define the organizational unit being considered. At one extreme they apply to the individual person who receives information (material), sends out information (product), and keeps his or her own files containing notes and other items produced just 'for the file' (system information). At the other extreme they apply to the organization as a whole.

A hypothetical example will help to clarify the nature of these three kinds of information. In this example, the organizational unit is a whole company—a credit card company. This company needs to receive a wide variety of information to operate effectively, for example: information on card transactions, information on bank interest rates, information about individual customers relating to their credit status, information about the long-term prospects for credit-card companies, and so forth. All of this is material information.

Product information is all the items of information output, for example: statements to account holders informing them of the balances in their accounts, information on rules and procedures, information on special offers for account holders, information output from the advertising department on services the company offers, and so on. In between, all the memoranda, internal reports, and other items which are produced internally for use solely by company personnel make up the system information.

System information forms one component—usually the major one—of the 'price' extracted by the system used by the organization in converting material information into product. It is analogous to the heat generated by a transformer in converting electrical energy in one form (say, 240 V) into electrical output in a more useful form (say, 9 V). Another component is that part of the material information which does not become incorporated in the product but is simply wasted.

A further type of information which needs to be distinguished at this stage is that required to maintain an organization made up of many individual units (or a larger system, such as society, made up of many organizations). This is metasystem information. It is similar to system information but, unlike system information, it extends beyond the boundaries of the individual organizational unit and serves to link different units together. A request from the finance department to the marketing department, or from the personnel department to all departments, can be regarded as examples of metasystem information if the individual departments are regarded as the organizational units of primary concern.

These four types of information—material, product, system, and metasystem—are shown diagramatically in Figure 3.1

44

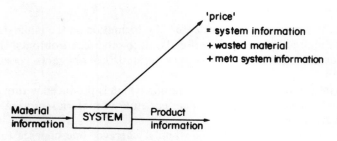

Figure 3.1.   Material/product and system information.

Returning to our general formula for the classification of items of information, and considering only the second of our four key dimensions, we can now write the following as examples of possible types of information:

$$I = D_1 + M + D_3 + D_4,$$

which means an item of material information, i.e. information being input to the organizational unit being considered;

$$I = D_1 + S + D_3 + D_4,$$

which means an item of system information, i.e. information that is produced within and never leaves the organizational unit being considered, and so on.

Item Content

An item's value on the third of our key dimensions specifies whether the item contains 'programme' information or 'data' information.

'Programme information' and 'data information' are analogous to the 'program' and 'data' of data processing. Data information is words, numbers, shapes, or other symbols which are manipulated or otherwise acted on. Programme information specifies how the data information is to be acted on. In contrast to the normal situation in data processing, data information is very often in a very loose, arbitrary and unpredictable format. Programme information is just as often imprecise, vague and difficult to interpret unambiguously.

A typical example of programme and data information might be:

"Please have a look through these files and see what you can find on the company that could give us a basis to work on."

In this example, the files are the data information and the rest is the programme information. The example is hypothetical but not especially unusual in business communications, and it serves to illustrate the lack of precision which is characteristic of such communications. Unambiguous interpretation of the programme information depends heavily on context, and one can imagine that the files referred to contain papers in all sorts of different formats. A heavy load is put on the human.

A similar degree of imprecision and freedom of format in the data processing environment would probably mean the program would not run or that many errors would be made in reading and manipulating the data. An interesting characteristic of electronic office systems as they are evolving is that they are designed to accept information 'as it is found'; at the present time they usually require the information to be input through a typewriter-like keyboard, but there are usually few constraints on format—in a few years, voice input will remove even the need for key-boarding.

Two types of data information need to be distinguished:

- basic information, and
- meta-information

which correspond roughly to Schreider's 'semantic' information and 'meta-infor-mation', as discussed by Belkin (1978). Basic information is what the message or text is actually about. Meta-information is information about how the basic in-formation is organized. For example, the contents page of a book can be considered meta-information relative to the rest of the book (which is the basic information) since it contains only information about how the basic information is organized.

The distinction between basic information and meta-information is of practical importance in the design of electronic systems. For example, in videotex systems (see Chapter 5), most frames displayed carry some meta-information in the form of instructions to the user concerning the options available or other information about the information available (e.g. 'no such page exists—try again'); some frames contain nothing but meta-information.

There are various levels of meta-information. In the videotex case, specifically British Telecom's Prestel service, user directories are published giving the frame locations of the organizations putting information in the system. The directories themselves can be considered to contain both basic information (the Prestel page numbers) and meta-information (an index to help the user find the appropriate part of the directory).

(It is of incidental interest to note that this is an example of how electronic sys-tems—Prestel—and paper systems—the directories—do not have to compete but can be used in combination for more effective Type B communication.)

Returning to our general formula for the classification of items of information, we can now write the following examples:

$$I = D_1 + D_2 + P + D_4,$$

which means an item of programme information (e.g. 'see page 93');

$$I = D_1 + D_2 + B + D_4,$$

which means an item of basic information (e.g. 'snow is expected in parts of the north-east this evening'), and so on.

Technological Fit

The fourth of our four key dimensions is likely to become less important during the 1980s as electronic systems become capable of handling a wider variety of types of information. At the present time, however, it is useful to distinguish between four main types of information in regard to this dimension. They are listed below with examples of the kinds of electronic or other systems that can handle them at the present time:

- data (large quantities of numerical information), e.g. traditional data-processing equipment, mini- and microcomputers;
- text, e.g. word processors, videotex systems, microfiche;
- image (photographs, charts, handwriting), e.g. facsimile machines, microfiche; slow-scan video;
- voice, e.g. dictation machines.

These types of systems are described in Chapter 5. During the 1980s systems will become more readily available which will be capable of handling various combinations of these types of information simultaneously, including developments such as direct voice input into word-processing systems.

In terms of our classification formula, we may write:

$$I = D_1 + D_2 + D_3 + T$$

for information in the form of text; and so on.

General Comments On The Model

It will be apparent that the elements in the classification formula are not additive in a simple algebraic fashion, that is the values on the various dimensions cannot be combined according to the rules of simple arithmetic to yield a single, easily interpretable value for I. In this sense, the formula is more like a chemical formula than an algebraic or arithmetic equation.

It will also be apparent that, depending on how narrowly one defines any given item of information, different values on some of the dimensions may not be mutually exclusive. For example, it was noted above that some items of information, e.g. videotex frames, can contain both basic information and meta-information. This can, however, be dealt with simply by assigning proportions, for example:

$$I = 0.5O, \quad 0.5Pl; 0.5NB, 0.5A_{\text{act}} + S + 0.1M, .09B + T$$

means an item of system information (S) which is 90 per cent basic information (B), is in text form (T), is concerned equally with orientation (O) and planning (Pl), and bears equally on normative belief (NB) and attitude toward the act (A_{act}).

The proportions assigned will inevitably depend to some extent on one's point of view. The formula is therefore a psychological one rather than a physical one, and reflects the view taken by some information scientists (see Belkin, 1978) that information is a relationship between a person and an item.

These points will be explored further in the next chapter.

CONCLUSIONS

The psychologist often uses the term 'information' without feeling any need to describe the type of information involved in much if any detail. We, however, are concerned with describing the variety of information. We are concerned to do this at a level of generality corresponding roughly to the definition of items of information as individual documents, pages of text, paragraphs, books, floppy discs, and so forth, i.e. at a 'macro' level. We find ourselves hampered by a proliferation of concepts and lack of agreement concerning definitions and classification schemes. Very little research has been done on the empirical structure of information at the macro level. We have been forced to take a pragmatic approach, describing items of information in terms of their values on salient dimensions. We have identified four dimensions which seem likely to be especially important in most contexts with which we shall be concerned. These are: relation to behaviour; organizational penetration; item content; and technological fit.

Chapter 4

The value of information

There is a well-known phrase in computer circles: 'Garbage in, garbage out'. It means that no matter how sophisticated or clever the computer program, if it is fed useless data it will yield useless outputs. The same sort of thing applies to information more generally. No matter how sophisticated or clever the electronic information system, if the information it is handling is useless performance will be low. Put another way, one might say there is no sense in improving the efficiency with which information is handled if the information itself is of no value.

This is being recognized increasingly by organizations which are automating their office functions. Many of these organizations recognize that their paper-based information systems are overloaded with much information that is either redundant or of little value, or both. Rather than automating such information, these organizations prefer to assess the value of the information currently flowing through their offices, and then automate only that which is valuable. A large multinational consumer-products company which recently completed such a 'weeding-out' project found that over 90 per cent of the papers currently being processed and stored could be dispensed with entirely, leaving only 10 per cent that there was any real point in automating. This particular example may be extreme but it serves to illustrate the kind of inefficiency that can develop if the value of information in an organization is not audited regularly.

It is important that value is assessed accurately. Clearly, there is no sense in wasting resources on processing and storing valueless information; equally, one does not want to 'throw out the baby with the bath water'. The important thing is to get the balance right. The question is how to do this.

It surely is indisputable that at least some information has some value. Many lines of evidence indicate this. For example: People buy books, and the price they are prepared to pay presumably reflects in part the value of the information to them; people keep records—both official and personal; companies and government organizations spend large amounts of money producing and storing files of papers, libraries of books and other documents, and so forth. Other examples can be given as well. The author was recently told of a case where a company was taking delivery of a large quantity of chemical. When the chemical was emptied into the designated storage vats it ate right through them, destroying the vats, wasting the chemical, and causing considerable damage. It was a costly mistake. Interestingly, the relevant information was already available in the company's own files. In a similar vein, instances have been recorded where devices of various sorts have been completely re-invented from scratch, simply because the people concerned did not have access to, or felt no need to refer to, the relevant information. The cost of wasted effort in such instances can be very high. Conversely, a principle of certain kinds of industrial espionage is that it may be less expensive to acquire information from a competitor, even if unwilling, than to go through all the research and development work oneself. In some cases, the value of information can be measured in terms of lives; this is part of the reason for marking chemical containers on lorries so that in the event of an accident emergency teams will know what to do and what not to do.

These examples may serve to demonstrate that information can have some value, but they do little more than that. In particular, they do not show how the value of any particular items of information can be assessed adequately. Take videotex as a practical example. In a videotex system, information is made available in the form of 'pages' displayed on a television screen. The user pays to read the information, and the information is charged on a page-by-page basis.

At first glance, the price charged would seem to provide a useful measure of the value of the information. To the extent this is true, it is true only as an average—an average both over a large number of people using the system, and over significant periods of time (since the value of the information may depend upon circumstances, e.g. traffic information is likely to be more valuable if one is about to travel than if one is not). Even with this proviso price provides only a very rough guide. Some of the most valuable information provided on Prestel (British Telecom's videotex service) is provided free of charge by government bodies and, in some cases, private companies. The cost of providing the information on Prestel is also unreliable as a guide to value because it depends on many factors (e.g. whether it is already being provided through some other medium) and is unlikely to bear a very close relationship to its value to the user. Finally, price considerations do not help an organization very much to decide what information, if any, to put on a system like videotex—especially if it is an 'in-house' system for use only by the organization's own personnel, where the concept of charging people to read the information does not apply very well.

Measuring the value of information accurately is a task for the psychologist because the value of information depends ultimately on the people who use the information and the circumstances in which they use it.

In this chapter we shall review some of the concepts that have been proposed in connection with assessing the value of information, and see how far we can go toward developing a model which has fairly general applicability.

CONCEPTS RELATING TO VALUE

The Shannon and Weaver Model

The Shannon and Weaver 'bit' index is probably the best-known measure of information and has had a significant impact on the work of psychologists in several different areas. It is therefore worthy of our attention but we shall see that it actually has rather limited applications in our present context, for reasons we shall discuss.

Weaver (1949) distinguishes between communication problems at three levels:

(A) The accuracy with which the symbols of communication can be transmitted (the technical problem).
(B) The precision with which the transmitted symbols convey the desired meaning (the semantic problem).
(C) The effectiveness with which the received meaning affects conduct in the desired way (the effectiveness problem).

The 'bit' measure applies to the technical problem (Level A), and is a measure of the amount of information. As Weaver puts it:

> "To be sure, this word information in communication theory relates not so much to what you *do* say, as to what you *could* say. That is, information is a measure of one's freedom of choice when one selects a message. If one is confronted with a very elementary situation where one has to choose one of two alternative messages, then it is arbitrarily said that the information, associated with this situation, is unity."

In general, the amount of information is measured by the logarithm to the base 2 of the number of available choices (possible events). One of two possible events conveys one 'bit' ('binary digit') of information; one of four conveys 2 bits; one of eight conveys 3 bits; one of sixteen conveys 4 bits; and so on.

An example given by Weaver illustrates the basic limitation to this model from the psychological point of view. The example deals with the binary situation:

> "The two messages between which one must choose, in such a selection, can be anything one likes. One might be the text of the King James Version of the Bible, and the other might be "Yes". The transmitter might code these two messages so that "zero" is the signal for the first, and "one" the signal for the second."

The 'bit' measure ignores the 'content' of the message entirely, together with all the psychologically significant factors associated with that, e.g. 'usefulness', 'informativeness', and other factors considered below.

The measure can be applied to the question of value, but primarily in relation to the value of media. Indeed, it is normal practice for equipment suppliers to measure the capacity of the storage media and other items they offer in terms of bits. For example, a 'floppy disc'—about half the size of an A4 sheet of paper (but about the thickness of a 45 r.p.m. record)—can carry many more bits of information than a typed sheet of paper. In fact, a floppy disc used in a word processing system often carries as much information as 60–150 A4 sheets of typed paper. We can rate the value of the floppy disc as higher than the value of paper, in this sense.

Relevance

One might suppose that relevant information is more valuable than irrelevant information, and that relevance might therefore serve as a useful index of the value of information. In practice, there are some complications.

First, one has to specify, relevant to what—and when? Information that is relevant to finding entertainment is not of much real value if it deals only with films currently showing at suburban cinemas when I am interested only in plays that will be running in the West End next week. Some information I have available that is relevant to the psychology of motivation is not of much value to me in connection with a research paper I am writing if it does not address the particular aspect of motivation with which I am concerned.

Secondly, it has been argued (Kent, 1974), that relevance judgements—at least those made by users of information retrieval systems—are too influenced by motivational levels to provide a reliable index of value. Once a user receives an item which is sufficient for his or her purposes, it is argued, further items may be disregarded as being somehow 'irrelevant' even though they may in some other sense be even more relevant than the item accepted.

Thirdly, relevance depends upon one's point of view. In this connection, Harmon (1970) distinguishes between 'user relevance' and 'system relevance'. User relevance is the user's judgement of the strength of the relationship between his or her need and the response of an information retrieval system. System relevance, on the other hand, is the system's assessment of the degree of relationship between the information it has available and the user's query. Harmon does not specify the criteria by which a retrieval system should make this assessment but one can see that the two measures of relevance would be likely to diverge in practice.

Usefulness

Kent (1974) suggested that 'usefulness' might provide a better index of value than 'relevance'. Unfortunately, apart from saying that it should not depend on users' judgements, he does not indicate how it should be measured. Kegan (1970) does provide some guidance in this regard. He has pointed out that usefulness is a multidimensional concept, and he has suggested five ways in which an item of information might be considered useful, as follows:

(a) The item itself is cited.
(b) The information in the item is reported.
(c) The item causes the user to take some action other than citing or reporting.
(d) The item has some other effect on the user, e.g. changing his or her confidence in a research finding.
(e) The item is used in some other way.

These five uses of information fit readily into a research environment where researchers are retrieving information from libraries or automated retrieval systems for use in writing research reports or in other research related activities. However, they also apply in general management situations and uses (c)–(e) apply very generally indeed, even to applications in the home.

Informativeness

One could argue that information does not have to be useful to be of value—it can simply be informative. Informativeness was used as an index of value by Ravensborg (1970), in assessing the effectiveness of automated nursing notes. In this study, automated nursing notes (ANN) were compared with traditional notes (TNN) as to efficiency in recording and transmitting information and ability to preserve the identifiability of individual patients' behaviour. The study was conducted in an adolescent psychiatric unit.

Two observers filled out ANN twice weekly on four male and four female adolescents. After an observation period of one month, a stenographer copied all the TNN which had been made during the month and edited them to remove references to specific persons. Then two nursing education instructors summarized both the ANN and TNN. The completed summaries were then submitted to ten members of the relevant medical records committee with instructions to compare the summaries (paired) and judge which was the more informative. Identifiability was assessed by asking four staff members of the adolescent unit to try to identify the patients concerned from the summaries.

The ten judges compared the summaries on the eight patients observed, making a total of 80 judgements. Of these 80 judgements, 61 were in favour of ANN (a statistically significant difference). In terms of identifiability, patients were identified correctly 10 times on the basis of ANN and 9 times on the basis of TNN (not a statistically significant difference). These results suggest that the ANN were more informative and no more likely than the TNN to reveal the identities of the patients concerned.

Information Utility Estimates

McKendry, Enderwick, and Harrison (1971), suggest that in many 'operational situations' (and they are thinking primarily of military contexts) it is impossible to measure the utility of information on a rational basis, and subjective estimates

Figure 4.1.   McKendry *et al.*'s information utility estimates.

---

1. $b = \sum\limits_{j=1}^{n} (k_j * a_j),$

where b = worth of information contained in a message;

n = number of content areas in a message;

k_j = number of items in the jth content area;

a_j = average perceived value of items of information in the jth content area.

2. $B = \sum\limits_{i=1}^{N} b_i,$

where N = number of messages;

B = the total information value of the N messages.

---

are the only feasible alternative. They propose two formulae, shown in Figure 4.1, for estimating the worth of information in a single message and in a set of messages. Though they talk of messages and refer to military applications, the formulae could obviously be applied to other information items, such as memoranda, letters, videotex pages, even bulky reports (or pages of reports), just as easily.

The researchers report on several experiments which demonstrate the value of the information utility measures in predicting task performance. In a typical experiment air crew being trained in antisubmarine operations worked in a simulator to seek out target submarines. They were provided with a sequence of 'sensor returns' (items of information) which had been scaled previously using paired-comparison judgements of experienced tactical coordination officers. Results showed that the proportion of search area remaining per unit time decreased as a linear function of perceived information value, indicating that the utility estimates were psychologically meaningful, at least in this situation.

Yovits and Abilock's Model

Yovits and Abilock (1974) propose a model for considering the value of information which links information to human decision-making; indeed, they define information as 'data of value in decision-making'. More precisely, they regard information as that which changes the probability distribution representing the decision-maker's overall inclination towards each or all the possible courses of action open to him or her (his or her 'decision state'). They propose a measure, I, of the amount of information 'contained in' a decision state, as follows:

$$I = m \sum\limits_{i=1}^{m} \{P(a_i)\}^2 - 1,$$

where m is the number of possible courses of action available to the decision-maker, and $P(a_i)$ is the probability of each course of action.

The value of I is zero when all the $P(a_i)$'s are equal to $1/m$, i.e. a state of complete uncertainty. It will assume its maximum value of $m - 1$ when one of the $P(a_i)$'s is unity and all the others are zero, i.e. a state of complete certainty.

When there are only two possible courses of action, I varies from zero (complete uncertainty) to unity (complete certainty). Yovits and Abilock choose this situation to define a unit of information which they call a 'binary choice unit' or 'b.c.u.'.

In general, the maximum amount of information for any given decision state will be $m - 1$ b.c.u.'s. The value of information can therefore be assessed in terms of the number of b.c.u.'s reduction in uncertainty reflected in the change in the distribution of the $P(a_i)$'s resulting from receipt of the information.

The b.c.u. is a psychological measure because, as Yovits and Abilock say, the value of any items of information, measured in b.c.u.'s, 'must be time and situation dependent since the same data will have different significance to different decision-makers at any point in time or to the same decision-maker at different times'.

General Comments

The foregoing six approaches to the question of value are illustrative of the broad range of theoretical concepts which have been proposed in the literature, although no attempt has been made to be exhaustive. They fall into two main classes which can be referred to as 'actual' and 'potential', as follows.

Those in the 'actual' class are concerned with the effect of information on actual behaviour or its assumed immediate precursors. The three models in this class are:

* Shannon and Weaver's 'bit' model, where the value of information is reflected in the correlation between the inputs to a system (stimuli) and the outputs (responses);
* McKendry, Enderwick and Harrison's 'information utility' estimates, where the estimates are shown to predict objectively measurable performance;
* Yovits and Abilock's 'b.c.u.'s.', where the value of information is directly related to the impact of the information on the probability distribution of observable behaviours (decisions).

The remaining three—relevance, usefulness, and informativeness—belong in the 'potential' class because they assume that information can have high value (e.g. be highly informative or relevant) even though in some instances it may be very difficult to see how exactly the information affects observable behaviour, or whether it does so at all, i.e. the information may have 'potential' rather than 'actual' value (though it may on occasion have both).

All of these concepts of value have something in their favour, and this points to an important conclusion: 'value' is a multidimensional concept, i.e. items of information can be valuable in different ways.

A MULTIDIMENSIONAL MODEL

The multidimensionality of value can be related to the classification formula discussed in the previous chapter. For example, the distinction between actual and potential value can be applied to each level of the first dimension of the classification formula ('relation to behaviour') to give a description of the value of an item which might look like this:

$$I = 0.5 \, O \quad \text{(low actual, high potential)}, 0.5 \, Pl \text{ (high actual, low potential)}$$

which indicates that this particular item is concerned equally with orientation and planning activities, has high actual value for the planning activities (because it helps directly to decide on a particular plan of action) but low actual value for the orientation activities (although it has high potential value).

Consider the case of a researcher doing work supported by a grant from a research council. He incurs unexpected expenses and has to ask the council for some extra funds. His request to the person concerned has:

- high actual value for that officer in relation to his programmed activities (deciding whether he can authorize the extra funds or not);
- medium potential value in relation to planning activities for the board concerned with planning how to share the council's resources for the coming quarter (because it helps to indicate the likely level of over-expenditure on research grants, but needs to be combined with information about all the other grants current at the time);
- low potential value in relation to the orientation activities of the council (because it helps the council to see what level of demand there is for research funds as compared with, say, postgraduate grants—but its value is rather limited);
- and so forth.

A complete description of the relevant items, I, in the above example might look like this:

$$I = 1.0Pr; 0.8A_{\text{act}}, 0.2NB + M + 0.1Prg, 0.1Me, 0.8B + t$$

$$(\text{value} = 3Pr, 0Pl, 0or)$$

for the officer dealing with the request. This means that the item is treated as relating to programmed activity, is mostly concerned with the researcher's justification of the request (0.8) but also serves to indicate the researcher would be pleased to receive the extra funds (0.2), is material (i.e. input) information, is mostly basic information (about the amount of money involved, and reasons for needing it) but also contains some meta-information (about how the basic information is organized) and some programme information (in the form of a request for certain actions to be taken), and the item is in the form of text. Its value, on a scale of 0 (= none) through 1 (= low), and 2 (= medium) to 3 (= high) is high as programmed information and none in other respects.

There are two points to notice about the formula. First, it takes up much less space than the verbal explanation, so it is a useful shorthand. Secondly, it will be slightly different for, in this example, the board (e.g. $I = 1.0$ planning) and the council (e.g.

I = 1.0 orientation), illustrating again that the relationship of the item to the person or body using it is important in being able to describe it adequately.

It is possible, of course, to combine the formulae for different people or bodies to produce an aggregate description of an item or sets of items of information. This will often need to be done in an information audit, described below.

THE INFORMATION AUDIT

Two main points were made earlier which point to the need for information audits:

- much information in an organization is of relatively little value;
- the value of information is not necessarily related directly to the costs associated with it.

In deciding how best to improve efficiency by weeding out unwanted information, an organization normally will need to take account of the costs associated with the information as well as its value. The costs will include such items as:

- price paid for material information items, e.g. how much the organization paid for the market research reports, books, and other materials used in producing a set of forecasts;
- staff time spent on analysing and working with the material information to produce the product (the forecasts);
- deterioration of any equipment used, e.g. calculators;
- costs of office space, heating, and other overheads involved;
- any other relevant costs.

Figure 4.2 presents the results from a hypothetical audit of a single department of a large organization. More detailed results could be presented based on a breakdown of the individual cells, e.g. looking at the various types of programmed activities in detail. More general results could be presented by collapsing various cells together, e.g. all those relating to orientation activities regardless of the technological fit of the information. The level of detail shown in Figure 4.2 is appropriate for bringing out the following points about this hypothetical example:

- The potential value of the information—especially data and voice—is low but the storage costs are high. The department should consider destroying the information rather than storing it, or finding a very cheap way of storing it commensurate with its low value.
- The actual and potential value of image information in this department is at best medium but the costs associated with it are high. The department should consider dispensing with image information except in cases where it is really considered necessary.

Type of in-formation		Value		Costs (except storage)	Storage costs
		Actual	Potential		
Data	O	low	low	medium	high
	Pl	low	low		
	Pr	high	low		
Text	O	medium	high	low	high
	Pl	medium	medium		
	Pr	high	low		
Image	O	low	medium	high	high
	Pl	low	low		
	Pr	medium	low		
Voice	O	low	low	very high	very high
	Pl	medium	low		
	Pr	high	low		

Figure 4.2.   Value and cost of information—a hypothetical example.

O = orientation activities.
Pl = planning activities.
Pr = programmed activities.

- The storage costs of text are high but this information has potential value. The department should continue to store its text information but should consider reducing costs by using a less expensive medium, e.g. using microform if this is not already being done.

The reader will no doubt be able to draw further conclusions from the table which could be of practical use to the department concerned.

What the table does not make clear is whether the information currently handled adequately meets the needs of the department concerned. For example, if the department feels a strong need for orientation information, then the table suggests this need is not being met very well. For example, suppose the 'department' were the psychology committee of a research council, and suppose the committee had been asked by the council to prepare a policy statement concerning the future use of funds by the committee; in this event, the table shown in Figure 4.1 suggests the appropriate information needed by the committee for this orientation activity is largely missing.

The information audit therefore has two main aspects:

- value of information in relation to costs;
- value of information in relation to needs.

Both of these aspects need to be considered in any adequate survey of the effectiveness of information management in an organization.

CONCLUSIONS

A variety of methods has been proposed for assessing the value of information. They all have something in their favour, and this points to an important conclusion: 'value' is a multidimensional concept, i.e. items of information can be valuable in different ways. This multidimensionality can be related to the classification formula discussed in the previous chapter, and provides a practical basis for developing an 'information audit'. Such an audit has two main aspects: the value of information, assessed multidimensionally, in relation to its costs, and its value in relation to needs. Both of these aspects need to be considered in developing plans, perhaps involving the use of electronic systems, to improve the effectiveness of information management in an organization.

Chapter 5

Information systems

In the previous two chapters we discussed information in the abstract. We saw how it is possible to classify items such as reports, memoranda, notes and other materials according to the types of information involved. And we saw how it is possible to evaluate the worth of information. In this chapter, we turn our attention to electronic systems for handling information. If they are fed information of high value, these systems can help enormously to support human decision-making and related behaviour in the office and in the home.

The systems selected are those which in the author's opinion are the most pertinent. They are described at a macro level and mainly in terms of their capabilities from the user's point of view, rather than in terms of their technical details. The systems are concerned with the production, storage, retrieval and communication of information, primarily text. They are not concerned with systems designed for the transmission or processing of large quantities of largely numerical information ('data'), or direct person-to-person communication. For a more comprehensive view of telecommunications, with a somewhat greater emphasis on technical aspects, the reader is referred to Smith, R. (1979).

The systems considered include:

- videotex;
- traditional STI (scientific and technical information);
- microform;
- word processing;
- computer conferencing;
- personal computers.

In the information society, systems such as these will form an increasingly important aspect of the environment, E, in the psychological equation:

$$B = f(E, P).$$

VIDEOTEX

Videotex is a family of electronic systems which having started in Britain during the last year or two will spread throughout the world during the 1980s and 1990s to provide more information to more people more quickly than ever before in the history of the human species. One can reasonably expect its impact to be as great as that of the printing press or, more recently, radio and television.

A Definition

There are a number of different systems in the videotex family. The most important are: The British 'Viewdata' (on which British Telecom's 'Prestel' service is based); the German 'Bildschirmtext'; the French 'Antiope'; the Canadian 'Telidon'; and the Japanese 'Captain'. These all have the following features in common:

- use of a television screen for displaying the information;
- storage of the information in a central computer or network of computers until it is called for by the user;
- transmission of the information from the computer to the user's screen over telephone lines;
- use of a numeric or alphanumeric keypad or keyboard by the user to request particular items of information from the computer.

These can be considered defining features of videotex, an example of which, as indicated above, is the viewdata system on which is based British Telecom's Prestel service. People in Britain (or, indeed, elsewhere) who have a suitably adapted television set can connect it to their telephone (just by pressing a button) and by pressing the appropriate buttons on their keypad call up information from British Telecom's computers. The information is supplied to British Telecom by a wide variety of organizations and covers weather, entertainment guides, recipes, 'best buys', government statistics, stocks and shares, railway timetables, and all sorts of other information. Prestel is discussed further below.

The term 'videotex' is sometimes used to cover a rather different sort of system as well, called 'teletext'. Examples of teletext are the BBC's 'Ceefax', and the IBA's 'Oracle'. These systems are like those described above in that they store information in computers and display it on the television screen. They differ in that the information is sent to the television receiver 'over the air', in spare lines associated with but not used for the broadcasting of television pictures. This means the user cannot communicate directly with the computer. Instead, the information is sent out in a continuous stream, over and over again. The user presses buttons on a keypad to tell the television set what information to grab and hold on to and what to let pass by. This in turn means the set has to wait for the appropriate part of the stream of information. This can take many seconds and imposes a limit (of a few hundred screenfuls—or 'pages') on the amount of information that can be made available in this type of a system. Beyond that limit, the stream becomes so long as to make the waiting period for some of the information in it intolerable. In addition to this limitation, the lack of interaction between the user and the computer means the extra functions shown in Figure 5.2 cannot be supported.

The term 'videotex' will be used in this book to refer to the interactive type of system based on communication between user and computer by means of the telephone line or similar transmission medium. The main differences between videotex, teletext and word processing (described below) are shown diagrammatically in Figure 5.1.

Main Videotex Features

In addition to the defining features indicated above, videotex systems are characterized by several other features as follows:

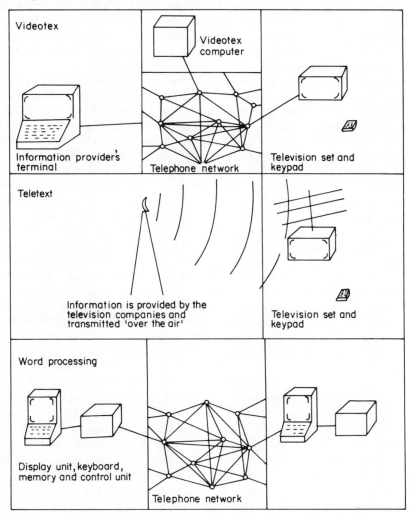

Figure 5.1. Videotex and its relatives.

(a) The information is stored and displayed in the form of pages. A page is made up of one or more frames, where a frame is whatever is on the screen at any one time. Multiframe pages are usually used where the complete page forms a meaningful unit of information, e.g. a description of a job vacancy, but there is more information than can be displayed on the screen all at once. The user simply presses a 'continue' key to move from one frame of the page to the next.

(b) A single frame is made up of a relatively small number of character-spaces (in viewdata, a frame is 40 characters wide by 24 characters tall) so the number of words is limited. The characters can be upper or lower-case, and colours can be used (up to seven in Prestel). Simple graphics can also be displayed.

(c) The amount of information is virtually unlimited. At the time of writing, over 150 000 pages are available on Prestel. (This compares with about 600 on Ceefax and Oracle combined.)

(d) A very simple retrieval scheme is used based on a tree structure. Upon entering the system and at any subsequent point the user is given a maximum of ten options (eleven, if one includes the 'continue' button). These are written out on the screen, and numbered from 0 to 9. For example, option 1 might be 'restaurants', 2 might be 'wine bars', and 3 might be 'pubs'. The user simply presses the appropriate key on the keypad, say '2' for information on wine bars. This might result in further options being displayed, e.g. for different parts of the city, from which the user continues to select until obtaining the information required.

(e) As well as being an information retrieval system, videotex supports a variety of other functions as well. For example, the branching tree structure where what is displayed depends upon the user's response to the previous set of options lends itself readily to programmed learning and trouble-shooting (where the system guides the user to a correct diagnosis by asking questions which depend upon the answers to previous questions). Users who have an alphanumeric keyboard can also write messages on special, blank pages for other users to read. There is also an interactive capability whereby by pressing the right keys in response to certain pages users can order goods or request brochures or other materials to be sent through the mail. The range of functions possible is illustrated in Figure 5.2.

(f) By connecting a personal computer to a videotex set the user in principle can take data and computer programs from the videotex computers and use his or her personal computer to work with these. Even without a personal computer, (s)he can use the videotex set for limited data processing by using it as a terminal to access the remote computing power of the videotex computer.

It can be seen from this that videotex is a flexible system which whilst being primarily an information retrieval system also supports many other functions including sending of messages and even data processing. It therefore represents a point of convergence of several main streams (information, communications, and data processing).

Figure 5.2.   Videotex functions.

A videotex system can serve a number of different functions, especially:

- *Retrieval of information*, e.g.:
  - consumer advice
  - news and weather reports
  - sports information
  - information for business
  - and so forth
- *Standard format messages*, e.g.:
  - to indicate when the person concerned can be expected to arrive, by simply entering the time into a standard message
- *Open format messages*, e.g.:
  - almost anything requiring an alphanumeric keypad
- *Order entry*, e.g.:
  - shopping from home
- *Enquiry entry*, e.g.:
  - to businesses
  - to government departments
- *Training*, e.g.:
  - standard training packages for businesses
  - home courses
- *Problem solving and trouble shooting*, e.g.:
  - supplementation to engineering manuals
  - DIY in the home
- *Calculations*, e.g.:
  - mortgage repayments
- *More complicated computations*
- Games

Prestel

Prestel is the world's first public service based on videotex technology, specifically the British viewdata system, and it serves well to illustrate the kinds of services that are likely to become common during the coming decade.

Figure 5.3 shows the relationships between the main parties involved, which are as follows.

Equipment manufacturers. These produce the computers, telephone lines, switching equipment, television sets, and other equipment needed for a videotex system to operate. This equipment often passes through 'middlemen' not shown on the diagram, such as the television set rental companies who supply about 60% of television sets in the UK. Investment decisions made by the equipment manufacturers limit the number of sets available and therefore the growth of the system as a whole.

The main incentive for the manufacturers and 'middlemen' is revenue accruing from the supply of equipment.

64

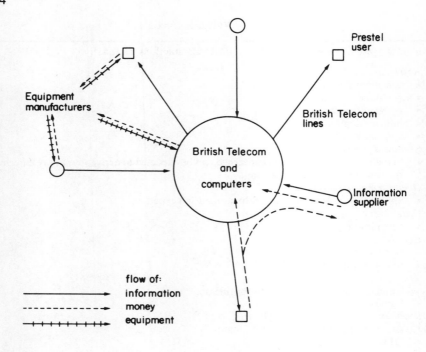

Equipment
manufacturers

Prestel
user

British Telecom
lines

British Telecom
and
computers

Information
supplier

flow of:
information
money
equipment

Note: The same general model might apply where the
videotex operator is not British Telecom,
i.e. to videotex systems other than Prestel.

Figure 5.3.   Prestel overview.

British Telecom. British Telecom operates in two distinct roles. First, it provides
the telephone lines. Secondly, it operates the Prestel service, which means setting
up a network of computers and doing all the administration and marketing involved.
British Telecom's revenue comes from: use of the telephone lines; users' payments
for use of the service (over and above the telephone charges); information providers'
payments for use of the service. British Telecom has a monopoly in the UK for the
supply of telephone lines, but there is nothing in principle to stop other companies
operating services similar to Prestel using their own computers, and some companies
are planning to do just this.

The information providers. These are private companies, government departments,
and individuals who rent computer space from British Telecom in order to write
their own Prestel pages. Users pay the organizations concerned when they want
to read those pages. Payment is done through British Telecom on a single Prestel
bill. (This is part of the administration involved for British Telecom.)

Some organizations, including some government bodies have elected to make their information available free of charge. Some examples of the sorts of information that have been put on to the Prestel computers are given in Figure 5.4.

The users. Prestel has been designed to be of use to business as well as people at home. Business use is expected to develop first. The domestic market will eventually be very much larger in terms of the number of sets, because there are many more homes than there are offices. Business may still turn out to be the larger user in terms of amount of use, but this will depend on the value of the information made available. As the previous chapter has indicated, the question of value is complex and at this early stage all one can confidently say is 'time will tell'. An important influencing factor may be the extent to which international, or large national, videotex projects are successfully implemented, as discussed below.

This overview can do little more than hint at the complexity of what is involved in launching something as grand as Prestel. Success depends crucially on a harmony of efforts and yet there are inevitable difficulties. To give just two examples:

(a) Set manufacturers may be more interested in the domestic market, because that is where the greatest potential for sales of sets is, but British Telecom might be more interested in business because business sets are likely to be used more and so contribute more to revenue from telephone charges.

(b) The price of sets will influence their sales and to reduce price manufacturers would like to sell viewdata sets abroad, but internationally viewdata is in direct competition with other systems such as Antiope and Telidon.

Figure 5.4.   Typical videotex information suppliers.

Well over 160 companies are supplying information through Prestel. This list therefore is merely illustrative:

- Travel guide companies
- Credit card companies
- Newspapers
- Airlines
- Utilities
- Information/advice organizations
- Classified advertisement magazines
- 'Councils' and 'Boards' (e.g., Sports Council)
- Local Government agencies
- Development corporations
- Transportation executives
- Educational institutions
- Government departments
- Government research centres
- Consumer magazines
- Private companies of many sorts

British Telecom has been criticized for the way it has gone about the marketing of Prestel, yet on balance one must concede that it has been a tremendous achievement to launch the world's first videotex system and the world's first public videotex service. Whether Britain will be able to capitalize on this lead internationally, however, is not certain; there is strong competition from other countries.

International Videotex

Videotex has much to offer Europe as a means of rapidly sharing information internationally in specialized areas. It is part of the remit of the Agricultural Community, for example, to share scientific and technical information concerning agriculture among the member countries. Information on pest-control methods, crop diseases, weather, market prices, farming methods, and so forth, could be supplied to farmers and agricultural advisory workers very well through videotex, and updated much more rapidly than with conventional media such as newsletters. International projects of this sort would need to address such questions as automatic translation of information into the various languages of the member countries, and effective interworking of different videotex systems, including viewdata, Bildshirmtext, and Antiope. If such projects are undertaken and these questions resolved satisfactorily, they would help to put videotex on a very firm footing, at least in Europe.

National Projects

National projects will also have an important influence on the development of videotex, even relatively small projects undertaken by private companies. An example is the Sealink project in which Sealink subsidizes viewdata sets for travel agents so they can get information on Sealink services faster and more effectively. Of course, once the travel agents have their sets they are able to use them to access Prestel and any other services based on viewdata. In this way, subsidized sets can help to build up the number of users to a level where videotex becomes a commercially attractive proposition for all concerned.

Teletext

Teletext, as explained above, is similar to videotex but is non-interactive because the information is broadcast 'over the air' and although the user can instruct his or her set to 'watch out for' a particular page as it is broadcast, he or she cannot communicate with the computer. Ceefax and Oracle are the chief examples of this type of system.

Various possibilities have been suggested for overcoming these limitations. One possibility is to broadcast a very long stream of pages overnight for them to be captured by the user's set automatically for storage in a local memory and accessed later using a personal computer. Another possibility is to broadcast an ever-changing stream of pages, according to requests made by users who could make their requests using a keypad connected by telephone to the teletext computer. In this scheme, requests would come in by telephone and information would be sent out 'over the air'.

These possibilities indicate some of the ways in which the distinctions between videotex, teletext and personal computers may tend to break down in the future.

General Comments On Videotex

Videotex could have impacts as great as those of the printing press or television. For this to happen there will need to be meaningful support from national governments, creative initiatives by individual organizations, and cooperation internationally. The outcome will be an electronic infrastructure tying homes and offices together in a common information network of unprecedented sophistication and extent. It is anticipated that the market for videotex sets and services by the late 1990s could be as high as the present combined revenues of the telecommunications and publishing sectors.

It is because videotex is potentially so important that we have discussed it first and have devoted more space to it than to the remaining types of systems described below.

TRADITIONAL STI SYSTEMS

Computers containing large quantities of information, especially scientific and technical information (STI), have been around for many years. These can often be accessed through international communications networks. Psychologists, for example, can search for references and abstracts in the computerized version of psychological abstracts that is available online through the Lockheed Dialogue service. The computer is in California, but the terminals can be anywhere in the world. The National Science Library in London provides access for those who do not have their own terminal.

In addition to the major STI systems and services, of which the Lockheed Dialogue service is but one, universities and other organizations sometimes develop their own, such as the Syracuse University Psychological Abstracts Retrieval Service (SUPARS) mentioned in a later chapter.

Traditional STI systems differ from videotex in several ways. They usually use conventional computer terminals rather than adapted television sets for display, the databases are very large but come from a relatively restricted range of information providers (e.g. Psychological Abstracts, Chemical Abstracts, and others), and they operate on a tight profit margin compared with that promised by videotex. Probably the most important difference, however, is the procedures used to call up information, and the way it is displayed on the screen or printed out.

To use a traditional STI system, the user normally has to be familiar with a relatively complicated 'log on' procedure (to gain access to the system), a 'language' for communicating with the computer (to be able to tell it, for example, to print out just the titles of the first fifty relevant items, and to sort them by author), and a manual of keywords which can be used in combination to define items the user wants. This is normally much more complicated than the simple videotex tree search where the user simply selects an option from those presented, and continues in this way until (s)he finds the information required.

The display of information also differs from videotex. In particular, it does not usually follow the 'page' form. It is often organized around lists, such as lists of titles—as long as need be (printed out on a continuous roll of paper, or shown on a screen with a 'scrolling' facility so the user can scan down the list). In many cases only some of the information, e.g. titles, is printed out at the time of the search and the rest, e.g. abstracts, is printed 'off-line' later to save costs and delivered to the user through the mail.

The disadvantage of the complexity is the training needed to use the systems properly. A special operator is often employed to help users, acting as a 'human buffer' between the system and the person wanting information. The main advantage is the flexibility provided. One can simply ask the computer for all references after 1965 that have to do with human development and the EEG. The reader is invited to work out a corresponding videotex tree structure for such a search, bearing in mind the wide range of topics apart from EEG and human development likely to be in the database, and remembering that the maximum number of options at any stage of the search is ten.

The flexibility of STI systems is illustrated by ARIANE, which is a system used by the French building industry. At any stage of a search using ARIANE, the user may be presented with a series of options from which to choose, or can enter keywords to help narrow down the search. In this way, ARIANE combines the 'option' approach with the 'keyword' approach.

Euronet

During recent years there has been an increasing awareness of a need to link different STI systems together to facilitate access to their information by users spread over wide geographic areas, even different countries. Such linkages in principle can also simplify the interface between the user and the mass of information held in computerized form.

A particularly significant milestone in Europe was 18 March 1975 when the Council of Ministers of the European Communities adopted an action plan to implement EURONET. This network, now operational, links computers in all the main European countries. At the time of writing, it offers over 25 information services giving access to over 100 bibliographical databases and factual databanks in several different languages. It is anticipated that the number of public users in

Europe will increase markedly as a result of EURONET which, amongst other things, offers a distance independent tariff (the user pays the same no matter how far (s)he is from the particular computer holding the information needed). This is consistent with one of the aims of the project, which is to create a European information-conscious society.

The Commission of the European Communities has examined the feasibility of linking videotex into Euronet. In some application areas, e.g. agriculture, this could make the accessing and display of information held in Euronet computers much simpler and, because the terminals are based on television sets which many people have anyway, could make low-cost terminals feasible. The information currently held on Euronet computers would have to be re-formatted to fit in with the videotex page format but this could be done automatically using appropriate computer programmes.

MICROFORM

Some organizations are using automated systems based on microform. In these systems, papers are photographed on to microform which can be stored in much less space than paper, e.g. a complete journal article can be held on a microfiche about a quarter the size of an A4 sheet. The microform is automatically labelled as the photography is done so that it can be easily identified later. The labelling is done magnetically or in a similar way so that it can be read automatically. Computerized search procedures typical of some of the STI systems discussed above can then be applied. When a microfiche is retrieved it can be automatically displayed on a screen or printed out on to paper. An added feature of some systems is to have the microform produced directly by computer in the first place so there is no need for photography.

WORD PROCESSING

Basic Word Processors

Word processing (sometimes called text processing) in its simplest form can be thought of as computerized typewriting. Typically the operator uses a typewriter keyboard with some extra keys and sees what (s)he is typing printed out or displayed on a screen. Traditional uses have been for highly repetitive typing, such as standard letters that need to be personalized or legal documents that need only minor revision, or documents that need to be redrafted several times. In such cases, the basic text can be stored electronically and revisions made very easily, a perfect copy being produced every time. Word processing has made significant inroads in many countries and has been growing in popularity in British offices during the last few years.

Basic word processors differ from one another in terms of three main functional dimensions:

70

- power typing;
- information storage and retrieval;
- communications.

The majority of current word-processing systems emphasize power typing. They typically offer such features as:

- automatic closing of spaces following deletion of words or lines
- automatic adjustment of margins;
- ease of changing line spacing;
- automatic cursor control from memory to guide the typist to parts of the text (e.g. standard letter) which may need to be tailored to the individual who will be receiving it;
- and many other features.

These features account for most of the productivity increases typically claimed for these machines. (They are often claimed to be able to do the work of up to about four conventional typists, but obviously this depends on particular circumstances.)

They are relatively poor on the information storage and retrieval side. Typically they hold only a page or two of text in main memory and depend upon removable stores—usually 'floppy discs'—for the rest. (A 'floppy disc'—about the size of a 45 rpm singles record—typically holds about 60–150 pages of text.) Retrieval normally depends upon the individual items (e.g. pages of a document, or letters) being numbered, so the machine can search for the numbers specified.

Some machines are better than this on information retrieval. At least one machine currently available allows the user to tag up to about thirty identifiers on to each item stored. If the items are, for example, descriptions of personnel employed in the company, the identifiers can be such things as age, sex, time with the company, qualifications, departments worked in, rank achieved, and so on.

The machine can then be asked to search for all personnel who conform to certain characteristics, e.g. over forty years of age, with the company at least three years, and of all but the lowest two ranks. This obviously compares very favourably with other machines that require the user to specify the unique identifying numbers of the personnel concerned (which often involves some manual searching through lists). In any case, once the machine has been told who to search for it can then be told to take certain elements from the descriptions, e.g. the home addresses and favoured form of address (e.g. 'Mr Smith', or 'Bill') and attach these to a standard letter. At this stage all the operator need do, having prepared the letter once, is let the machine automatically type personalized versions of the letter for each of the people involved, including addressing the envelopes.

Machines which are relatively good on information retrieval tend at the moment to be poorer on power typing. For example, the machine alluded to above does not have a full-size screen—the typist can only see the particular line (s)he is typing, which can be inconvenient.

Communication between word-processing stations (individual typing consoles) is limited at the moment but many new systems offer this possibility and it is likely to become more visible as the cost of physically carrying paper from one place to another increases.

Basic word-processing systems support just one or a very small number—say, up to three—consoles.

Advanced Word Processing

Advanced word-processing systems are beginning to appear and will become more common during the 1980s, especially in medium and large organizations. The description given here is of a typical system one might expect to see towards the latter half of the decade, although many elements are already incorporated in existing systems.

An advanced word-processing system is much nearer to a complete office information system than a basic word processor. It supports up to 20–30 workstations in one system, and different systems can be connected by telephone lines or cable. Each work station looks like the typing console of a basic word processor in that it has a typewriter keyboard (with extra keys) for input, a screen to see what is being typed or is held in store, and possibly a printer to produce paper copy. There is only possibly a printer because the emphasis is much more on the electronic, paperless office.

The key difference between advanced word-processing systems and basic systems is the much greater intelligence in the advanced system. In current systems this is located in a central control unit which is the 'brain' for the 20–30 work stations connected to it, but the intelligence could in principle be distributed among the work stations. In addition, there are a number of other differences, especially:

- much greater on-line storage, so that hundreds of thousands of pages of text can be held in the system for instant access;
- larger removable stores for information not requiring immediate access;
- greater use of screens and less of printers;
- special printer stations for high-speed, high-quality production of papers when necessary;
- direct connection to special output devices such as phototypesetting for brochures, pamphlets, and so forth;
- connection to computer systems where required.

The emphasis in these systems is very much on electronic information and to ensure that papers received from outside the organization, or already on file, can be converted into electronic form, two special kinds of input device are used:

- optical character recognition units (OCR) which can recognize special type fonts and convert the text rapidly into electronic form with few errors;
- facsimile input which does not intelligently recognize individual characters, as

FAX

OCR does, but simply treats them as pictures and converts them into electronic images.

The OCR units in particular also mean that any original typing needed can be done on inexpensive, conventional typewriters, leaving the work station typists free to do revisions, editing, corrections, and compilation of new documents from existing pages already held in electronic form. Direct voice input will become increasingly important as well, so that managers will be able to dictate to a work station rather than to a secretary. Elementary systems capable of voice recognition already exist.

The use of facsimile—for output as well as input—also means that 'image' and 'text' information can be handled together by these systems. In this way, a report containing mainly text but with some graphs and diagrams can be printed out as a complete document, or held electronically as such. This is in contrast to the existing situation where text and diagrams have to be handled separately and combined manually as part of the final collation process.

Finally, but perhaps of greatest significance of all, such systems allow for intelligent inter-office communication. This is achieved by the control units, and is most easily explained by example. Suppose Mr Smith, a manager, comes into his office prior to going to a meeting. He wants to know what is in his 'in-tray'. He presses the 'in-tray' button on his work station and up on the screen comes a list of titles ('headers') with priorities attached. The priorities have been attached by the people producing the memoranda, notes, reports, or other items concerned, or by default by the control unit according to previous programming (e.g. 'Mark all downward communications "high priority" and all communications from divisional directors to subordinates "top priority" unless other priorities are assigned by the authors concerned'). Mr Smith does not have to accept these priorities, but they do determine the order in which items are sent through the system to his work station.

In this particular example, let us suppose that Mr Smith is interested in only one item, a report he needs for his meeting. He sees it has arrived and presses a few more buttons to see the contents page and executive summary on the screen. Satisfied this is what he wants, he instructs the machine to have it printed out in his divisional printing centre; he asks for six copies (which will be automatically collated, including all diagrams), with the appendices on blue paper, as he will need to distribute the report at the meeting. Ordinarily he would not have the report printed but he is going to a client's premises and this makes it difficult because:

(a) British Telecom regulations make it difficult to send information electronically between organizations, and
(b) in any case, the client does not have display units in the conference room, nor even a system that is capable of communicating with Mr Smith's.

However, he will keep an electronic copy of the report on file so that it can be read by others in his own organization who have the correct security clearance (the control unit is told the pass numbers of those who are authorized to read the report), and it will also be useful as a basis for preparing updates or similar reports in the future.

Before leaving for the meeting, Mr Smith dictates a short note addressed to members of the 'Office Accommodation Working Group'. The note is displayed on the screen and he corrects two errors made by the voice-recognition unit before he sends the note out at 'ordinary priority' by pressing the appropriate button. The control unit knows who is on the working group and ensures that an electronic copy is sent to the work stations concerned. There is some uncertainty about which work stations are involved because Mr Smith's colleagues move around a lot. It locates the correct work stations by referring to the electronic diaries for the people concerned. Two of the people concerned are working at home so the unit automatically instructs the organization's viewdata computer to store the following message in the 'messages' part of the database: 'Ms Bartholomew, Mr Hinde: Please contact your secretary for a note on the OAWG from J. Smith'. (Alternatively, the computer could reformat the note into videotex format for display on Ms Bartholomew's and Mr Hinde's home videotex sets.)

This example is hypothetical but many of the elements described are already available and most will be incorporated in some office systems of the mid 1980s. Experimental systems very similar to the one described probably already exist in the offices of some of the world's leading equipment manufacturers. They are very far removed indeed from the simple concept of a machine to do standard letters, and they indicate one important way in which the twin concepts of 'information' and 'communication' are being brought together by electronic technology.

COMPUTER CONFERENCING

Computer conferencing at the moment seems likely to have less impact than the developments described already but it is worth mentioning as another bridge between 'information' and 'communication'.

In a computer conference, a number of people (typically half a dozen up to about thirty) sit at their individual computer terminals and type in messages. If everyone is on-line at the same time, the messages may look rather like the comments people make when seated around the table in a conference room. If different people tend to be on-line at different times, the messages may look a little more like letters, memoranda, notes or telexes.

The terminals which in principle can be spread world-wide are linked through a common computer which decides who should receive which messages. There are two main classes of messages: 'public' (which everyone receives), and 'private' (which are received only by people specified by the person writing the messages). The messages are organized into a conference 'script', with each message numbered for ease of reference. The 'script' to date can be accessed at the convenience of the individual participant. The script can serve as a convenient form of recording the minutes of such a 'meeting'.

The involvement of a computer allows other things to be done as well. For example, the chairman can have a questionnaire distributed on-line, and receive a computer-analysed summary of the results with minimum delay. The technique lends itself quite well to Delphi enquiries. The computer in principle can also be used to access databases available through other computer networks, allowing the computer conference participants to benefit from convenient access to relevant information.

Computer conferencing has tended to be used mostly by government or quasi-government agencies in the USA, often for the monitoring and coordination or actual conduct of research activities. For example, NASA have used it for coordinating work on space experiments being done by scientists at locations spread over a wide area making face-to-face meetings difficult. Similarly, it has been used to supplement other forms of communication between government officials, outside consultants, and field teams working in remote parts of Alaska.

PERSONAL COMPUTERS

The power of a personal computer available today for about £1,000 would have cost about £40,000 ten years ago (in 1981 pounds). For the reader who is not computer-minded, one can get an inkling of what this means by considering that for as little as £16 one can buy a pocket calculator that is programmable and can calculate a range of statistics such as chi-square, Student's t or the product-moment correlation coefficient, or play simple games (but not store data). One can see that £1000 buys quite a powerful machine.

Of the two most popular types of personal computer, one comes with a small, integral screen and the other is used in conjunction with a conventional television set. Both types offer as add-on features:

- cassette units for storage of data (relatively slow and inconvenient, but inexpensive);
- small 'floppy disc' units for storage of data with very rapid access;
- printers of various sorts for producing paper output.

As well as offering the capability of storing data and doing calculations, personal computers offer:

- complex games for entertainment;
- communication with other personal computers over telephone lines;
- capability for basic word processing;
- capability for writing, storing, and searching through viewdata pages;
- capability for computer conferencing.

The use of the television for display points very much in the direction of the television taking on a much wider role in the home of tomorrow, acting for example as:

- an intelligent typewriter;
- a source of entertainment apart from television programmes;

- a source of videotex information;
- a communications link with other homes or with the office.

The personal computer is likely to find a place in many homes, but there are also strong indications that many organizations will see it as an important way of inexpensively bringing many of the concepts we have discussed into the office.

TOWARDS AN INTEGRATION

Some people see a gradual merging of the various streams of development we have discussed into a single, all-embracing system serving many different functions. The present author feels it is more likely that in the foreseeable future the various concepts we have discussed will jostle for positions and gradually settle into niches which might result in a situation such as the following:

- a continuing role for special-purpose data-processing systems;
- a continuing role for direct voice communication by telephone, and emerging person-to-person media such as teleconferencing (see Short, Williams, and Christie, 1976);
- advanced word-processing systems for reports and similar documents, and the bulk of inter-office memoranda, including an important part of information retrieval in the office;
- videotex for information services to the office and information within organizations, and as a link between the home and office;
- personal computers for 'personal' use in offices and as an important component of the work station at home, enabling more people to spend more time working at home.

As each of these types of systems becomes established, so it is likely that flexible links between them will emerge. The results will be an electronic network of very high complexity, not understood in its totality by any one person, linking homes and offices together in a system that by its very redundancy will ensure greater flexibility and reliability than any single system existing today. More information will be more readily available, and more of it will be electronic. The question arises as to how the performance of systems in such a network can be properly evaluated.

SYSTEM PERFORMANCE

System performance is to be distinguished from organizational performance discussed in the next chapter. System performance refers to the performance of individual systems such as those described in this chapter, or other systems where the handling of information is a key function. It will be limited by the value of the information handled by the system since, in general terms at least, system performance cannot be very high if the information received, stored, processed, retrieved, communicated, or otherwise handled, is low. On the other hand, high-value information is not sufficient for high system performance. A system may perform poorly by handling in an ineffective or inefficient way information that is of high value.

This is reasonable in general terms. The difficulties arise when one attempts to be more specific, perhaps by giving examples. At this stage, one must decide precisely what counts as 'high performance' and what does not. The difficulties become especially apparent when trying to compare different systems, especially complex systems that vary along several different parameters. For example, how does one compare the performance of a viewdata system with that of a shared logic document handling system?

This kind of difficulty has been discussed by several writers (e.g. Smith, P. C., 1976; Swanson, 1975), and has become known as 'the criterion problem'.

The Criterion Problem

The criterion problem essentially is this: The purposes of evaluation of a system require that there exist performance specifiers by which the system can be measured, but in the case of real information-communication systems it has proved very difficult to identify appropriate specifiers.

One method of proceeding which in principle provides a solution to the criterion problem is to compare 'what is' with 'what should be' (e.g. Olsen, 1977). Unfortunately, it is rarely possible to specify what an 'ideal' system should look like, with any degree of certitude, unless one has definite criteria in mind, which makes it difficult to avoid circularity in this approach.

An approach having greater generality might be structural-functional analysis, or 'functionalism' for short. Farrace et al. (1977) set out five main stages to such an analysis, as follows:

(a) All the parts of the system which are to be included in further analysis must be specified.
(b) Relevant parts of the system's environment must be clearly noted.
(c) The attributes or traits of the system which are considered essential for its continued existence must be determined.
(d) The different amounts or values which each trait may assume must be indicated, especially the range of values within which the trait must stay for the system's continuation.
(e) The mechanisms by which the system's components keep the traits within the limits required must be discovered and understood in terms of the potential impact of internal system changes or of changes in the environment.

Performance measures can be derived from a knowledge of the relevant traits and their acceptable limits. The difficulty in practice, in regard to information-communication systems is that not enough is known about the human behavioural context for these systems for the relevant traits or their acceptable limits to be identified properly. Consequently, it is conceivable that more or less arbitrary measures are applied which correlate poorly if at all with the real effectiveness of the system. For example, measures of the accuracy of information provided to users may result in quite misleading comparisons between different systems if the differences are sufficiently small as to be inconsequential from the user's point of view; speed of delivery might be a much more meaningful measure under such circumstances.

No completely satisfactory set of criteria having sufficient generality to cover all systems has so far been proposed. The nearest seems to be a scheme set out in an unpublished paper by Krumm et al. and presented by Baker (1970). This is shown in Figure 5.5. This goes some way towards systematizing observable system features and related performance measures, but in practice real systems can be distinguished from one another in terms of more traits than can easily be accommodated by this scheme. Some key criteria that need to be considered are set out below.

Some Indices Of Performance

The complexity of the criterion problem suggests that no single index of performance is likely to be entirely satisfactory by itself. What constitutes a suitable index will vary according to context, and it may often be useful to use various indices in combination. It may help to see the relationships between the various indices if we think of them in terms of the 'information cycle' shown in Figure 5.6.

The information cycle. It will be shown in Chapter 6 that users' behaviour in relation to information-communication systems of the type we are considering can be thought of as relating to two main kinds of process: Putting information into a store, and taking information out of a store. This formulation suggests four main kinds of activities where measures of performance can be applied:

(a) *Production* of information, e.g. the use of the power-typing capabilities of word-processing systems;
(b) *Commitment* of information to store, e.g. the creation of electronic files in word-processing systems or the transmission of videotex pages to the videotex computer store;
(c) *Retrieval* of information from store, e.g. using the 'index-number hunting' typical of current word-processing systems or the search tree of videotex;
(d) *Use* of information retrieved, e.g. by incorporating it in new documents, perhaps using the 'text merge' capability offered by many word-processing systems or the 'copy' facility of videotex, or reading the information and perhaps making decisions based on it.

In this formulation the use of existing information and the production of new information are conceptually quite close and can be thought of as completing a cycle.

Figure 5.5. The Krumm scheme.

Information processing function	System performance measures		Information quality measures	
	Thoroughness	Responsiveness	Completeness	Accuracy
Dissemination	Percentage of messages which arrive at the proper destination.	Speed of message preparation, processing, and routing.	Resistance to information losses during dissemination.	Correctness of disseminated information.
Computation		Speed with which computational reports are requested and prepared.	Completeness of computational reports.	Correctness of computational reports.
Compilation		Speed with which summary reports are compiled.	Completeness of compiled summary reports.	Correctness of compiled summary reports.
Retrieval		Speed with which queries yield responses.	Completeness of responses to queries.	Correctness of responses to queries.

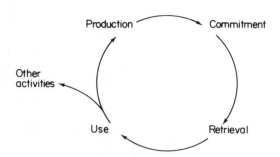

Figure 5.6.   The information cycle.

In this very simple model, the net gain is the contribution to 'other activities' not tied in to the information cycle itself.

The communication of items from one place to another does not appear explicitly in the information cycle but it is implicit in the model because communication can and often does occur between each stage and the next. For example, pages of a document required in the production of a report may be retrieved from an electronic store in Edinburgh and communicated to a word-processing unit in London where they are used to form an appendix to the report. The completed report may then be communicated to various storage devices located in all the regions covered by the organization concerned for retrieval by the people who need to see it.

The following are among the chief approaches to assessing performance that have been proposed.

Precision and recall. These are concerned with the retrieval of information from store. They are the two most frequently used measures of the effectiveness of this function (e.g. Salton, 1969). They represent the proportion of retrieved material actually relevant (precision) and the proportion of relevant material actually retrieved (recall). For valid comparisons, the measures have to be made under standard conditions (e.g. unchanging search procedures, no learning by either the computer or the human, no optional stopping) and measures of relevance have to be available. Relevance is often assessed by human judges. Typically, a negative correlation is observed between the two measures, i.e. the greater the proportion of relevant items in the sample retrieved the lower the proportion of all relevant material actually available that is retrieved. Reasons for this have been discussed by Robertson (1977) who has also discussed the relationship between these measures and those generated by signal-detection theory (discussed below). This concept of relevance and similar concepts have been discussed in Chapter 4.

Signal-detection theory. This also relates to the retrieval function. A clear presentation of the theory has been given by Swets, Tanner, and Birdsall (1961). Briefly, the theory is concerned with the detection of signals which are more or less buried in noise. Two normal distributions, equal in variance, are assumed, corresponding to the probability distributions of observations (e.g. values of a meter, spot on an oscilloscope, presence of a relevant item of information) given: (a) just noise, and (b) noise plus a signal. The theory yields two independent measures. The first, d', indicates the distance between the means of the two distributions (which usually overlap to some extent—the less the overlap the easier it is to detect a signal). The second, β, indicates the criterion the person is using. This is the cut-off point: Observations of value less than the criterion are judged to result just from noise; observations of greater value are judged to result from noise plus signal. The criterion used by a person depends on many factors, principally interest in detecting any signals that might occur even at the expense of many 'false alarms' versus interest in minimizing false alarms even if it means missing some signals.

Hutchinson (1978) has discussed the application of this theory to the measurement of the effectiveness of the retrieval function of information systems, and examples of such applications are provided by Brooks (1968) and Swets (1963). It seems to the present author that the main difficulty with this type of measure is its reliance on an appropriate definition of 'relevant item' (signal) and 'non-relevant item' (noise), a problem which has been discussed above, and in Chapter 4.

Amount produced in unit time. The number of pages produced per hour, or similar measures (e.g. lines of text or words per minute), is frequently used to assess the performance of a system in relation to the production of new items. Word-processors, for example, typically rate about 3 or 5 times as fast as conventional typewriters. A great deal depends upon the precise circumstances under which the measures are made, e.g. how much of the material is already stored electronically, how much can be input through an optical character reader (OCR) or similar device, and so on. The measure usually implies that the same level of accuracy is achieved as with conventional typing. Apart from accuracy, other features relating to the general quality of presentation (e.g. right-hand justification) could also be taken into account.

Measures of production relate closely to measures of retrieval and of use. For example, difficulties in retrieving appropriate items from store will slow down production. In relation to use, poor layout of material at the production stage may make it less easy to use later. This aspect of the information cycle has been discussed in detail by Wright (1977) in relation to the presentation of technical information. Some systems allow more flexibility than others. For example, conventional methods of producing paper reports allow greater flexibility in this regard than, say, videotex.

Speed and accuracy of communication. These are the usual indices of performance applied to the communication function at any stage of the information cycle. The usual measure is the number of bits transmitted per second. Signal-to-noise ratios and other measures can be used to provide additional, related information on the technical performance of communications channels.

The 'bit' index. The concept of the 'bit' of information has been discussed in Chapter 4. The various measures based around this concept are usually applied at the very 'technical' level, i.e. they are concerned with questions such as the speed and accuracy with which electronic signals (in the form of strings of bits) produced by, say, a word-processing operator are, say, reproduced on a floppy disc at some remote location, or the number of bits that can be stored by a given volume of storage medium, or similar questions.

Measures relating to use. The close connection between information and decision-making suggests that one index of the performance of an information system could be the decision-making that results. Various measures of decision-making are possible. For example, Ekehammer and Magnusson (1973) measured the time taken to reach a decision and subjects' confidence in their decisions as a function of the amount of information available. In this experiment, the decisions were ratings of interviewers on four personality variables. The judges were allowed to watch the interviews through one-way screens. Amount of information was varied by varying interview length (8, 16, 24 and 32 minutes). The judges took longer to make their decisions the more information they had, but their confidence was greater. Either these or other results could have been expected on theoretical grounds and it is not clear to what extent the findings have relevance for other contexts, e.g. information in the form of documents or abstracts, but clearly the question of how much information a system should provide in response to a user's needs is an important one.

The kind of decision made is at least as important as the time taken to make it, and this has been studied by Streufert (1973) in relation to a distinction she made between information relevance and information load (the amount of information received per unit time whether or not the information is relevant). In this experiment, 12 pairs of undergraduate students played a war game against an 'opponent nation' (actually, unknown to the subjects, this was the experimenter who fed all teams the same fixed input programme). Two measures of 'simple' decision-making were made: The number of retaliating decisions and the number of decisions related to information search. One measure of 'complex' decision-making was made: The number of 'integrations' (presumably of different pieces of information).

The results were tentatively interpreted to suggest that relevance of information affects complex decision-making whilst information load affects simple decision-making. Again, more research is needed before conclusions can be drawn for the design of information systems but clearly 'relevance' of information is affected by the precision and recall characteristics of a retrieval system, as is the amount of information and therefore information load.

The 'integrations' in Streufert's experiment were intended to measure 'the integrative quality of decision-making'. A substantial amount of work has been done on how people combine different items of information to arrive at a decision. It is not really appropriate to go into it here and the reader is referred to Louviere and Norman (1977) or Fishbein and Ajzen (1975) for recent overviews.

Users' attitudes. The various indices of performance considered above are likely to influence the attitudes of users toward the systems in many contexts. We shall not spend time considering this aspect of system evaluation here as we go into it in detail in later chapters.

COMPARISONS BETWEEN SYSTEMS

The Nature of the Comparisons

We are not concerned here with detailed comparisons between different information-retrieval systems for scientific and technical information or between different models of word-processor or even between different types of videotex systems (e.g., the French 'Antiope' compared with the British 'viewdata'). These are important questions for the manufacturer or potential user of such systems, but we are concerned here with much broader comparisons, such as between videotex and word-processing.

Figure 5.7. Approximate relative performance of the main systems at different stages of the information cycle (intuitive generalizations).

Type of system	Production	Commitment to store	Retrieval	Use	Communication	Overall
• large, shared-logic word processing systems	***	***	***	**	***	***
• communicating word processors	***	**	**	**	**	**
• stand-alone word processors	***	**	**	**	*	**
• videotex	**	*	**	*	*	**
• teletext	**	*	*	*	—	*
• computer conferencing	*	**	*	**	***	**
• unintelligent communications systems, e.g. facsimile	—	—	—	—	**	*
• specialized computer access systems (generally speaking)	*	*	variable	variable	variable	variable

Key: *** = high
     ** = medium
     * = low
     — = not useful

We shall consider in very general terms the following types of systems:

- stand-alone word-processors;
- communicating word-processors;
- large shared-logic word-processing systems;
- videotex;
- teletext;
- unintelligent communications systems, e.g. facsimile;
- specialized computer-access systems, e.g. for scientific and technical information;
- computer conferencing;
- manual methods.

We shall compare these systems in terms of their performance at different stages of the information cycle. The research which has been done and which has been outlined above has not been directly concerned with these sorts of comparisons, nor has it been organized specifically in terms of the information cycle or in any other way which makes it easy to draw general conclusions about the relative performance of different types of systems at different stages of the cycle. Our judgements must be made therefore on a general knowledge of the systems and their capabilities, and a rational analysis, rather than hard empirical evidence.

The Comparisons Themselves

The systems are most easily compared by referring to Figure 5.7. This sets out the author's judgements of the relative performance of the different systems at different stages of the information cycle. It should be noted that the rank order of the systems varies according to the stage of the cycle.

These judgements should be regarded as hypotheses rather than facts and should be interpreted with extreme caution. Much research is needed before they can be confirmed or disconfirmed even as broad generalizations, and—as we have seen—much depends upon specific contexts.

The judgements are based on an overall evaluation of the systems, taking account of their typical capabilities, and intuitively averaging over a range of typical applications. In the case of production, for example, word processors are rated highly because it is generally reckoned that one word-processing operator can normally be expected to do the work of up to three or four conventional typists. Videotex is given a medium rating because it incorporates some of the features of a word processor which aid the operator, e.g. being able to correct mis-spellings easily by simply typing over the word, and being able to copy pages easily, but simple videotex systems at least do not incorporate many others, e.g. easy movement of individual paragraphs. Computer conferencing is rated low for production of information because the sort of person who typically operates a terminal (e.g. a researcher) would normally write or dictate into a dictation machine rather than type.

The judgements, being intuitive averages over a range of applications, will not reflect effectiveness for all applications equally well. This is particularly true of the 'specialized computer access systems', where there is also an intuitive averaging over a range of such systems. These systems can vary tremendously as their only defining characteristic is that they involve a computer and a special application, e.g. airline reservations or banking systems. Many systems in this very heterogeneous category are not of primary interest to us as we are concerned here with systems dealing with 'files' of information of various sorts, including letters, documents, reports, and so forth, but not with systems designed for the transmission or processing of large quantities of numerical information ('data processing').

It would not be reasonable for an organization to select a system on the basis of Figure 5.7. For some applications, videotex, for example—especially where emphasis is on retrieval of information—may be more than adequate and anything having greater capabilities would be a waste. Similarly, of course, it would be foolish to invest in, say, communicating word processors if much less expensive systems such as telex or facsimile would be adequate.

Finally, the scheme set out makes no allowance for the possible combination of different systems, e.g. word processing linked into the telex system, or videotex linked into the main computer system. This again illustrates the difficulty of evaluating performance without considering specific applications in specific contexts.

CONCLUSIONS

In this chapter we have seen that a wide range of electronic systems are available for handling information at various stages of what we have called the information cycle. It seems unlikely that there will be a complete merging of these systems into a single, all-embracing system concept serving many different functions, although some people see a trend in this direction. What is more likely is that very complex networks will emerge, overlaid on one another and incorporating many different kinds of systems. These will provide many links between different organizations and between offices and homes.

Evaluating the performance of systems in such networks is a complex matter. Many specific indices of performance have been proposed, as well as more general schemes, e.g. structural–functional analysis. A significant amount of work has been done on measuring the performance of different variants of similar systems, e.g. scientific and technical information systems, in terms of narrowly-defined criteria. Very little work has been done on comparing different types of systems, e.g. videotex against manual methods or word processing. We have made some broad judgements of the relative performance of different types of systems at various stages of the information cycle, based on a general knowledge of the systems' features. Such global evaluations, independent of particular applications or contexts, are of limited value. To assess performance properly it is necessary to take a more fundamental approach and examine the roles which the systems play or could play in relation to the behaviour of individual users and organizations. This we do in the following chapters, starting with a discussion of the basic concepts involved.

Chapter 6

Information in organizations

In the preceding chapters we have seen that there are different types of information, that information is available in different ways, and that it can be associated with a wide range of different electronic systems, as well as existing in paper form. The purpose of this chapter is to examine what role information plays in organizations, how the flow of information through organizations can be described, and how the performance of organizations in relation to the management of information can be assessed.

The relationship between information management and organizational performance is bound to be far from simple, if only because both 'information' and 'organizational performance' are complex concepts. We have discussed some of the complexity relating to the concept of information in previous chapters. The complexity of organizational performance is evidenced by the wide range of variables that have been said to index it. For example, Campbell (in Campbell et al., 1974) identified 19 different variables that have been used in studies of organizational performance. Steers (1975) reviewed 17 studies and concluded that there was a major lack of consensus as to what constitutes a useful and valid set of measures of organizational performance.

The multidimensionality of organizational performance is made even clearer by the factor-analytic studies which have been done (e.g. Seashore, Inoik, and Georgopoulos, 1960; Yuchtman and Seashore, 1967; Friedlander and Pickle, 1968). These studies generally have observed many low, and some negative, correlations between the measures of effectiveness made. Even when positive correlations are observed, they may vary significantly in magnitude from one organizational unit to another (e.g. Seashore, Inoik, and Georgopoulos, 1960). Even when stable factors have been identified, there may be many of them. For example, Yuchtman and Seashore (1967) identified ten main factors based on 76 measures of the effectiveness of 75 life insurance agencies, measured repeatedly over eleven years:

- business volume;
- production cost;
- productivity of new members;
- youthfulness of members;
- business mix (unit size of transactions);
- labour-force growth;

- management emphasis;
- cost of maintaining clients;
- member productivity;
- market penetration in terms of estimated population potential.

Apart from the number of factors that need to be considered and their relative priorities, there is the further complication that people do not always agree on the polarity of the factors, i.e. whether it is good to be high or good to be low on a particular factor (e.g. Yuchtman and Seashore, 1967).

We can see that the role of information in organizations is bound to be a complex topic. We need a model to make our task manageable. All models are, by definition, simplifications of reality and whatever model we choose we must be aware from the outset that it will not deal with all organizational phenomena equally well. We must find a model that will deal well with those particular phenomena that are of most interest to us, i.e. those relating most clearly to information.

The model we shall elaborate here—we can call it the 'information model' of organizations—is best understood by regarding it as a general model containing a set of more specific models, e.g. the source–store–sink model. This is analogous to other areas in psychology. For example, Eysenck's model of personality (e.g. Eysenck, 1970) can be considered to comprise a general model (the factor structure of personality) and a set of more specific models (e.g. a neurological model, an arousal model, a conditioning model, a genetic model, and so forth).

THE GENERAL MODEL

The general information model is proposed as an alternative to Katz and Kahn's (1978) energy model of organizations, and was suggested in large part by that. Katz and Kahn adopt a very broad definition of 'energy' in developing their model, and the reader may wish to regard the information model as a special case of the energy model.

Katz and Kahn's Energy Model

The energy model is based on the notion that organizations are open systems that survive only as long as they are able to maintain negative entropy, that is, 'import in all forms greater amounts of energy than they return to the environment as product'. Katz and Kahn drawn an analogy with electric motors, transformers, and other physical devices. These all extract a price—usually in the form of heat—in changing electrical energy to mechanical, alternating current to direct current, and so forth. Even the silicon chips and other components in the electronic systems of particular interest here pass on less energy than they receive.

Following their analogy, Katz and Kahn suggest it is appropriate to ask of organizations, as of electrical transformers, how much of the energy input into the system emerges as product. The ideal—never attained in practice—would be 100 per cent. They recognize that organizations are more complicated than transformers but feel that many or all of the complications can be accommodated by their model, and concern such things as the varied forms in which energy is input.

Especially important forms of energy input include: people, as sources of energy (e.g. in carrying loads, operating machinery); materials which have already extracted what Katz and Kahn call an 'energy price' in the processes of their manufacture and distribution; and energy proper in the form of steam, electricity, and so forth.

The concept of efficiency plays a central role in the energy model. The immediate consequences of a gain in efficiency are, other things being equal, said to be the creation of a surplus in some form. The surplus can be used in various ways, e.g. increased profit, growth, survival over time, and so on. The particular ways in which the surplus is used depend upon organizational goals. These in turn help to define what is effective for the organization. Efficiency therefore, in this model, is central to an understanding of other important organizational variables, including effectiveness.

The Information Model

It may be that Katz and Kahn's model can be applied to all kinds of organizations but we need to consider an alternative viewpoint that suggests itself: an 'information model' rather than an 'energy model'.

The energy model is based on the notion that organizations need 'energy' (in various forms) to survive. The information model asserts that organizations do not even exist, let alone continue over time, without information. Organizations are not accidental, random concatenations of components and processes. They are organized. They 'contain information' in the same sense that a document or a picture may be said to 'contain information' by comparison with a random array of words or picture-elements. An information view of organizations therefore seems inherently more suited to the complexity of organizations than the 'energy' view, which may be better suited to relatively simple systems such as transformers. That is the first point.

The second point is more important. The energy model seems suited best to manufacturing organizations, those characteristic of industrial society. This is supported by Katz and Kahn's choice of practical examples. They compare, for example, two hypothetical companies concerned with manufacturing baseball bats; they discuss automobile manufacture; and they compare hypothetical companies manufacturing television sets (see Katz and Kahn, 1978, pp. 220 ff.). These sorts of organizations lend themselves readily to the energy model as they are primarily concerned with using energy to make gross changes in the physical form of materials. But we have seen that our society is changing. We are moving rapidly to a post-industrial or information society, where the predominant type of organization deals in information, not energy and materials. The information model therefore seems better suited to the type of organization which is becoming predominant in our society. Even in the examples given by Katz and Kahn, one can argue the information model is as important as the energy model. In the manufacture of television sets, for example, there are many information-related aspects of what goes on, such as: The design of the sets, the ordering of materials, stock control, marketing activities, the personnel function of the company concerned, and many others.

The two models are closely related. The differences, although important, are mostly a matter of emphasis and precise definition. If defined sufficiently broadly, 'energy' could certainly be taken to include information as one particular form. If so, we would argue that information is the most important form in the post-industrial society. The relationship between the two models is shown in Figure 6.1.

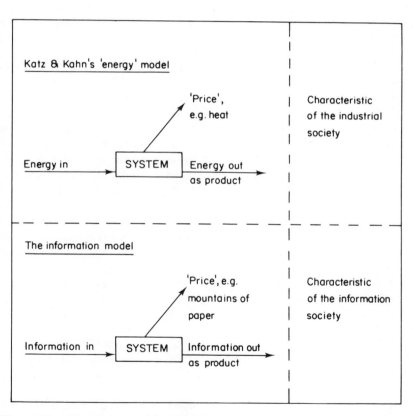

Figure 6.1.   The energy model and information model of organizational efficiency compared.

Impacts of Electronic Systems

The information model suggests that electronic systems will have three main impacts on organizational efficiency, as follows:

1. *On information input.* All other things being equal, and assuming constant output from the organization, electronic systems will tend to reduce the amount of information input, for the following reasons.

   The economics of handling information in paper-based systems mean that the units of information input are often quite large. For example, it is easier and less expensive to buy a complete book of railway timetables—even though the book will contain many pages of unwanted information—than to make repeated visits to a library to photocopy individual pages as and when needed. Electronic systems will help to overcome this difficulty with paper-based systems. For example, the whole of the Prestel database is designed on a page-by-page basis. Someone needing to know about trains to Edinburgh on weekdays can access that information when it is needed without having to receive information about all other train services as well.

2. *On output.* All other things being equal, and assuming constant information input to the organization, electronic systems will tend to increase the amount of information output from organizations, for the following reasons.

   Electronic systems will make it easier to handle information. Word processors, for example, even today make it easier to merge information from different documents, edit text, delete columns and rows from tables of numbers, and so forth. Reports can be tailored to the needs of particular readers. In other words, it becomes feasible to produce several different reports based on the same information, rather than a single report aimed at the 'average' reader, which fits on-one's needs perfectly. As systems become more sophisticated—for example, allowing easier retrieval of information—the possibilities will increase still further. At the moment, organizations currently collect a lot of information—and generate more internally—which is subsequently discarded as waste. Much of that information could be of use to other organizations but is not made available because it is uneconomical to package it. Of course, some information is confidential but in future organizations will find it easier to package their non-confidential information and instead of simply throwing it away will be able to sell it.

3. *On the 'price' of processing.* All other things being equal, electronic systems will tend to reduce the 'price' of processing information, for the following reasons.

   Many factors associated with paper-based systems seem inevitably to result in mountains of paper being created. Two factors seem to be especially important: an extraordinarily high value placed on immediate access, which in practice means people keeping many personal files (usually duplicating information held elsewhere); and an extraordinary reluctance on the part of many organizations to throw anything away.

Electronic systems will help with access by making it possible for different people in widely separate locations simultaneously and immediately to access the same information held on central, electronic files. They could help with the second problem by imposing a new discipline on office workers at all levels. Procedures and guidelines for the storage of information will tend to be more explicit. Unfortunately, some education will also be needed to achieve this. If the apparent 'hoarding instinct' shown by many managers were allowed to continue unchecked the low cost and easy availability of storage could simply mean that even more information would be stored for even longer periods than is the case with paper-based systems. A better understanding of the value of information is needed at all levels of the organization.

To understand the impacts of electronic systems in more detail, we need to consider the more specific structural models contained in the general information model and discussed below.

THE SPECIFIC MODELS

Five specific models of increasing complexity need to be considered, as follows:

- the source–channel–sink model;
- the source–store–sink model;
- the network model;
- the information sphere;
- the conflict–harmony model.

The Source–Channel–Sink Model

In its most general form, this model contains just three elements. Information is transmitted from the source to the sink when variations in the state of the sink are correlated with and lag behind (in time) variations in the state of the source. No information is transmitted when the state of the sink does not vary despite variations in the state of the source, or when the two are uncorrelated. It is mediated by a channel, which can take a variety of forms.

This simple model can be applied both at the level of organizations, where variations at the organizational boundary precede correlated organizational responses (e.g. placement of an order is followed by delivery of goods), and at the level of individual persons.

The model can be elaborated in various ways. In Figure 6.2, for example, we have taken a model of a typical man-machine system (from McCormick, 1976) and shown how it can be analysed into various source–channel–sink components at different levels of generality. The figure illustrates how it is important to distinguish between:

92

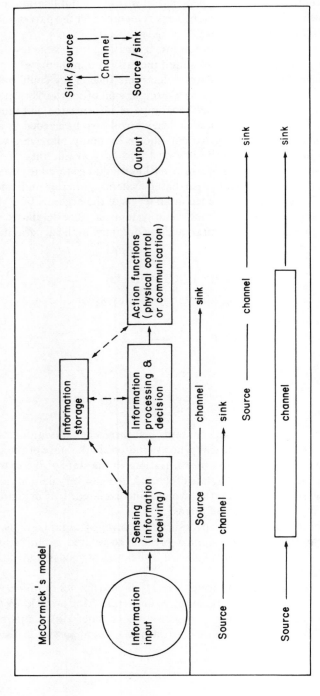

Figure 6.2. The source–channel–sink model applied to man–machine systems. (The figure shows how the source–channel–sink model can be applied to McCormick's (1976) model of the types of basic functions performed by man or machine components of man–machine systems.)

- the physical components of an information system, and
- the logical components or roles.

The roles of source, channel and sink can be played by different physical components at different times, and any given component can often be regarded as playing more than one role, depending on one's point of view.

The simple source–channel–sink model needs to be elaborated in another way. In many cases, both at the individual and organizational levels, the relationship between any given information input and response may be modified by other information inputs.

This can be demonstrated even in quite simple situations, such as a rat pressing a bar for food. The fact the bar is available is important information but so is the fact that the light is on if the act of pressing the bar only results in food when the light is on. In operant-conditioning terms, the light acts as a 'discriminative stimulus'. Other examples of discriminative stimuli include:

- the 'ready—enter your card' sign on cash card machines;
- the 'thank you—now enter your pass number' instruction in videotex;
- the 'system down' type of instruction;

and all other instances where the probability of reinforcement for a given behavioural act (e.g. logging on to a computer system) is affected by an instruction, sign or other stimulus (e.g. the 'engaged' tone). Reinforcement may for the sake of simplicity of presentation here be regarded as 'successful outcome', and operant conditioning theory suggests that this concept also needs to be included in a model of information-related behaviour (whether of individuals or, by analogy, organizations). Behaviour not reinforced will eventually be 'extinguished' (i.e. its frequency of occurrence will return to a baseline value, buried in what we might think of as 'behavioural noise'). The main concepts are shown diagrammatically in Figure 6.3.

The Source–Store–Sink Model

A particularly important elaboration of the simple source–channel–sink model concerns the concept of a store. McCormick (1976) uses this concept in describing the fundamentals of any man-machine system (see Figure 6.2).

The store can be regarded as a special type of channel which involves noticeable and significant delay in the communication between source and sink, or as a special type of source, or as a special type of sink. There is some value, however, in treating it as a concept at the same level of generality as the other three and distinguishable from them.

Doing this, we can create a symmetric model of Type B communication composed of two main parts, commitment and retrieval, which come together at the store. This is shown in Figure 6.4.

According to this model, the primary difference between Type B communication

94

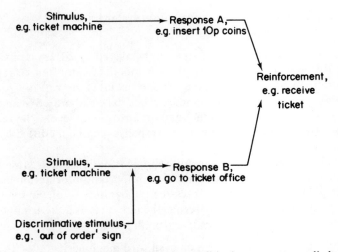

Figure 6.3. Some simple operant conditioning concepts applied to the source–channel–sink model. (For an elementary discussion of operant conditioning and other models of behaviour, see Hilgard and Bower, 1966.)

and Type A is not in terms of the delay involved in communication, though Type B normally will involve greater delay than Type A. Rather, it concerns the relative 'decoupling' of commitment and retrieval. At the time of commitment it is not normally known which sinks or how many will retrieve the information. In this regard, Type B communication is similar to mass communication: for example, a message may be sent out by television but generally it is not known who or how many people will switch on their sets and pay attention.

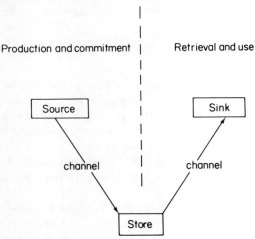

Figure 6.4. The source–store–sink model.

The decoupling creates difficulties in the design of retrieval systems because the probability of any given sink retrieving the information will be influenced by how the information was committed to store—the way it was 'tagged'—and this normally will have been done without knowing who the ultimate sinks would be. Confidentiality is another problem. One of two solutions is usually adopted: either certain information is never committed to store or certain people are barred access to the information. The first solution suffers from the risk that the information may be forgotten or its existence denied at a later time. The second suffers in at least two ways. First, it is necessary to indicate that the information exists (and has special value) in order to bar access to it, and secondly it is usually necessary for practical reasons to bar access to relatively large chunks of information (e.g. whole files or even whole buildings) which may contain much useful information of an essentially non-confidential nature.

Electronic systems can help to overcome these problems. For example, taking the commitment problem, it is feasible to commit the information to store in many more different ways (e.g. using many more identifiers) than could be done manually.

On the confidentiality problem, it is easier to edit out sensitive information automatically (providing it has been tagged at the time of commitment) at the time of retrieval, adjusting the level of 'censorship' to the 'security level' assigned to the person concerned, so more information can be made available than in manual systems. It is also possible to make the censorship completely invisible, so that not even the fact the information exists is revealed. A particular example of the latter is the use of 'public' and 'private' messages in computer conferencing. Each participant receives an apparently uncensored transcript of the conference but in fact each transcript could be different because a person does not receive a 'private' message (and is not told it exists) unless the person writing the message names him or her as an authorized recipient at the time the message is committed to store.

Stanfield (personal communication) has suggested that the source–store–sink model provides a useful way of describing the configuration of an information system, the main possibilities being shown in Figure 6.5.

The Network Model

Networks can be regarded as many Stanfield configurations linked together. They can vary in several ways, for example:

- the number of components;
- the heterogeneity of components, e.g. different types of stores, different communications media, and so forth;
- the frequency of role changing, e.g. sinks becoming sources.

Some of these variables can be important in practical situations. Heterogeneity of stores, such as a mixture of paper-based files and electronic files, is a particular

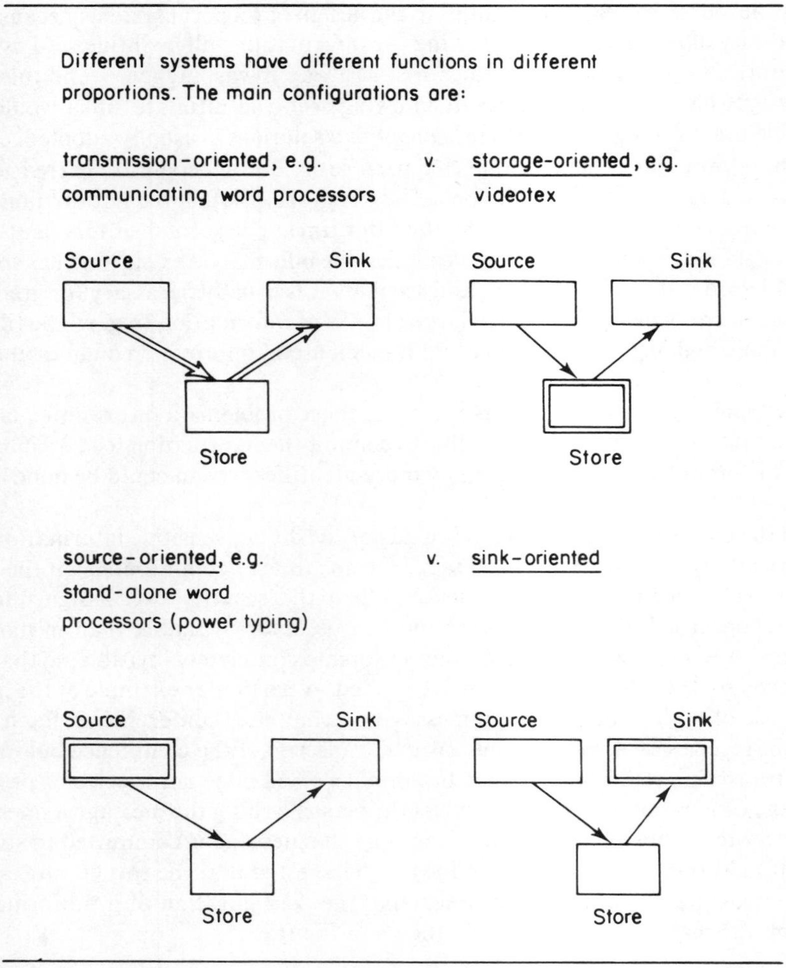
Different systems have different functions in different proportions. The main configurations are:
transmission-oriented, e.g.
communicating word processors
v.
storage-oriented, e.g.
videotex
Source
Sink
Store
Source
Sink
Store
source-oriented, e.g.
stand-alone word processors (power typing)
v.
sink-oriented
Source
Sink
Store
Source
Sink
Store

Figure 6.5. Stanfield's configurations (adapted from Stanfield, personal communication).

example; this can require careful attention to the design of the interfaces between the various kinds of files.

Psychological research in this area has focused on rather simple networks where the number of components is relatively small, they tend to be homogenous, and the frequency of role changing is low. In particular, they have usually been based on the simple source–channel–sink model, failing to treat stores as explicit components of the system. Some of the networks which have received special attention are illustrated in Figure 6.6.

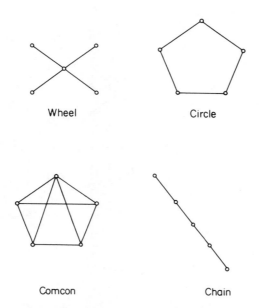

Figure 6.6. Some networks which have received special attention from researchers.

Experimental research on these simple networks has shown that both task performance and the attitudes of the people involved, especially attitudes to their own roles, are affected by the type of network set up. Some types of networks are more appropriate for some kinds of tasks than others, and the complexity of the task seems to be important in this regard. Groups which can set up their own networks tend to gravitate toward particular kinds of networks depending on the type of task being done. For a review of this research, see Baird (1977).

Field studies of networks have produced a number of important findings, especially: the existence of both formal and informal networks (e.g. see Baird, 1977); and the existence of 'gatekeepers' and other special communicators who seem to be specially important in influencing the flow of information (e.g. Bass, 1969; Whitley and Frost, 1974). Olsen (1977), discusses some other factors affecting information flow.

The Information Sphere

The work alluded to above which shows reciprocal influences of information flow in networks on task performance and attitudes points to the need to incorporate psychological factors such as attitudes into the general information model. This is done in the information sphere, shown in Figure 6.7.

The information sphere, like all models, is a simplification of reality and does

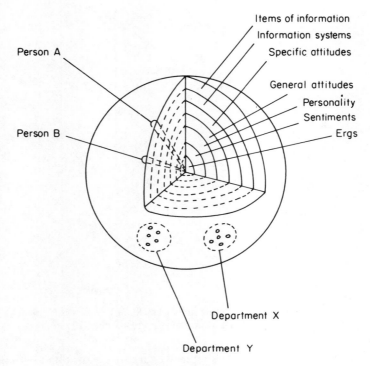

Figure 6.7. The information sphere.

not deal well with all organizational phenomena. On the other hand, in trying to understand phenomena as complex as organizations it may be necessary to focus on models which are quite considerable simplifications of reality. It is in this spirit that the information sphere is offered. It has several interesting features, as follows:

(a) The organization is seen as an 'onion' having seven main levels, as shown. Those nearer the surface are more readily observed than those nearer the centre.

(b) The most directly observable layer comprises the stimuli and responses needed to describe behaviour. These come in a variety of categories, but in this book we are only concerned with items of information—Type B communication. People respond to items of information (stimuli) and they produce items of information (responses).

(c) The form the stimuli and responses take is strongly influenced by the information systems being used. For example, a viewdata system allows for the use of colour but current word-processing systems do not. In either case, the item concerned takes quite a different form from that in a paper-based system, although in all cases it could be basically the same item, e.g. notification of recent staff changes.

(d) The main concepts introduced up to now (types of information, value of information, sources, stores, sinks, networks, and related concepts) apply most directly to the two outermost layers of the sphere, but not exclusively to these layers; 'value', for example, also relates to the 'attitude' layers.

(e) The production of one particular item of information rather than another, the decision to use one source of information rather than another, the choice of information system used in a particular instance, the decision by a company to install one kind of word-processing system rather than another, and other behaviour relating to items of information and information systems depends on the attitudes of the people concerned. Attitudes are discussed in detail in later chapters, but it is necessary at this stage to point out that the sphere includes two 'attitude' layers:

- specific attitudes, e.g. toward an IBM word-processing system compared with a Wang system; and
- general attitudes, e.g. toward office automation in general.

(f) The attitudes, and associated behaviour, evidenced in any particular situation will reflect personality and motivation (sentiments and ergs). To give some examples, we would expect:

- Managers scoring high on 16PF personality factor Q1 ('Radicalism') to support the introduction of electronic systems;
- word processing (as an occupation) to be more acceptable to A− (sizothymic) than to A+ (affectothymic) people, especially where the system is arranged such that the operator does nothing but word processing;
- people scoring high on Factor C (ego strength) to cope with word processing better than people lower on C, especially where the system is fed work from several managers;
- people scoring high on MAT motivation factors Na (narcism erg) and Sw (spouse sentiment) to support the introduction of systems allowing more work to be done at home;
- people scoring high on the unintegrated component of motivation factor As (assertiveness erg) to be amongst the most likely to acquire a personal computer.

  These are all hypotheses which await empirical research. One could easily enumerate many more. The important point is that personality and motivation structure will have definite influences on the specific and general attitudes related to behaviour in regard to information and information systems.

(g) People are represented as rods running from the surface of the sphere to the centre. This means they converge towards the centre. This reflects psychological reality. At the surface, for example in regard to the particular information systems used and items of information produced or referred to, people may differ widely, but underneath we are all driven by the same sentiments and ergs ('drives' or 'motives').

(h) Departments, sections, divisions of a company, and so forth, are treated as collections of people.

(i) The levels of the sphere interact. For example items of information received can affect attitudes. Conversely attitudes will affect the items of information a person or department produces (and see the discussion of Janis and Mann's model in Chapter 10).

(j) The concept of 'task' does not appear explicitly in the model but is there as a derivative of information and attitudes. For example, if I receive information (in a form which I may regard as an implicit or explicit request or order) that my immediate superior would like me to prepare a summary of current market research on product Z, and I have a favourable attitude toward complying with my superior's wishes in this regard, then I shall regard preparing the summary as my 'task' (which I may choose to delegate).

The Conflict–Harmony Model

The conflict–harmony model is a derivative of the information sphere and is explained by means of a hypothetical example in Figure 6.8. This shows that individuals or groups can be in conflict or in harmony at all levels of the sphere. In the particular example:

- Department X has information that sales are up on last year but Department Y has contrary information (level 1) (for several possible reasons, e.g. one may be dealing with figures on total revenue whilst the other may have figures only on the total number of sales);
- the two departments have difficulty communicating because their information systems are incompatible (level 2);

Figure 6.8. The conflict–harmony model.

Level of sphere	Person A (or Department X)	Person B (or Department Y)	Result
1. Items of information	sales are up	sales are steady	conflict
2. Information systems	IBM system	incompatible system	conflict
3. Specific attitudes	go for viewdata	go for personal computers	conflict
4. General attitudes	automate	automate	harmony
5. Personality	A+, I−	A−, I+	conflict
6. Sentiments	high Ca (career)	high Ca (career)	harmony
7. Ergs	high Pg (pugnacity)	high Pg (pugnacity)	conflict

- they agree on the need for further automation of the company's office functions (level 4) but disagree about whether to go for viewdata or personal computers (level 3);
- the key person involved in Department Y is rather reserved and aloof (characteristic of the $A-$, sizothymic person) and shows a dislike of 'crude' people, preferring gentleness and kindness (characteristic of the $I+$, premsic person), but the key person in Department X is just the opposite—easygoing and outgoing ($A+$, affectothymic) and 'masculine' and 'no-nonsense' ($I-$, harric) (level 5);
- these two agree in their desire to succeed in their work (career sentiment) (level 6); but
- they are both high on the unintegrated component of Pg (pugnacity), although this manifests itself in different ways, and this is apparent in the mutual hostility which seems to characterize their interactions with one another (level 7).

The overall impression one might get from a situation such as this hypothetical example might be one of tension and unfriendly competitiveness between the two departments concerned, and the two key people in particular, but one would need to analyse the situation in terms of the seven levels of the information sphere to best decide what steps to take to improve the situation. Without such an analysis, one might assume that making the information systems compatible would solve the difficulty—or resolving the difference of opinion about sales figures, or deciding on the form of future automation, or whichever element one happened to focus on. Such 'solutions' might result in short-term or partial improvements, but sustained and significant improvements would depend on a more complete, 'systems' approach being adopted. Such an approach would, amongst other things, distinguish between:

- short-term goals, e.g. compatibility of information systems to improve communications (and help to reduce misunderstandings or differences of interpretation in relation to such things as sales figures); and
- long-term goals, e.g. recruitment and training policies to ensure that people who need to work together are compatible and are the appropriate sort of people for an automated office environment. (This would involve personality and motivation factors discussed in Chapter 16.)

CONCLUSIONS

Organizations can be thought of as processors of information. The information systems involved form networks made up of 'sources', 'channels', 'stores', and 'sinks', which can change roles. These elements can be machines or people or combinations of the two (e.g. a word-processing work station and its operator). The information systems and the items of information flowing through them are the most directly observable features of the organization in regard to Type B communication. They can be thought of as forming the outer layers of a sphere, representing the people and associated systems in an organization. To fully understand what goes on in these surface layers, it is necessary to look deeper into the sphere—at attitudes, personality, and motivation structures. Although there is great variety at the surface, the deeper one goes the more similar people become.

PART 3
Behaviour

Chapter 7

The surface structure of office activity

The theoretical significance of Type B communication in organizations, discussed in the previous chapter, is reflected in its practical importance when one examines the surface structure of office activity. By 'surface structure' is meant the way in which time is allocated to easily observed, non-overlapping categories of activity (e.g. 'meetings', 'other activities'). In this framework, studies have shown that Type B communication consumes a significant amount of managers' time, generally from about 15 per cent to as much as 45 per cent of their time, and more for some other office workers such as secretaries or (in some organizations) clerical workers.

Surface structure is to be distinguished from 'deep structure', which is the way in which specific office activities are related to one another in the normal course of events, i.e. which activities 'go with' which others. This is examined in Chapter 8, where it is shown that several different dimensions of behaviour relating to information (e.g. 'reading and evaluating'; 'using information, local'; 'using information, remote') need to be considered in describing the psychological framework in which information activities occur in the office.

A PACTEL STUDY

During September and October of 1979, the author and his colleagues at PACTEL examined the surface structure of office activity in the offices of The Commission of the European Communities in Brussels. The Commission is a large organization of about 8000 officials and forms the administrative heart of the European Economic Community (EEC). The purpose of the study was to measure approximately how much time officials spent on the following basic office activities:

- on the telephone;
- in meetings, discussions, chats, etc.;
- reading, writing or dictating letters, reports, memos, etc.;
- all other activities.

This was seen as a first step towards defining officials' needs for support systems, such as filing systems. Only when the needs of officials were understood could appropriate improvements in their support systems be identified.

Procedure

Self-completion questionnaires were distributed to 1000 officials covering the three main grades (A, B, and C) and all the main parts of the commission ('DGs' or 'Directorates General') in Brussels, except for the 'cabinets' which were considered special cases. Respondents were asked to indicate on a scale from 0 to 100 per cent what proportion of their time in the office was spent on each of the four groups of activities listed above. Both French and English versions of the questionnaire were distributed and the respondents were asked to complete the version in their preferred language. There were 178 usable returns, a response rate of 18 per cent.

Results

The questionnaire returns suggested that about 35 per cent of officials' time was spent on Type B communication ('reading, writing, . . .'), or more if one assumes that some of the 'other activities' involved Type B communication. This is a weighted average of the results which takes account of the fact that the mix of grades in the sample was biased towards the 'A' grades (the most senior) relative to the numbers in the Commission as a whole. The differences between grades were statistically significant and are shown in Figure 7.1. There were no statistically significant differences between the questionnaire language versions or between the DGs (based on comparing eight groups of DGs which were derived by pooling the data for DGs considered to be 'similar' on *a priori* grounds).

Discussion

The results suggest that at least in this particular organization Type B communication is the single most time-consuming activity in the office. The results of other studies considered below indicate that Type B communication is also a very significant consumer of time in other types of organizations, including commercial organizations. The other studies do indicate, however, that organizations vary considerably in the precise amount of time involved.

OTHER STUDIES

The Engel et al. Study

Engel et al. (1979) report a study done by an IBM team in a commercial environment. The company concerned was a multinational corporation with a consumer and industrial product line. The study was done in the corporate and divisional headquarters, where over 1700 people were employed in a decentralized administrative environment. The purpose was to specify requirements for a prototype electronic office system. As in the PACTEL study above, it was felt that a system could be defined with confidence only after the needs of users, in this case managers and other office workers, had been examined.

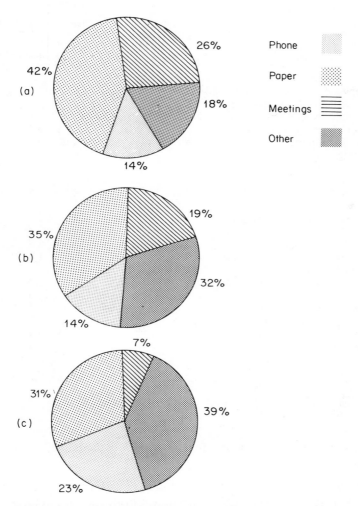

Figure 7.1. Percentage of time spent on office activities by grade
of official.

Engel et al. unfortunately do not explain how the questionnaire they used was
developed, its precise form, or how the data were treated, but their results are
especially interesting in that they compare principals with secretaries and clerical
workers. Figures 7.2 to 7.4 are based closely on the tables presented by Engel et
al. but the activities have been sorted and subtotals inserted to make the distinction
between Type A and Type B communication clear.

Two very striking findings emerge from the results in Figures 7.2 to 7.4:

• Type B communication consumed significantly more time than Type A, and was
the most time-consuming class of activities at all grades; and

Figure 7.2. Time spent by principals in the study by Engel *et al.* (1979).

Activities	Level 1	Average percent of time Level 2	Level 3	All
Type A communication	38.2	26.8	19.5	26.5
• telephone	13.8	12.3	11.3	12.3
• conferring with secretary	2.9	2.1	1.0	1.8
• scheduled meetings	13.1	6.7	3.8	7.0
• unscheduled meetings	8.5	5.7	3.4	5.4
Type B communication	38.3	0.4	44.2	44.2
• writing	9.8	17.2	17.8	15.6
• proofreading	1.8	2.5	2.4	2.3
• searching	3.0	6.4	6.4	5.6
• reading	8.7	7.4	6.3	7.3
• filing	1.1	2.0	2.5	2.0
• retrieving filed information	1.8	3.7	4.3	3.6
• dictating to secretary	4.9	1.7	0.4	1.9
• dictating to a machine	1.0	0.9	0.0	0.6
• copying	0.1	0.6	1.4	0.9
• mail handling	6.1	5.0	2.7	4.4
Other	23.3	25.9	36.0	29.4
• calculating	2.3	5.8	9.6	6.6
• planning or scheduling	4.7	5.5	2.9	4.3
• travelling outside HQ	13.1	6.6	2.2	6.4
• using equipment	0.1	1.3	9.9	4.4
• other	3.1	6.7	11.4	7.7
	100%	100%	100%	100%
Total number of principals	75	123	130	329

Level 1 = upper management.
Level 2 = other management.
Level 3 = nonmanagement.

• Lower grades spent even more time on Type B communication than did the principals.

The PACTEL study considered above did not include secretaries or strictly clerical workers, and so the Engel et al. study provides useful complementary information about these. In general, the two studies show marked agreement even though one was done in a government environment and the other in the commercial environment. They suggest that managers in both environments may spend around 30–40 per cent of their time on Type B communication. Other studies provide further support for the hypothesis that Type B communication takes up a significant part of a manager's day.

Other Studies

Goddard and Pye (1979) have reviewed several earlier studies of the way time is spent in offices. The methods which were used to conduct the studies were time

Figure 7.3.   Time spent by secretaries in the study by Engel *et al.* (1979).

Activities	Average percent of time
Type A communication	14.8
• telephone	10.5
• conferring with principals	4.3
Type B communication	79.9
• writing	3.5
• mail handling	8.1
• bulk envelope stuffing	1.4
• collating/sorting	2.6
• proofreading	3.9
• reading	1.7
• typing	37.0
• copying or duplication	6.2
• taking shorthand	5.5
• filing	4.6
• pulling files	2.8
• keeping calendars	2.6
Other	5.5
• pick-up or delivery	2.2
• using equipment	1.3
• other	2.0
	100%
Total number of secretaries	123

consuming so it is not surprising that relatively small numbers of people were studied, usually fewer than in the PACTEL and Engel et al. studies considered above. This by itself would make it difficult to compare the results of the various studies, but this difficulty is made even worse by the fact that different ways of categorizing time were used. Furthermore, the emphasis in many of the studies was on Type A rather than Type B communication. The following are examples.

Liujk (reported by Copeman, Liujk, and Hanika, 1963) observed 25 directors over a five-day period, and found that over 50 per cent of their time was spent on Type A communication (leaving a maximum of about 50 per cent for Type B). In an earlier case study of a Chicago manager in 1942, Notting (reported by Carlson, 1951) found that about 59 per cent of time was spent on Type A communication (leaving a maximum of 41 per cent for Type B). In another case study, this time of a personnel manager, Palmer and Beishon (1970) found 60 per cent of time was spent on Type A communication; of the remainder, 20 per cent was spent on 'private activities' (e.g. thinking), 15 per cent on what could definitely be classed as Type B communication ('writing and dictating' and 'reading'), and the remaining 5 per cent on 'observing'. Carlson (1951) studied ten managing directors and found that

Figure 7.4.   Time spent by clerical workers in the study by Engel *et al.* (1979).

Activities	Average percent of time
Type A communication	11.1
• telephone	9.2
• meetings	1.9
Type B communication	68.2
• filling out forms	8.3
• writing	7.3
• typing	7.8
• collating/sorting	5.2
• checking documents	10.5
• reading	2.9
• filing	5.9
• looking for information	10.2
• copying or duplication	3.9
• using a terminal	6.3
Other	20.7
• calculating	10.3
• pick-up or delivery in HQ	0.8
• scheduling or dispatching	1.2
• other	8.4
	100%
Total number of secretaries	115

the amount of time spent on Type A communication varied from 65 per cent to 90 per cent (leaving a maximum of 10 per cent to 35 per cent for Type B).

The variability is illustrated well in a study by Burns (1957). He used a diary technique on a sample of 76 managers drawn from seven companies. The amount of time spent on 'spoken communication' (Type A communication) varied from 42 per cent to 80 per cent. Time spent on 'written communication' (Type B) varied from 12 per cent to 35 per cent. Between 8 per cent and 29 per cent was spent on 'interpretation'.

A more detailed study was done by Stewart (1967) using a diary technique on a sample of 160 managers. Her results are shown in Figure 7.5. They show that, excluding 'figure work', 'inspecting' and 'social activities', 56 per cent of time was spent on Type A communication and 28 per cent on Type B.

A Point Of Methodology

The studies considered above paint a broad and roughly consistent picture but there is some degree of variability and some of that variability would seem to be due to the methods of data collection used, especially between self-completion questionnaires and direct observation of behaviour. The evidence for this comes from a study by Klemmer and Snyder (1972).

Figure 7.5.   Results of Stewart's (1967) study.

Type A communication		
	96	
informal discussions	43	
committees	7	56%
on the telephone	6	
Type B communication		
writing, dictating or reading company material	26	
reading material originating outside the company	2	28%
Other activities		
figure work	8	
inspecting	6	18%
social activities	4	

Klemmer and Snyder organized spot check observations on what 3,132 personnel at Bell Telephone Laboratories at Holmdel and Murray Hill were doing. Their sample included professional, technical, administrative and clerical personnel. In addition, approximately 4000 questionnaires were distributed, with 2626 (66 per cent) usable returns. Figure 7.6 presents the main results obtained and highlights the differences between the two types of data. As can be seen, the questionnaire respondents tended to underestimate the amount of time they actually spent on Type A communication (except for telephone contacts) and overestimate the time spent on Type B. This effect is quite large. The questionnaire data would suggest

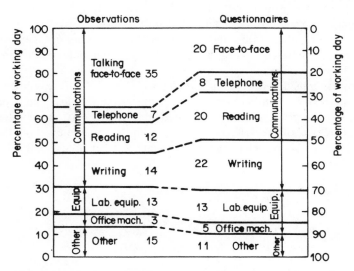

Figure 7.6.   Average percentage of the working day spent in various activities by employees of a research and development laboratory.

that more time was spent on Type B communication than on Type A but the observational data indicate that in fact the reverse was the case. This possible source of distortion should be borne in mind when considering the results of the studies of office activity considered above.

CONCLUSIONS

The studies considered in this chapter were concerned with the surface structure of office activity, and have been considered with special reference to Type B communication. It seems clear that this kind of communication consumes a significant proportion of office workers' time. There is considerable variability between different organizations and the difficulty in drawing general conclusions is further complicated by the different category systems used in the various studies and the apparent tendency for questionnaire respondents to overestimate the amount of time spent on Type B communication relative to Type A. In broad terms, the studies suggest that managers spend something of the order of 30–40 per cent of their time on Type B communication and some other office workers, including secretaries, may spend more than twice that amount. Type B communication therefore is a significant aspect of behaviour in the office environment and a worthy subject for the attention of psychologists. It is also an area where electronic systems offer obvious possibilities for savings. Even a modest reduction in the amount of time required to achieve a given level of Type B communication could release valuable working time.

For example, an electronic office system reducing the amount of time involved in writing and re-writing reports, preparing letters, and other aspects of Type B communication by, say 10 per cent, could save a typical manager about an hour and a half a week which (s)he could spend on other activities or on upgrading the quality of work done. For an organization of, say, 100 managers, this amounts to about 150 hours a week.

The studies considered were concerned only with a broad breakdown of office activity into a small number of mutually exclusive categories. The psychologist normally likes to go beyond arbitrary divisions of this sort and investigate the 'natural structure' of the domain in question, in this case to examine the way in which specific pieces of behaviour relate to one another functionally. This is the concern of the next chapter.

Chapter 8

The deep structure of office activity

The studies reviewed in Chapter 7 were concerned with what we may call the 'surface structure' of office activity. They showed that Type B communication forms a significant proportion of office workers' time. In this chapter we examine the structure of office activities in more detail, to see which specific activities 'go with' which others in the normal course of events. We may call this the 'deep structure' of office activities.

The general hypothesis of a 'deep structure' to office activities is based on the idea that specific, observable office activities derive their psychological meaning from more basic needs or processes. A telephone call, for example, may reflect a need to communicate. But how many psychologically distinguishable communication needs do we have to take account of to 'explain' the wide variety of specific behaviours we can observe in the office environment—behaviours such as persuading, giving advice, writing memoranda, filing personal notes, using a library, and so forth?

We would not expect the deep structure of office activity to be related to the surface structure in a very simple way, any more than symptoms of disease are related to particular, underlying disease processes in any simple way. A cough, for example, may be symptomatic of a cold or something more serious. This is why doctors look for patterns of symptoms when deciding on a diagnosis. In factor-analytic terminology we can say that specific symptoms, e.g. a cough, 'load on' different diseases, e.g. a cold, to varying extents.

Factor analysis seems well suited to the study of the deep structure of office activity. The factor-analytic approach assumes that office workers are capable of an infinite variety of specific attitudinal and behavioural responses within an office environment. For example, one would have a hard time just trying to make a comprehensive list of all the many specific kinds of telephone calls that are possible (e.g. short, long, self-initiated, other-initiated, urgent, angry, one of a series, etc.), let alone covering all the other kinds of office activities. The factor-analytic approach—or, more precisely, the common factor approach—does assume, however, that the generation of this open-ended variety of specific behaviours is governed by a finite set of rules. Specifically, the infinite variety of specific office activities can be thought of as representing weighted combinations of a large but finite number of basic psychological factors.

A simple and rough analogy is the location of spots on a sheet of paper. A spot can be anywhere, the possible number of specific locations is infinite. Despite this, we do not have to have an infinitely long list of possible spot locations in order to describe or 'explain' the position of any particular spot—in fact, we only need to refer to two dimensions: the vertical and horizontal axes. This principle is used in some facsimile machines, electrowriters and other devices used for transmitting pictures from one location to another. By placing spots according to appropriate vertical and horizontal coordinates it is possible to build up an accurate representation of the picture being transmitted. The same principle is used in giving map references.

In psychological research, and the study of office activities is no exception, we normally require more than two dimensions (or 'factors') to describe or 'explain' the variety of behaviours in which we are interested. Furthermore, since we are usually interested in psychologically meaningful factors rather than just arbitrary axes, we often find the factors are correlated—that is, they 'vary together' or if represented geometrically are seen to be not at right angles to one another. This is because they are often not functionally independent of one another.

For example, in the study reported in this chapter, it was found useful to distinguish between a factor representing use of local sources of information (e.g. one's own files) and a factor representing use of remote sources (e.g. libraries), but the study also showed these factors to be slightly positively correlated—because people who needed to use remote sources a lot also had a slight tendency to use local sources more than average (reflecting a more general dimension of need for information).

The relative importance of particular factors depends upon the particular set of behaviours being considered in a study. For any psychologically meaningful set of specific behaviours the number of important factors is less than the number of behaviours.

Thus, for any particular response, R (observable piece of behaviour or response to a questionnaire item), the following equation applies:

$$R = F_1W_1 + F_2W_2 + F_3W_3 + \ldots + F_kW_k,$$

where F_1-F_k are 'factor scores'—the amounts of the factors which are characteristic of the person concerned—and W_1 to W_k are the weights which apply to the factor scores to determine the value of R. The factor scores are characteristic of the person concerned, the weights (or 'factor loadings') are characteristic of the response concerned.

Factors can be identified by observing the kinds of responses they influence and the kinds they do not (given by the factor loadings).

As there are fewer important factors than there are responses (there are infinitely many responses) for any psychologically meaningful domain it follows that understanding the factor structure of a domain is the key to understanding the rules governing responses in that domain.

It is important to distinguish between the psychological model of behaviour implied in the description given above and the variety of particular mathematical techniques used to apply the model. Any mathematically defined factor resulting from a factor analysis is only an estimate of the 'true' (but hypothetical) psychological factor. Different mathematical techniques will yield slightly different results. Usually the differences are of no practical importance and in any case we assume that they are due to error in estimating the 'true' psychological factors, not that there are really different factors indicated. An important aspect of the science of factor analysis is selection of an appropriate mathematical technique. The techniques used in the study presented in this chapter are believed to be the best available at an economic cost.

The factors which emerge from a particular study depend on the particular variables measured. The computer adage 'garbage in, garbage out' applies well to factor analysis. It is important to sample the variables to be included as carefully (arguably, more carefully) as the respondents. In the study considered in this chapter this was done on the basis of a conceptual analysis of the main facets of office activity.

METHOD

The study presented here was done by the author and his colleagues at PACTEL in parallel with the study described in the previous chapter. As explained in that chapter, the organization concerned was the Commission of the European Communities in Brussels, the administrative heart of the European Economic Community. The study was seen as a first step towards defining officials' needs for information-support systems, such as filing systems. Only when the needs of officials were understood could appropriate improvements in their support systems be identified.

A basic assumption of the study, as explained above, was that a natural structure to office activities exists which can be discovered by analysing the relationships between the amounts of time spent on various facets of office activity, especially:

- use of various communications media, e.g. telephone calls and meetings;
- time spent on various 'process' or 'content' areas, e.g. answering queries or solving problems;
- use of various sources of information.

Procedure

Self-completion questionnaires were distributed to 1500 officials covering the three main grades (A, B and C) and all the main parts of the Commission ('DGs' or 'Directorates General') in Brussels, except for the 'cabinets' which were considered special cases. The questionnaires were distributed independently of the questionnaires used in the study described in the previous chapter, i.e. no account was taken in the distribution or analysis of the questionnaires of whether the respondent had received the questionnaire described previously.

The questionnaire was structured around three main sections dealing with:

- media used, e.g. telephone calls, meetings;
- process and content, e.g. answering queries;
- information sources used, e.g. libraries.

The items in the first part of the questionnaire (called 'General Overview') were selected to cover the range of media, including teleconferencing, known to be available in the Commission. Item No. 7 (on 'equipment') was included following Klemmer and Snyder (1972). The items were as follows:

(1) reading letters, documents, computer printout, notes, books or anything else;
(2) filling in forms, questionnaires or any similar materials;
(3) writing or dictating or making amendments to letters, documents, computer printout, notes, books or anything else;
(4) talking on the telephone;
(5) participating in or attending meetings, informal discussions, seminars, or anything similar *other than* teleconferences;
(6) participating in or attending teleconferences;
(7) using a calculating machine, computer, photocopier, a facsimile machine, or any other kind of equipment *other than* a telephone or conferencing system;
(8) doing anything else.

Many of these items could have been broken down into a series of more specific items but it was felt that this would have made the questionnaire too long. The same applies to the remaining two sections of the questionnaire.

The items in the second section ('Type of Work') were selected to cover the range of content areas and processes involved at a similar level of generality and taking account of the work done on face-to-face (Type A) communication reported by Short, Williams, and Christie (1976), and considered in Chapter 3. Particular note was taken of the main dimensions of 'functions' and 'activities' found in that work. The 'atmosphere' dimensions (e.g. 'angry', 'cautious') were ignored because they were felt to be of less interest and including them would have added significantly to the length of the questionnaire. This is a facet of office activities that could well be explored in future studies. The items were as follows:

(9) dealing with unsolicited items, e.g. documents, papers or other materials you have not specifically requested;
(10) dealing with items you have specifically requested;
(11) answering questions of any kind from any source;
(12) asking questions of any kind in any form of any person or group or organization;

(13) providing information of any kind in any form to any person or group or organization;

(14) solving problems of any sort;

(15) making decisions of any kind;

(16) giving instructions or orders or making requests of any kind in any form to any person or group or organization;

(17) receiving instructions, orders or requests of any kind in any form to any person or group or organization;

(18) giving advice to anyone;

(19) receiving advice from anyone;

(20) actively searching for information of any kind;

(21) bargaining, persuading or negotiating;

(22) forming impressions of others;

(23) allocating work, coordinating tasks or coordinating different stages of a project;

(24) giving presentations of reports or draft reports or anything else;

(25) appraising another department's or organization's work or services;

(26) reviewing or checking subordinates' or others' work;

(27) doing anything else.

The items in the remaining section ('Need For Files') were selected largely to span the range of information sources used. Items 29–34, which dealt with turnaround times (e.g. items needed 'immediately' compared with items needed 'within a day') are not included below because they proved to be so ambiguous they had to be dropped from all of the analyses. The remaining items were as follows:

(28) papers, documents, notes or other items that are put on file somewhere, either in your own office or anywhere else.

Using the following:

(35) your own or your secretary's files;

(36) files kept by other officials or their secretaries;

(37) your divisional files;

(38) files in *other* divisions of your own DG;

(39) the central records department of your own DG;

(40) files in other DGs;

(41) Agence Europe (Europe Agence Internationale D'Information par la presse);

(42) CELEX (computerized information system);

(43) ECDOC (computerized information system);

(44) SCAD (a system for requesting documents);

(45) documents centres, e.g. COM, SEC;

(46) one of the libraries;

(47) any other sources.

All the items asked what proportion of time the respondent spent on various types of activity. Responses were always in the form of a mark on a 21-point scale extending from 0 per cent to 100 per cent, with the 10 per cent intervals marked. Both French and English versions of the questionnaire were distributed and the respondents were asked to complete the version in their preferred language. There were 225 usable returns, an overall response rate of 15 per cent. (A questionnaire was regarded as usable if no more than two of the 47 items had been missed.)

RESULTS

The data were analysed by computer to answer the following main questions:

- How many functionally separable factors are needed to describe the range of office activities on which officials report, and how do these relate to the need for information?
- What are these factors?
- How do officials in different DGs and at different grades differ in relation to their office activities and use of information? (Only the differences between grades are reported here.)

The analysis necessary to answer these questions was conducted in five main stages, reported below:

- calculation of correlations;
- first-order factor analysis;
- second-order factor analysis;
- analysis of variance;
- construction of profiles.

The Primary Correlation Matrix

The primary correlation matrix required for the first-order factor analysis was computed using the SAS statistical package. Items 29–34 inclusive (dealing with the turnaround time officials felt necessary in gaining access to papers) were excluded from this and all subsequent stages of the analysis because of obvious differences in the way officials had interpreted this particular set of items, making their responses to these items very difficult to interpret unambiguously.

Of the $41 \times (41 - 1)/2 = 820$ correlations, a total of 438 (about 53 per cent) attained the 5 per cent level of statistical significance (two-tailed tests), indicating that the responses to the questionnaire items 'overlapped' or 'varied together' more than would be expected by chance and that an underlying psychological structure could be found by analysis of the correlations.

	FACTOR									
	I	II	III	IV	V	VI	VII	VIII	IX	X
21. bargaining	-.85	-.02	-.01	-.01	-.01	-.05	-.10	-.02	-.01	-.05
16. instructions	-.81	.01	.00	.00	.08	.14	-.06	-.21	.01	.16
15. decisions	-.78	.00	.08	-.06	.13	.28	-.04	.04	-.03	.12
23. coordinating	-.76	.01	-.07	-.11	-.21	.01	.07	-.13	.07	.08
24. presentations	-.71	-.02	.10	.08	.04	.05	-.15	.12	-.01	-.12
22. impressions	-.68	-.04	-.16	.10	-.13	-.10	.30	.03	-.01	.00
26. reviewing	-.57	.05	-.02	-.17	-.29	-.02	.09	-.23	.15	-.03
18. advice	-.55	-.00	.07	.12	.11	.39	-.01	.11	.00	-.00
19. advice	-.39	-.04	.00	.22	-.10	.03	.33	-.02	-.33	.06
42. CELEX	.03	.94	-.07	.12	.07	-.14	-.05	.15	.02	.06
43. ECDOC	.05	.87	-.00	.08	.11	-.12	-.04	-.18	-.14	-.00
41. Agence E.	.00	.79	-.09	.14	-.01	.00	-.11	-.07	-.04	.01
38. files	-.27	.75	-.08	.16	.04	-.20	-.13	.07	-.02	-.05
40. files	-.00	.73	.03	.02	-.20	.08	-.04	-.13	.11	-.00
44. SCAD	.08	.71	-.06	-.18	-.15	.08	-.07	-.11	.18	.08
46. libraries	.03	.68	.17	-.17	.07	.08	.28	.05	.02	.04
39. cent. records	.11	.59	.08	.07	-.08	.04	.28	-.36	-.01	-.02
47. other sources	-.07	.58	-.07	-.18	-.08	.22	-.03	.42	-.05	-.01
27. anything else	-.03	.10	-.80	-.15	-.03	.30	-.14	.12	.08	-.13
8. anything else	.04	-.01	-.79	-.08	.08	.15	.18	-.01	.12	-.10
3. writing	.03	-.02	.62	-.02	-.29	.16	-.07	-.01	.26	-.11
36. files	.03	.23	.14	.67	.09	.06	.27	.09	.24	-.03
35. files	-.14	-.03	.12	.58	-.02	-.02	.05	.00	-.15	.01
37. files	-.08	.16	-.06	.58	.04	.05	-.00	-.45	-.04	-.24
28. on file	.29	.07	-.01	.53	-.18	.21	-.01	.17	.01	.39
1. reading	.10	.07	.18	-.05	-.83	-.08	.07	-.10	-.16	-.04
25. appraising	-.38	-.02	-.19	.08	-.58	-.38	-.09	.16	-.03	-.00
13. information	-.07	-.03	-.03	.06	.11	.85	.00	-.07	.04	-.02
11. queries	-.06	.00	-.10	-.08	.17	.82	.11	-.14	.01	-.04
14. problems	-.43	.02	.03	-.04	.05	.62	-.07	.07	-.09	.04
17. instructions	-.17	-.09	-.20	.16	.09	.58	.24	-.15	-.04	.03
9. unsolicited	.10	-.13	-.10	.21	-.27	.47	-.33	-.39	-.06	.13
12. questions	-.12	-.00	-.08	.11	-.29	.32	.27	.19	.01	.09
4. telephone	-.09	-.07	.02	.11	-.02	.02	.69	-.16	.18	-.03
7. equipment	.16	-.01	-.08	.11	.15	.04	.64	.10	-.20	-.07
20. searching	-.20	.01	.08	.06	-.32	.24	.48	.08	-.06	-.09
5. meetings	-.33	.02	.32	.12	.11	.00	.43	-.06	.21	-.05
45. documents	-.06	.29	.08	-.20	-.00	.18	.02	-.74	-.25	-.05
2. forms	.02	-.01	-.03	-.05	-.03	-.09	.07	-.32	-.81	.15
10. requested	.02	-.02	.09	.02	-.27	.28	-.11	.05	-.66	-.25
6. teleconferen.	-.17	.06	.11	-.02	.06	-.01	-.18	.06	-.02	.89

Figure 8.1. Factor pattern matrix.

The First-order Factor Analysis

The primary correlation matrix was factor-analysed using the SAS statistical package. The number of factors was determined by conducting a principal components analysis with unities in the diagonals and rejecting all components (factors) with eigenvalues less than unity, i.e. all factors which contributed less than the average variable to the total variance. This gave ten first-order factors. These were

120

		I	II	III	IV	V	VI	VII	VIII	IX	X
I	people		-.096	-.057	-.211	.205	-.329	-.039	-.016	.001	.143
II	remote inform.			.043	.153	-.105	.176	.029	-.101	.098	-.137
III	other activit.				-.042	.063	-.123	-.172	.170	-.007	-.104
IV	local inform.					-.056	.105	-.005	.068	-.172	.020
V	appraising						-.383	-.113	.117	-.113	-.030
VI	prov. inform.							.228	-.007	-.080	.009
VII	clerical								-.112	-.158	.068
VIII	doc. centres									-.257	-.103
IX	forms										-.028
X	teleconferenc.										

Figure 8.2.   Intercorrelations between the first-order factors.

identified by rotating them to oblique simple structure using the Promax Criterion.

The factor loadings are given in the factor pattern matrix in Figure 8.1. These loadings show to what extent the factors 'explain' or 'predict' the individual judgements given by the respondents. For example, the most important factor influencing responses to item 1 (proportion of time spent reading letters, etc.) is Factor 5 (with a loading of −0.83). An interpretation of the ten factors is given in the 'discussion' section below.

The Second-order Factor Analysis

As explained above, psychologically meaningful factors are often correlated with each other to some degree. The correlations between the first-order factors that emerged in the study being described here were judged sufficiently high to warrant a further stage in the analysis to determine broader factors. These second-order factors, of which there were four, were identified by analysing the intercorrelations between the first-order factors, shown in Figure 8.2, according to the same procedures described above for the analysis of the primary correlation matrix.

The factor loadings are shown in Figure 8.3 and the inter-factor correlations in Figure 8.4. Interpretation of the factors is discussed below.

The Analysis of Variance

The factor analyses described above showed that officials' office activities could

	S1 person- oriented	S2 forms	S3 other	S4 use of in- formation
VI providing information	.79	.09	.10	.03
V appraising	-.71	.22	-.04	.11
I people	-.60	-.09	.30	-.19
IX forms	.00	-.80	-.17	-.10
VIII document centres	.00	.69	-.41	-.11
III other activities	-.02	.13	-.67	-.12
X teleconferencing	-.15	.01	.60	-.06
VII clerical	.39	.16	.51	-.12
IV local information	-.06	.25	.11	.82
II remote information	.09	-.34	-.12	.64

Figure 8.3.   Loadings on second-order factors.

be understood in terms of ten main factors which, in turn, could be understood in terms of four broader, 'second-order' factors. The purpose of the analysis of variance was to determine whether there were any differences between the DGs or grades of official. For the purposes of this analysis, an *a priori* grouping of the DGs into eight groups was made on the basis of their similarities and these eight groups were then compared in the analysis of variance.

	S1	S2	S3	S4
S1 person-oriented		-.011	.061	.197
S2 forms			.046	.043
S3 other				-.049
S4 use of information				

Figure 8.4.   Intercorrelations between the second-order factors.

The analysis was performed using the SAS statistical package GLM program. The data supplied to this programme were the factor scores derived from the first order factor analysis. (These scores represented the officials' standing on each of the ten factors.) Factor scores were computed only for those respondents who had returned absolutely complete questionnaires, a total of 105 respondents, and the analysis of variance therefore was based on this number of respondents.

The analysis was designed to decide whether the scores on the ten factors depended at a level of statistical significance (P <0.05) on:

- the respondent's DG group (DG);
- the respondent's grade (G);
- the language version of the questionnaire (L);

and whether any differences between the DG groups were influenced by the respondent's grade ($DG \times G$). Any such interactions would have complicated interpretation of the analysis.

A summary of the analysis is presented in Figure 8.5.

The Profiles

Profiles were prepared to show graphically the differences and similarities between the various DG groups and various grades. Only those for the grades are presented here, in Figure 8.6(a)–(c). They should be interpreted bearing in mind the results of the analysis of variance (Figure 8.5) which show where the main differences lie and where apparent differences could be due to chance variation, e.g. in sampling respondents.

The profiles show deviations from the average and are based on factor scores which have been corrected to take account of the numbers of respondents contributing to each profile and the corresponding numbers in the Commission itself.

Figure 8.5.   Analysis of variance summary.

Factor	DG Group (DG)	Grade (G)	Language (L)	$DG \times G$
1. Dealing directly with people			*	
2. Using information (remote)				
4. Using information (local)				
8. Using document centres		*		
5. Reading and evaluating				
6. Providing information				
10. Teleconferencing	*			
9. Filling in forms		*		
7. Clerical activities	*	*		
3. Other activities	*			

* Indicates a statistically significant effect (P <0.05) on the factors concerned.

Figure 8.6(a). Profiles (Grade A officials).

Factor	Factor score	sten	Standard ten score (sten)				Average						High-score description; Spends much time:
			1	2	3	4	5	6	7	8	9	10	
D1	0.240	6	•	•	•	•	•	•	•	•	•	•	Dealing directly with people — bargaining, giving instructions, allocating work, giving presentations, forming impressions, reviewing or checking subordinates' work
D2	0.057	6	•	•	•	•	•	•	•	•	•	•	Using information (remote) — CELEX, ECDOC, Agence Europe, files in other divisions or other DGs, SCAD
D4	-0.259	5	•	•	•	•	•	•	•	•	•	•	Using information (local) — own files, files in own division
D8	-0.056	5	•	•	•	•	•	•	•	•	•	•	Using document centres — e.g. COM, SEC
D5	0.023	6	•	•	•	•	•	•	•	•	•	•	Reading and evaluating — reading letters or other documents, appraising work or services
D6	-0.180	5	•	•	•	•	•	•	•	•	•	•	Providing information — answering queries, dealing with unsolicited items
D10	-0.015	5	•	•	•	•	•	•	•	•	•	•	Teleconferencing — participating in or attending teleconferences
D9	0.457	6	•	•	•	•	•	•	•	•	•	•	Filling in forms — filling in forms, questionnaires or other materials
D7	-0.768	4	•	•	•	•	•	•	•	•	•	•	Clerical activities — on the telephone, using a calculator, photocopying, using other equipment
D3	-0.741	4	•	•	•	•	•	•	•	•	•	•	Other activities — doing other miscellaneous things

Office activity profile (factors D1–D10)

Grade A officials
$n = 46$

A sten of about

1	2	3	4	5	6	7	8	9	10
2.3%	4.4%	9.2%	15.0%	19.1%	19.1%	15.0%	9.2%	4.4%	2.3%

was characteristic of officials

124

Fig. 8.6(b). Profiles (Grade B officials).

Office activity profile: (factors D1–D10)		Grade B officials $n = 28$

Standard ten score (sten)

Factor	Factor score	Sten	1	2	3	4	5	6	7	8	9	10	High-score description; Spends much time:
D1	−0.046	5					•						Dealing directly with people: bargaining, giving instructions, allocating work, giving presentations, forming impressions, reviewing or checking subordinates' work
D2	0.500	7							•				Using information (remote) CELEX, ECDOC, Agence Europe, files in other divisions or other DGs, SCAD
D4	0.093	6						•					Using information (local) own files, files in own division
D8	−0.259	5					•						Using document centres e.g. COM, SEC
D5	−0.004	5					•						Reading and evaluating reading letters or other documents, appraising work or services
D6	−0.140	5					•						Providing information answering queries, dealing with unsolicited items
D10	−0.104	5					•						Teleconferencing participating in or attending teleconferences
D9	−0.066	5					•						Filling in forms filling in forms, questionnaires or other materials
D7	−0.080	5					•						Clerical activities on the telephone, using a calculator, photocopying, using other equipment
D3	−0.323	5					•						Other activities doing other miscellaneous things

A sten of about	2.3%	4.4%	9.2%	15.0%	19.1%	19.1%	15.0%	9.2%	4.4%	2.3%	was characteristic of officials
	1	2	3	4	5	6	7	8	9	10	

Average

Figure 8.6(c). Profiles (Grade C officials).

Office activity profile: (factors D1–D10)

Grade C officials $n = 29$

Factor	Factor score	Sten	Standard ten score (sten)	High-score description; Spends much time:
D1	−0.155	5	5	Dealing directly with people — bargaining, giving instructions, allocating work, giving presentations, forming impressions, reviewing or checking subordinates' work
D2	−0.075	5	5	Using information (remote) — CELEX, ECDOC, Agence Europe, files in other divisions or other DGs, SCAD
D4	0.141	6	6	Using information (local) — own files, files in own division
D8	0.202	6	6	Using document centres — e.g. COM, SEC
D5	0.056	6	6	Reading and evaluating — reading letters or other documents, appraising work or services
D6	0.224	6	6	Providing information — answering queries, dealing with unsolicited items
D10	0.075	6	6	Teleconferencing — participating in or attending teleconferences
D9	−0.309	5	5	Filling in forms — filling in forms, questionnaires or other materials
D7	0.637	7	7	Clerical activities — on the telephone, using a calculator, photocopying, using other equipment
D3	0.765	7	7	Other activities — doing other miscellaneous things

(Average marked at sten 5 and 6)

A sten of about:

1	2	3	4	5	6	7	8	9	10
2.3%	4.4%	9.2%	15.0%	19.1%	19.1%	15.0%	9.2%	4.4%	2.3%

was characteristic of officials

The 'average band' (STENS 5 and 6) is therefore the estimated average over the commission as a whole, not simply the average of the particular sample of respondents in the study. The averages estimated in this way are shown in Figure 8.7.

DISCUSSION

We said at the beginning that we would not expect the deep structure of office activity to be related to the surface structure in a very simple way, and the results of the study bear this out. The ten first-order factors cut across the distinctions made at the surface between 'telephone', 'meetings', 'reading and writing', and so forth (see Chapter 7), and across the distinction between Type A and Type B communication. For example, we may suppose that Factor 1 ('Dealing Directly With People'—e.g. bargaining, giving instructions) mainly involves Type A communication and Factor 2 ('Using Information, Remote'—e.g. CELEX, ECDOC) mainly involves Type B, but it is likely that in regard to Factor 1 some instructions are given in writing and in regard to Factor 2 some face to face communication takes place in connection with using some remote sources of information. Factor 6 ('Providing Information') seems especially to represent a mixture of Type A and Type B communication. This makes sense. At the surface, people make use of Type A and Type B communication as these are available and as other factors, e.g. cost and expected effectiveness, are relevant. The underlying psychological factors are less dependent on the particular choice of communications medium. For example, a need to provide information may result in either Type A or Type B communication depending upon particular circumstances. Bearing this in mind, it may nevertheless be helpful in discussing the factors to group them according to their likely *emphasis* on Type A or Type B communication, as follows.

Figure 8.7.   Average amount of time spent on main office activities.

	Factor	Proportion of time spent (%)	
5	Reading and evaluating	21	
7	Clerical activities	16*	
6	Providing information	15	79%
1	Dealing directly with people	11	
4	Using information (local)	9	
9	Filling in forms	7*	
8	Using document centres	6*	
2	Using information (remote)	1	7%
10	Teleconferencing	0*	
3	Other activities	14*	

* Indicates that DG groups or grades of official differ to a degree that is statistically significant (see Figure 8.5).

'Type A' Factors

Dealing directly with people (Factor 1). This accounted for about 11 per cent of the time of officials in the study. It involves a variety of specific activities, including: giving instructions, allocating work, reviewing subordinates' work, giving advice, forming impressions of people, giving presentations, and in some cases bargaining, persuading or negotiating. It often involves attendance at meetings or informal discussions. The generality of the factor with respect to its content, covering a wide range of the 'functions' and 'activities' identified in the Short, Williams and Christie research considered in Chapter 3, suggests this may be a second stratum factor even though it emerged as a first-order factor in the study. (The term 'stratum' refers to a conceptual or theoretical level, the term 'order' to a level in a particular study. A second stratum factor may emerge as either a first- or a second-order factor in a particular study depending on particular features of the research design, e.g. the mix of variables included.)

Providing information (Factor 6). About 15 per cent of the time of the officials studied was concerned with this factor. This probably mostly involved Type A communication but there was probably also some Type B involved. The particular kinds of activities contributing most to this factor include answering queries and dealing with a variety of unsolicited documents, papers and other materials. The factor is often connected with helping to solve problems of various sorts.

Clerical activities (Factor 7). This family of activities includes using a calculating machine, computer, photocopier, facsimile machine or other equipment, often in connection with an active search for information. It is included here because it may often involve talking on the telephone (but is unlikely to involve attendance at a meeting of any kind). About 16 per cent of officials' time was consumed in this way in the study, although this figure was less (about 8 per cent) for 'A' grades and, as would be expected, considerably more (over 20 per cent) for 'C' grades.

Teleconferencing (Factor 10). The officials studied generally spent less than 1 per cent of their time on teleconferencing. It appears as a separate factor largely because it does not correlate significantly with any other activity, with the exception of a very small (+0.019) but statistically significant correlation with time spent on papers, documents, notes or other items put on file somewhere.

'Type B' Factors

Reading and evaluating (Factor 5). About 21 per cent of the officials' time was spent on reading letters, documents, computer printout, notes, books and other material. This was often associated with appraising another department's or organization's work or services. All grades were involved about equally, although we may assume there would have been differences in the detailed nature of the work involved. In terms of time consumed, this general type of activity emerged as being the single most important in the present study.

Filling in forms (*Factor 9*). This includes filling in questionnaires and other materials as well as forms as such, and often involves items which have been specifically requested or the filling in of forms that is required in order to obtain such items. About 7 per cent of time was consumed this way in the study, although it was less for 'A' grades (about 3 per cent) and more for 'C' grades (over 10 per cent).

Using document centres (*Factor 8*). About 6 per cent of the officials' time involved using document centres and some other information sources apart from the main sources on which the study focussed. 'C' grade officials spent a little more time (about 9 per cent) in this way.

Using information (*Local*) (*Factor 4*). About 9 per cent of the officials' time was spent using local sources of information, especially their own files and files kept at divisional level.

Using information (*Remote*) (*Factor 2*). 'Remote' sources include, for example: the computerized systems (CELEX, ECDOC), the journal 'Agence Europe', the document request system 'SCAD', a rather heterogeneous collection but even so it accounted for only about 1 per cent of the officials' time. Perhaps in organizations where the type of information sources involved are used more often more than a single factor might emerge.

Providing information (*Factor 6*). This factor is described above and is listed here again simply because it probably involves a mixture of Type A and Type B communication.

Other activities (*Factor 3*). The remaining factor, accounting for about 14 per cent of the officials' time, describes a variety of other activities not easily classifiable and not always involving Type B communication. It is included here because many of the activities concerned often do involve writing or dictating or making amendments to papers and other material.

The Second-order Factors

In factor-analytic research it is often found that the higher-order factors are the more generalizable across different contexts, in this case organizations. This is not surprising because they represent more general sources of variance, more fundamental psychological processes. Many of the particular questionnaire items used in the study being described here would be inappropriate in some other organizations. For example, the terms 'CELEX' and 'DG' are peculiar to the Commission.

However, there are more general concepts of which these terms can be seen to be particular manifestations. 'CELEX' is a computerized information system, and 'DG' refers to a way of dividing up the organization. It is reasonable to suppose, then, that the ways in which the specific behaviours tapped by the questionnaire items 'vary together' to form the factors observed reflect underlying patterns of behaviour which are not unique to the Commission but are likely to manifest themselves, though through different particular items, in many other organizations. If this is at all true of the first order factors, it is even more true of the second order factors which reflect even more general patterns of behaviour.

The second-order factors therefore describe a broader framework, and probably a more generalizable one, underlying the particular activities which made up the working days of the officials studied. There were four such factors identified, as follows.

Person-oriented activities (Factor I). Officials who scored high on this factor spent a lot of time providing information (Factor 6) and dealing directly with people (Factor 1). About 26 per cent of the working day was consumed in this way, on average. The factor can be seen to represent an amalgam of Factors 6 and 1. If Factor 1 is regarded as a second-stratum factor, i.e. a factor at a more general conceptual level than some of the other first-order factors observed, then person-oriented activity must be a third stratum factor, i.e. a factor at a very general conceptual level and one that might be expected to be observed in very many different kinds of organizations.

Dealing with forms (Factor II). The precise interpretation of this factor is not entirely clear although it may represent a paper-based background administrative activity. It is defined largely by the two first-order factors 9 ('Filling in forms') and 8 ('Document centres').

Use of information (Factor IV). This clearly represents a general use of information factor that could be expected to be observed in a wide range of organizations. It is discussed further in the next chapter, in relation to the origination of items of information. In this study it was defined largely by the two first-order 'use of information' factors, 4 ('local') and 2 ('remote'). Officials who spent a lot of time using 'local' sources of information, e.g. their own and other officials' own files also tended to spend more time using 'remote' sources such as CELEX, ECDOC, the libraries, and so forth.

Other activities (Factor III). This factor reflects the remaining types of activities as described by the first order factors discussed above.

CONCLUSIONS

The surface structure of office activity discussed in Chapter 7 can be seen to reflect a more complex 'deep structure'. This deep structure could be described in the present study in terms of ten first-order factors. There is no clear distinction between Type A and Type B communication in terms of these factors, but the factors are seen to differ in their emphasis on the two types of communication. The factors reflect psychological patterns that are more basic than the very specific behaviours tapped by the particular questionnaire items used. Many of the questionnaire items are appropriate only in the context of the study itself but the more general patterns indicated by the factors are likely to be generalizable to other organizations. This is especially true of the second-order factors, and two of these stand out as warranting special attention:

- person-oriented activities, where the emphasis is on Type A communication; and
- use of information, where the emphasis is on Type B communication.

The Use-of-information factor is examined more closely in relation to the origination of items of information in the next chapter.

Chapter 9

The origination and use of information— towards a first law of information behaviour

The study presented in the previous chapter suggested the possibility of a general Use-of-information factor. The possibility of such a factor being demonstrated empirically supports the general notion that people in the office environment, and possibly elsewhere, vary in their use of the information sources available to them. The study suggests that, although the pattern of usage may vary according to the particular needs of a given person, i.e. using a particular mix of information sources, over and above this some people will tend to use all sources more than other people will. Other research bearing on this is discussed in Chapter 10. The purpose of the present chapter is rather different. The study discussed in the previous chapter was concerned with the use of information only in rather general terms, not in relation to specific circumstances. The study presented in this chapter was concerned with the circumstances in which information is used, and the circumstances in which items of information are originated.

The study was designed to map out the domain in an exploratory fashion rather than to test particular hypotheses. Probably the most important aspect of the results therefore was serendipitous and consequently must be treated with some caution until replicated in future studies, preferably by other researchers working in other types of organizations.

It is for this very reason that it is felt important to present the results of the study here, so that future studies can have a clear starting point, a research framework and a clear hypothesis to test. The hypothesis is that a first law of information behaviour exists analogous to the first law of intelligence and the first law of attitude.

The First Laws of Intelligence and Attitude

Shye (1978, p. 2) has suggested that "the scientific effort may be described as the search for those combinations of normalized conceptualizations for data collection, on the one hand, and structural aspects of the data, on the other, which reveal regularities. Naturally, therefore, special value is attributed to a scientific theory which has been convincingly verified by empirical evidence, that is, to a theory that asserts that data observed in accordance with its definitional system should behave in a certain way, and data are subsequently consistently found to behave as specified by that theory. When such a theory is considered to be of sufficient generality of import, it may be called a law."

Shye points out and emphasizes the importance of defining the universe of observation with which one is concerned. This helps other scientists to focus on those elements of a situation that are essential for the replication of an experiment or testing of a law, and ignore those aspects that are not important. Shye discusses the 'mapping sentence' in this regard. Such a sentence describes the universe of content by specifying various 'facets' and the 'relationships' between them. The concept is easiest to explain by example, as in the mapping sentences which describe the universes of intelligence and attitude items given below (from Shye, 1978, pp. 17–19):

> "An item belongs to the universe of intelligence items if and only if its domain asks about a (logical/scientific or factual/semantic) rule, and its range is ordered from (very right to very wrong) with respect to that rule."

> "An item belongs to the universe of attitude items if and only if its domain asks about behaviour in a (cognitive/affective/instrumental) modality toward an object, and its range is ordered from (very positive to very negative) towards that object."

The facets in the mapping sentences above are the parts in parentheses and the relationships between them are indicated by the remaining parts of the sentences. The elements in the facets can be of various sorts. They can be semantic or they can indicate possibilities in regard to experimental conditions, e.g. day of week or sex of interviewer. Shye suggests that when a conceivable facet fails to appear in a mapping sentence or a research design this implies (rightly or wrongly) that the kind of item differentiation implied by the facet is irrelevant to the hypotheses under consideration.

The mapping sentence therefore serves to define the universe of observations appropriate for the replication of a study or testing of a law. The statement of a law is meaningful only if it is tied to a mapping sentence or similarly rigorous definition. The first laws of intelligence and attitude are tied to the mapping sentences above. They are basic laws of behaviour in that they refer to a simple and general aspect of empirical observations, the sign of the correlation coefficients computed between items defined according to the mapping sentences. The laws, generally credited to Louis Guttman, summarize phenomena observed by psychologists over a period of many years. The laws, as stated by Shye (1978, pp. 18–19), are as follows.

For the First Law of Intelligence:

"If any two items are selected from the universe of intelligence items, and if the population is not selected artificially, then the population regressions between those two items will be monotone and with positive or zero sign."

Similarly for the First Law of Attitude:

"If any two items are selected from the universe of attitude items towards a given object, and if the population observed is not selected artificially, then the population regressions between those two items will be monotone and with positive or zero sign."

These two laws can be restated more simply by saying that correlation matrices made up of the correlations between items that conform to the definitions given in the mapping sentences do not contain any negative correlations.

As Shye points out, the statement of these laws paves the way for systematic, meaningful research. For example, in relation to the first law of intelligence, the law "invites scientists to test its applicability in diverse contexts to find and characterize situations where the law does not hold. Such "failures" can lead to constructive sharpening of the experimental conditions and of the definitional framework—for example, by clarifying what constitutes a "non-artificial" or a natural population in the context of intelligence testing or possibly by further restricting the definition of intelligence items" (Shye, 1978, p. 18).

A mapping sentence, which we have seen is a necessary precursor to the statement of a law, may be constructed prospectively for theory construction, in advance of gathering data, or it can be constructed retrospectively to analyse data already gathered. In the latter case, new data must be collected subsequently to see if they support the retrospective hypothesis. The study presented in this chapter was not designed to test any particular hypothesis and so the hypothesis of the existence of a first law must be considered retrospective and in need of much further research, but it is likely that the results were so neat largely because the study was designed around very clear and explicit facets, as described below.

METHOD

The study was done by the author and his colleagues at PACTEL in parallel with the study described in the previous chapter. The purpose of the study was to ascertain the circumstances in which officials in the Commission of the European Communities in Brussels needed to refer to or originate items of information, and to do this within a framework that would allow systematic comparisons to be made between different parts of the Commission and different grades of official.

Comparability between different parts of the Commission and different grades was ensured by focusing on activities which were considered to be common to all parts of the commission (all 'DGs') and all grades, although varying in importance. The activities, providing a context in which reference to and origination of information could be studied, were:

- telephone calls;
- meetings;
- written communications;
- miscellaneous other office activities;

in other words, the surface structure of office activity. To this facet, two further facets were added to make the definition of circumstances more specific. These were:

- locus of initiation, e.g. making a telephone call compared with receiving a call; and,
- time, e.g. before, during or after a call.

It was felt that more specifically defined circumstances which might be of special importance to particular officials, e.g. meetings of particular (named) committees, would normally be locatable within this general framework.

Procedure

Self-completion questionnaires were distributed to 1000 officials covering the three main grades (A, B and C) and all the main parts of the Commission in Brussels, except for the 'cabinets'. The questionnaires were distributed independently of those discussed in previous chapters.

The 22 items in the questionnaire were constructed within a framework defined by the facets of information behaviour discussed above, i.e.:

- type of action (reference or writing);
- type of context activity (e.g. a meeting);
- locus of initiation (self or other);
- time (before, during or after).

Item No. 1, as an example, was:

"How often do you need to refer to papers, documents, reports, computer printout, or any other kinds of information before making a telephone call (i.e. initiating a call yourself or through your secretary)?"

In this item the type of action is 'reference', the context activity 'initiating a telephone call', the locus of initiation 'self', and the time 'before'.

The sequence of items in the questionnaire was such that the type of action changed most slowly and the time most quickly. Items 1–11 were as follows:

"How often do you need to refer to papers, documents, reports, computer printout, or any other kinds of information:

- before, during or after *making* a telephone call (i.e. initiating a call yourself or through your secretary)? (Items 1, 2, 3)
- during or after *receiving* a telephone call? (Items 4, 5)
- before, during or after attending or participating in a meeting, informal discussion, seminar, teleconference, or similar event? (Items 6, 7, 8)
- in order to deal with a letter, memorandum, document, report, or other item you have received? (Item 9)
- in general in order to write or dictate a letter, memorandum, document, report or other item (e.g. filling in a form)? (Item 10)
- in connection with any other activities apart from those considered above (e.g. using a computer, calculating machine, making photocopies, sorting and classifying material, and so forth)? (Item 11)"

Items 12–22 were essentially the same but began:

"How often do you need to write notes, write a paper, fill in a form, dictate a letter, or write or dictate any other item?"

The response required was always in the form of a 9-point scale ranging from "almost never (0 per cent)" to "almost always (100 per cent)" with the 25 per cent, 50 per cent and 75 per cent positions marked.

Taken together, the 22 items are probably representative of the broad range of circumstances in which officials were likely to refer to information or generate new items by writing or dictating. The items offer a description of officials' information behaviour at a general level. The study was not designed to examine information behaviour at the next level of detail, e.g. in relation to the content rather than the medium of communication, or the particular sources of information used. It was designed to relate the broad structure of the working day—in terms of meetings, paper-oriented activities, telephone calls, and so forth—to officials' need for and origination of items of information.

Two versions of the questionnaire were distributed, in French and English, and respondents were invited to choose according to their preferred language. There were 239 usable returns, an overall response rate of just under 24 per cent. (A questionnaire was regarded as usable if no more than 2 of the 22 items had been missed.)

MAIN RESULT

The main result in the present context concerns the primary correlation matrix, computed using the SAS statistical package. Of the $22 \times (22 - 1)/2 = 231$ product-moment correlations, a total of 225 (about 97 per cent) were statistically significant, i.e. the responses to different items 'overlapped' or 'varied together' more than would be expected by chance (P <0.05). All the correlations were positive. This pointed immediately to two general conclusions:

- officials who referred to information a lot also tended to originate a lot of new items; and
- officials who referred to or originated a lot of information in one context were likely to do so also in many other contexts.

This type of correlation matrix is exactly the type discussed above in connection with the first laws of intelligence and attitude and suggests the possibility of an analogous first law of information behaviour. The result is especially suggestive of this because the items included in the questionnaire were not a random, hodge-podge of items selected intuitively for their interest or relevance but were carefully selected according to the explicit facet design described above. Particular care was taken to ensure that a consistent response range was used (measuring frequency, from 'almost never' to 'almost always'), an important feature of mapping sentences and research based on them.

It must be emphasized that the law suggested by the data from this study requires much further research, preferably by other researchers in other organizations, if it is to be substantiated. Perhaps it will need modification, but this is often the case. As Shye (1978, p. 17) has said, "The justification of definitional systems for observations, on the one hand, and of technical manipulations of data, on the other, is their ability to enter into joint partnerships to form laws.

"The strengthening and improvement of laws requires continued testing through experimental replications, so that any one or both of their parts, the definitional and the technical, may be refined, modified, or altogether replaced. But clearly, even the crudest law is preferable to elaborate conceptual schemes and to sophisticated techniques that do not show a promise of becoming partners in the formation of laws."

It is in this spirit that the following law of information behaviour is proposed for testing and refinement by fellow researchers.

Like other laws, our new law requires a mapping sentence. As indicated earlier, mapping sentences can be constructed in advance of data collection or retrospectively. In the study being discussed here, we defined what we felt to be important facets of information behaviour, and an appropriate response range, in advance of data collection in order to provide a meaningful basis for the questionnaire, but we did not go so far as to write a mapping sentence as such. In retrospect, we may write the following mapping sentence.

Definition of Information Behaviour

An item belongs to the universe of information behaviour items if and only if its domain asks about the frequency of (reference to/origination of) items of information in relation to (face-to-face communication/telephone communication/

written communication/other communication/other behaviour) and its range is ordered from (very infrequent to very frequent).

This is highly analogous to the mapping sentences for intelligence and attitude items but has the advantage of more easily avoiding tautology. Especially in regard to attitude items, where the response range is from (very positive to very negative) it may be difficult, although not impossible, to decide which direction is 'positive' without reference to responses to other items in the same domain. This difficulty does not arise with information behaviour items as defined above where it is easy to decide which direction is 'more frequent' without reference to other items of behaviour.

This definition underlies the proposed First Law of Information Behaviour which follows:

A Proposed First Law of Information Behaviour

If any two items are selected from the universe of information behaviour items, and if the population observed is not selected artificially, then the population regressions between these two items will be monotone and with positive or zero sign.

Such a law would not preclude the possibility of functionally distinguishable dimensions of information behaviour, any more than the first law of intelligence means that functionally independent dimensions representing special abilities cannot be identified—clearly, they can be. The dimensions of information behaviour which emerged from the study being considered here are discussed below.

SUBSIDIARY RESULTS

The data were analysed further to answer the following main questions:

- How many functionally different dimensions of officials' behaviour are needed to describe the context (described at the level of generality used in the study) in which items of information are referred to and originated?
- What are these dimensions?
- How do officials in different DGs and at different grades differ in relation to the use and origination of information, as described by these dimensions? (Only the differences between grades are reported here.)

The analysis was done in four stages:

- first-order factor analysis;
- second order factor analysis;
- analysis of variance;
- construction of profiles.

The First-order Factor Analysis

The primary correlation matrix was factor analysed using the SAS statistical package. The number of factors was determined by conducting a principal components analysis with unities in the diagonals and rejecting all components (factors) with eigenvalues less than unity, i.e. all factors which contributed less than the average variable to the total variance. This gave six first-order factors. These were identified by rotating them to oblique simple structure using the Promax criterion.

The factor loadings are given in the factor pattern matrix in Figure 9.1. These loadings show to what extent the factors 'explain' or 'predict' the individual responses given by the respondents to the original 22 questionnaire items. For example, most of the variance in responses to Item No. 1 can be accounted for by Factor 5 (with a loading of -0.52). The correlations between the factors are given in Figure 9.2. Interpretation of the factors is discussed below.

The Second-order Factor Analysis

The correlations between the first order factors were judged sufficiently high to warrant a further stage in the analysis to determine broader factors. This was done by analysing the interfactor correlation matrix shown in Figure 9.2 according to the same procedures described above for the analysis of the primary correlation matrix.

A single factor emerged at the second order level, clearly related to the general use-of-information factor discussed in Chapter 8, confirming the conclusions reached on the basis of the primary correlation matrix. The factor loadings are shown in Figure 9.3.

The Analysis of Variance

The factor analyses described above showed that information behaviour in the organization concerned could be understood in terms of six first-order factors and a single second order factor. The purpose of the analysis of variance was to determine whether there were any differences between different parts of the organization (DG groups) or grades of official in regard to the first-order factors.

The analysis was performed using the SAS statistical package, using the GLM program. The data supplied to the program were the factor scores derived from the first order factor analysis, representing the officials' standing on each of those factors. Factor scores were computed only for those respondents who had returned absolutely complete questionnaires, a total of 166 respondents, and the analysis of variance therefore was based on this number of respondents.

The analysis was designed to decide whether the scores on each of the six factors depended at a level of statistical significance ($P < 0.05$) on:

- the respondent's DG group (DG);
- the respondent's grade (G);

	FACTOR					
	I	II	III	IV	V	VI
5. telephone	-.78	-.04	.11	-.16	-.14	-.18
3. telephone	-.77	-.07	-.12	-.08	-.21	.21
12. telephone	-.69	-.07	-.03	.14	.06	.09
14. telephone	-.68	-.05	.11	.23	.04	-.10
16. telephone	-.64	.03	.00	.23	-.01	-.13
6. meeting	.07	-.73	.11	-.07	.06	-.35
7. meeting	.17	-.73	.05	.07	-.11	-.21
17. meeting	-.22	-.66	-.20	.00	.11	.18
19. meeting	-.17	-.66	-.09	.11	.10	.03
8. meeting	-.33	-.66	.01	-.16	-.03	-.02
22. other activities	.11	-.01	-.82	.07	-.28	.12
21. to write	-.12	.00	-.63	.03	.17	-.38
11. other activities	.10	-.13	-.62	-.18	-.48	.02
20. deal with letter	-.20	.11	-.58	-.06	.16	-.52
15. telephone	-.07	.01	.05	.88	-.06	.02
13. telephone	-.14	.16	-.02	.83	-.09	-.01
18. meeting	.16	-.45	-.11	.70	.05	.02
4. telephone	-.03	.10	-.25	-.02	-.78	-.05
2. telephone	-.15	.08	.04	.23	-.66	-.12
1. telephone	-.17	-.17	.06	-.01	-.52	-.34
10. to write	.09	-.09	-.13	.02	-.10	-.81
9. deal with letter	.01	-.11	.07	-.01	-.18	-.76

Figure 9.1.   First-order factor pattern matrix.

	I	II	III	IV	V	VI
I telephone calls, a.		.360	.319	-.377	.221	.399
II meetings			.267	-.272	.236	.389
III writing other items				-.251	.064	.154
IV making notes					-.203	-.305
V telephone calls, b.						.125
VI letters						

Figure 9.2.   Inter-factor correlations.

• the language version of the questionnaire (L);

and whether any differences between DG groups were influenced by the respondent's grade (DG × G). Any such interaction would have complicated interpretation of the analysis.

A summary of the analysis is presented in Figure 9.4.

The Profiles

Profiles were prepared to show graphically the differences and similarities between the various DG groups and grades. Only those for the grades are presented here,

First Order Factors	Second Order Factor
I telephone calls, a.	.75
II meetings	.69
VI letters	.66
IV making notes	-.65
III writing other items	.53
V telephone calls, b.	.42

Figure 9.3.   Second-order factor pattern matrix.

Figure 9.4. Summary of the analysis of variance.

Factor	DG group (DG)	Grade (G)	Language (L)	DG × G
1. Telephone Calls, a				
5. Telephone Calls, b		*		
2. Meetings	*	*		
6. Letters		*	*	
4. Making notes			*	
3. Writing other items				

* Indicates a statistically significant effect on the factors indicated ($P < 0.05$).

in Figure 9.5(a)–(c). They should be interpreted bearing in mind the results of the analysis of variance (Figure 9.4) which show where the main differences lie and where apparent differences could be due to chance variation, e.g. in sampling respondents.

The profiles show deviations from the average and are based on factor scores which have been corrected to take account of the numbers of respondents contributing to each profile and the corresponding numbers in the Commission itself. The 'average band' (STENS 5 and 6) is therefore the estimated average over the Commission as a whole, not simply the average of the particular sample of respondents in the study. The averages estimated in this way are shown in Figure 9.6.

DISCUSSION

We saw in Chapter 8 that people in the office environment, at least in the organization studied, differ consistently in the use they make of the information sources available to them. Some people behave as if they have a greater need for information than do other people. The study described in this chapter extends this finding to show that people are also consistent in regard to their origination of information, and that this is linked closely to the use of information. Some people behave as if they have a greater need to originate items of information than do other people, and these people tend to be those who also use a lot of information. The consistency in behaviour goes beyond this because, as the present study shows, people who tend to originate or refer to a lot of information in one context, e.g. in dealing with correspondence, tend to do so also in other contexts, e.g. in relation to meetings. We may therefore speak meaningfully of a general information-orientation factor— some people are more information-oriented than others.

Within this general pattern of individual differences, people vary. In Chapter 8 we saw that individual differences in regard to the use of information sources and other office activities could be understood, in the organization studied, in terms of ten first-order and four second-order factors. The study described in this chapter suggests that individual differences in regard to the *context* of information behaviour can be understood in terms of six main factors, as follows.

Figure 9.5(a). Profiles (Grade A officials).

Information activity profile (factors B1–B6)

Grade A officials
$n = 86$

Standard ten score (sten)
Average

High-score description;
Often refers to information or writes in connection with:

Factor	Factor score	STEN	1	2	3	4	5	6	7	8	9	10	High-score description
B1	0.080	6	•	•	•	•	•	•	•	•	•	•	Telephone calls (a) especially follow-up activities
B5	−0.204	5	•	•	•	•	•	•		•	•	•	Telephone calls (b) referring to items before and during calls
B2	0.667	7	•	•	•	•	•	•	•	•	•	•	Meetings
B6	0.525	7	•	•	•	•	•	•	•	•	•	•	Letters
B4	0.103	6	•	•	•	•	•	•	•	•	•	•	And: Makes notes during telephone calls and meetings Writes other items
B3	0.177	6	•	•	•	•	•	•	•	•	•	•	including papers, filling in forms and similar activities

A sten of about	1	2	3	4	5	6	7	8	9	10	was characteristic
	2.3%	4.4%	9.2%	15.0%	19.1%	19.1%	15.0%	9.2%	4.4%	2.3%	of officials

Figure 9.5(b). Profiles (Grade B officials).

Grade B officials
n = 52

Information activity profile (factors B1–B6)

Standard ten score (sten)

Factor	Factor score	STEN	1	2	3	4	5	6 (Average)	7	8	9	10	High-score description; Often refers to information or writes in connection with:
B1	0.137	6	•	•	•	•	•	●	•	•	•	•	Telephone calls (a) especially follow-up activities
B5	0.330	6	•	•	•	•	•	●	•	•	•	•	Telephone calls (b) referring to items before and during calls
B2	0.505	7	•	•	•	•	•	•	●	•	•	•	Meetings
B6	+0.336	6	•	•	•	•	•	●	•	•	•	•	Letters
B4	0.073	6	•	•	•	•	•	●	•	•	•	•	And: Makes notes during telephone calls and meetings
B3	0.217	6	•	•	•	•	•	●	•	•	•	•	Writes other items including papers, filling in forms and similar activities
A sten of about			1	2	3	4	5	6	7	8	9	10	was characteristic
of about			2.3%	4.4%	9.2%	15.0%	19.1%	19.1%	15.0%	9.2%	4.4%	2.3%	of officials

Figure 9.5(c).   Profiles (Grade C officials).

Information activity profile
(factors B1–B6)

Grade C officials
$n = 25$

Standard ten score (sten)

Factor	Factor score	STEN	1	2	3	4	Average 5	6	7	8	9	10	High-score description; Often refers to information or writes in connection with:
B1	-0.146	5											Telephone calls (a) especially follow-up activities
B5	-0.045	5											Telephone calls (b) referring to items before and during calls
B2	-0.820	4											Meetings
B6	-0.608	4											Letters
B4	-0.124	5											And: Makes notes during telephone calls and meetings
B3	-0.269	5											Writes other items including papers, filling in forms and similar activities

A sten of about 1   2   3   4   5   . 6 .   7   8   9   10   was characteristic
of about 2.3% 4.4% 9.2% 15.0% 19.1% 19.1% 15.0% 9.2% 4.4% 2.3%   of officials

Figure 9.6 Average frequency of referring to or originating information in relation to the factors shown

Factor	Frequency (%) (of originating or using information)
2 Meetings	72*
6 Letters	68*
1 Telephone calls, a	43
5 Telephone calls, b	40*
3 Writing other items	33
4 Making notes	26

* Indicates that DG groups or grades of official differed to a degree that is statistically significant (see Figure 9.4)

Telephone calls, a (Factor 1). Officials who scored high on this factor responded as if they often needed to refer to information, and often made notes or originated other items, in following up on telephone calls which they received or initiated themselves. Individuals differed in terms of this factor but on average there were no differences between grades.

Telephone calls, b (Factor 5). Officials who scored high on this factor responded as if they often needed to refer to papers and other items before and during telephone calls. Officials who scored high on this factor were not always the same as those who scored high on the previous factor, Telephone Calls (a). The correlation between the two factors was only 0.22, i.e. they have only about 5 per cent of variance in common (0.22 × 0.22). Again, there were no significant differences between grades.

Meetings (Factor 2). High scores here indicate a need to refer to information in various forms before, during and after meetings, and to originate items in connection with meetings. The more senior grades, A and B, scored higher than the lower grade, grade C, on this factor. This probably reflects, amongst other things, the need that casual observation suggests for senior officials to be able to take papers and documents with them when they go to meetings.

Letters (Factor 6). The senior officials, grade A, scored high on this factor, indicating a need to refer to papers or other items in connection with writing letters. Grade C officials had relatively little need to do so, and grade B were intermediate. Despite the somewhat similar pattern of differences between grades, compared with the Meetings factor, there were marked individual differences between officials and the overall correlation between the two factors was only 0.13.

Making notes (Factor 4). High scores on this suggest a need to make notes during telephone calls and meetings. This may be a less formal, more personal kind of activity than that suggested by the previous factor. There were no significant differences between grades.

Writing other items (*Factor 3*). High scores on this factor indicate that writing memoranda, reports and other items, and possibly filling in forms, is an important part of the person's work, often involving the sorting and classification of material, use of a computer or calculating machine, and other activities. Officials who scored high on this factor tended to score high on Telephone Calls (a) and Meetings (i.e. often wrote items following a telephone call and wrote a lot in connection with meetings) but scored low on Making Notes (e.g. they tended not to be involved in making notes during meetings). This suggests a 'behind the scenes' kind of activity, possibly involving briefing other officials. This is probably a role which for many people varied in importance from time to time. There were no significant differences between the grades.

As explained above, these factors describe individual differences within a more general tendency for the officials studied to vary consistently in their information orientation. This more general tendency is brought out in the second-order factor analysis from which a single, general information-orientation factor emerged, indexed best by the first-order factors 1 (Telephone Calls, a) and 2 (Meetings). We might expect this factor even more than the first-order factors to apply to other organizations, for the reasons given in Chapter 8 in connection with the second-order factors described there. The emergence of a single second-order factor supports the general conclusions based on the primary correlation matrix and, in particular, the hypothesis of a First Law of Information Behaviour.

CONCLUSIONS

The study suggests that people in the office environment may differ quite consistently in regard to their use and origination of information. Whilst individual patterns can be described (in terms of six main factors in the organization studied) the consistencies are sufficiently high as to suggest the possibility of a first law of information behaviour, analogous to the first laws of intelligence and attitude. This law would be:

> "If any two items are selected from the universe of information behaviour items, and if the population observed is not selected artificially, then the population regressions between these two items will be monotone and with positive or zero sign."

> "An item belongs to the universe of information behaviour items if and only if its domain asks about the frequency of (reference to/origination

of) items of information in relation to (face-to-face communication/ telephone communication/written communication/other communication/other behaviour) and its range is ordered from (very infrequent to very frequent)."

It is for fellow researchers to test the generalizability of the proposed law and to establish more clearly the conditions under which it holds.

In the next chapter, we examine some of the other research done on information behaviour.

Chapter 10

A further analysis of information behaviour

The close association between the origination and use of information discussed in the previous chapter emphasizes a point made in Chapter 6 that people are not passive in regard to information. In Chapter 6, it was suggested that to understand information systems properly one must look not just at the items of information involved or the electronic or manual systems involved, but one needs to look deeper into the 'information sphere'—at the attitudes, personality and motivation structures of the people involved. The people involved do not act simply as passive receivers of information, 'sinks' which passively absorb information presented. Neither do they act simply as unintelligent 'switches' in a system, routing items of information from one node in a network to another in an unthinking way. They do not inevitably forward items of information received, and to this extent they can be regarded as 'sinks', but they are 'active sinks'. In this chapter, we shall examine the concept of the 'active sink' and the nature of the activity involved, especially in regard to information seeking.

THE ACTIVE SINK

The human in an information system can be regarded as a sink into which information flows, but the sink is active in many ways, especially in:

- selecting sources;
- coding inputs;
- evaluating information (as coded);
- selecting overt behavioural responses (and so the amount of information transmitted).

At a relatively elementary level, the 'cocktail-party effect' provides a simple demonstration of selective attention: One hears one's own name mentioned (and perhaps some of the following, and even preceding, parts of the conversation) though other words with similar physical characteristics are completely lost in the general babble. This effect operates 'automatically' and 'unconsciously' so far as the person concerned can judge. Similarly automatic effects can be observed also at the level of coding: The '1' in Figure 10.1 is physically the same stimulus as the 'I' but it is automatically coded according to one's 'perceptual set', to the extent that not only does it elicit a different *overt* (verbal) response but it also elicits a different *implicit* response; i.e. it actually 'looks' different (until one begins 'consciously to analyse' the stimulus).

The example serves to illustrate a fundamental problem in psychology: The definition of what constitutes a stimulus. This has been discussed at length by Gibson (1960), but to take one aspect of the problem: if one defines a stimulus as that which elicits an overt or implicit response, it is clear in view of the examples above that the definition of what constitutes any particular stimulus depends partly on the nature of the response elicited. This circularity is also implied by those information scientists (see Belkin, 1977) who regard the definition of information as depending upon a situation-specific relationship between the user and part of his or her environment.

At a more molar level, a number of studies have demonstrated that humans do not passively receive information so much as actively seek it or, under some circumstances, avoid it.

Janis and Mann (1977) consider preferences for information in some detail in relation to decision making. They suggest that prior to the mid-1960s, psychologists generally believed that people censor their intake of messages in a highly biased way so as to protect their current beliefs and decisions from being attacked, and people actively seek information that supports their position. Deviations from this 'selective exposure hypothesis' were usually regarded as unimportant exceptions to the general rule, and the hypothesis became incorporated as a fundamental part of various attitude theories, especially cognitive dissonance theory. The hypothesis was called into question seriously by a number of studies done during the 1960s which showed that it was by no means as general as had been assumed. Janis and Mann suggest that the time has now come to look at the problem a different way: To specify the conditions under which people display selective avoidance. They propose a 'conflict model' which they believe addresses this and other relevant questions.

The conflict model postulates that a person can adopt different kinds of 'coping patterns' in dealing with a problem. Each pattern is associated with a characteristic mode of information processing which governs the type and amount of information the decision maker will prefer. Seven different coping patterns are postulated, as-

I　　Ⅱ　　Ⅲ　　Ⅳ　　V

F　　G　　H　　I　　J　　K

Figure 10.1.　A simple example of 'perceptual set' (see text).

150

sociated with five different information modes. These are summarized in Figure 10.2.

Some other factors apart from coping patterns which influence information-seeking behaviour are listed in Figure 10.3 and the subject is dealt with in more detail later.

The sink is also active in evaluating information received and in selecting appropriate behavioural responses. The responses selected can be thought of as mapping out a route through a 'behaviour tree', the route being dependent upon the information received and the way it is processed.

THE BEHAVIOUR TREE

A generalized behaviour tree is shown in Figure 10.4. This shows that at any given point in time a person has a range of behavioural options open. There are five main classes of these options:

- to wait
- to act
- to generate information
- to seek information
- to opt out of the situation.

Each of these classes can be broken down into finer groups, and eventually into the specific, concrete options available at a given point in time. But the general classes apply at all points of the behaviour tree.

The behaviour tree is analogous to the tree-like index used in viewdata systems to access information. At any particular stage of the process one finds oneself faced with a finite set of options. What exactly will result from selecting any given option is not entirely clear—there is an element of uncertainty, even risk (since page charges are involved). Once a particular option is selected, other options become available, but not until then. Furthermore, there is no going back. True, one can return to a page (and set of options) accessed previously but in this event it is not the original situation. One now knows something about the options available which was not known before, so the situation is different. It is in fact a highly similar situation to one already encountered, but at a later stage of the behaviour tree.

In real life, the consequences of selecting options are often much more significant. The choice of going to university or not, of which subjects to study, of which if any person to marry, generally affect the subsequent parts of the behaviour tree very noticeably. Opportunities once passed by are lost forever.

In fact, the 'analogy' between viewdata and real life is not an analogy at all. A viewdata session forms a tiny part of the user's overall behaviour tree and is just as real as any other part. In this connection, it is worth noting that the general classes of options noted above apply to this situation just as much as to any other. The user can wait before deciding what to do, can act on the information retrieved so far,

Figure 10.2.   The conflict model applied to information preferences (adapted from Janis & Mann, 1977).

Antecedents	Coping pattern	Dominant information mode	Characteristic information preferences	Level of interest in information
No serious risks	Unconflicted adherence or Unconflicted change	Indifference	Nonselective exposure	Low
High risk and little hope of a satisfactory solution	Defensive avoidance			
No deadline pressures	Procastination	Evasion●	Passive interest in supportive information; avoidance of all challenging information	Low
Strong deadline pressures plus possibility of delegating task	Shifting responsibility	Evasion	Delegation of search and appraisal to others	Low
Strong deadline pressures but no opportunity to shift responsibility	Bolstering	Selectivity	Selective exposure: search for supportive information and avoidance of discrepant information	Medium
High conflict, belief that a solution exists but serious lack of time	Hypervigilance	Indiscriminate search	Active search for both supportive and nonsupportive information, with failure to discriminate between relevant and irrelevant, trustworthy and untrustworthy information	Very high
Serious risks plus belief a satisfactory solution can be found in the time available	Vigilance	Discriminating search with openmindedness	Active search for supportive and nonsupportive information, with careful evaluation for relevance and trustworthiness; preference for trustworthy nonsupportive information if threats are vague or ambiguous.	High

152

Figure 10.3. Some factors influencing information-seeking behaviour.

Ease of using source, rather than the expected amount of information	Rosenberg (1967)
'Dogmatism' (as a measure of the person's 'cognitive style')	Lambert & Durand (1977)
Relevance of multiple sources and degree of conflict	Levine (1973)
Reliability of sources	Levine & Samet (1973)
Limitations on resources available	Levine, Samet, & Brahlek (1975)
'Coping pattern'	Janis & Mann (1977)

can generate information (e.g. by making notes, doing calculations) can seek information (by selecting one of the options presented by the system), or can opt out of the situation by switching off the set, walking away from it, kicking it, or falling asleep.

In some situations, especially command and control, the five main classes of options can be reduced to just two that really count:

- to take terminal action;
- to seek information.

Command and control situations include all sorts of emergency situations such as might involve police, ambulance, fire, military or other services. They can also be regarded as including the routine functioning of these services between emergencies, but here we are concerned with the response to crisis. In such circumstances

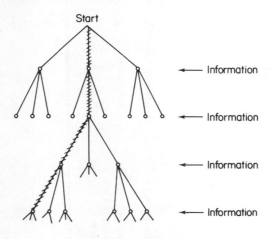

Figure 10.4. A generalized behavior tree.

each person's behaviour can be modelled fairly well by a robot that has just two possible modes of behaviour: terminal action and information seeking. For example, a fireman may run into a burning building to attempt a rescue (terminal action) or may ask bystanders if they can account for everyone who might have been in the building (information seeking). In a different context, a general might order an attack (terminal action) or seek further information about the enemy's moves (information seeking).

In situations such as these, the person is faced with a continuous stream of information. At some stage he or she must act on the information received, but has the option of when to do so. These situations are called 'optional stopping' situations. They began to be studied seriously with the advent of advanced military command and control systems, but the findings from the studies done have relevance in much broader contexts.

Optional Stopping

The 'optional stopping' studies emphasize the role of the human as a sequential processor of information who must choose between alternative courses of action. At each point in time, a decision must be made whether to gather additional information. Postponing terminal action may reduce the uncertainty associated with the choice but the delay involved may render the action ineffective. The critical decision is when to stop acquiring information.

Studies in this area have been concerned with:

- statistical parameters of the input information (e.g. Becker, 1958; Howell, 1966);
- payoff (e.g. Edwards and Slovic, 1965; Rapoport and Tversky, 1966; Irwin and Smith, 1957; Pitz and Reinhold, 1968);
- evaluation of strategies in terms of optimal models (e.g. Fried and Peterson, 1969; Pitz, 1968, 1969);
- conflicting and irrelevant inputs (e.g. Levine, 1973; Levine and Samet, 1973); and
- limitations on available information and the resources available for purchasing information (e.g. Levine, Samet and Brahlek, 1975).

Consumer Behaviour

Information seeking has also been studied intensively in relation to consumer psychology. It has been shown (e.g. Berning and Jacoby, 1974) that the amount of information sought prior to the decision to purchase can vary considerably, e.g. over a fifteen-fold range. A number of factors have been identified which appear to influence this behaviour, including:

- perceived risk (e.g. Cox, 1967);

154

- sociodemographic factors (e.g. Miller and Zikmund, 1975; Newman and Stuelin, 1972; Udell, 1966);
- decision rule utilized (e.g. Bettman and Jacoby, 1975; Payne, 1976);
- time pressures and distractions (e.g. Wright, P. L., 1974);
- dogmatism (Lambert and Durand, 1977);
- and miscellaneous other factors (e.g. Bucklin, 1966; Newman and Staelin, 1972; Udell, 1966).

CONCLUSIONS

The general conclusion to be drawn from the research seems clear: The sink is active and the factors influencing its activity are many and varied. Rather than attempt an exhaustive review of all the individual studies that have been done, what we shall do is present a selection of studies which are especially interesting because of their relatively applied nature, and see what general conclusions we can draw. This we do in the next chapter.

Chapter 11

Information seeking

It is important to understand the situation facing the person looking for information if one is to understand the factors which influence the suitability of electronic information systems. According to MacKay (1969), the person seeking information typically has an incomplete picture of the world, an inadequacy in his 'state of readiness' to interact purposefully with the world around him. Meadow (1970) has suggested the person typically:

- has only partial knowledge of the information (s)he wants;
- may have no knowledge at all of the way the information is structured in whatever information systems may be available;
- may not know the appropriate language for dealing with the available systems, especially if they are computerized, and may not know how to formulate his or her requirements;
- does not know what penalties may be imposed on his or her search strategies.

In view of these uncertainties it may seem surprising that people ever manage to find what they are looking for, yet they do. In the following sections we shall review some of the studies that have examined the strategies people use.

SOME SIMPLE EXAMPLES OF INFORMATION SEEKING

A very simple example is a lecture. Howe and his colleagues (e.g. Howe and Godfrey, 1977) have shown that even in such simple situations as this the human is an active rather than a passive sink. Note-taking is an important example of the activity concerned and Howe et al. have shown that the nature of the note-taking done has a significant influence on what the person learns in such a situation.

The next step up in complexity might be reading a magazine of classified advertisements, or one giving details of television and radio programmes. Dallos et al. (anon., 1978) have conducted experiments using this kind of a situation. Their subjects were asked to perform simple and complex search tasks using everyday information sources such as *Radio Times*, a cook book, and so forth. The details of the experiments are not available at the time of writing this book but the general conclusions are: people need to know fairly early on that the information they seek exists; people tend to scan more than one hard-copy page simultaneously; they sometimes mark previously accessed pages, e.g. by inserting a marker or tearing, for speedy re-access; and they use indexes heavily when these exist.

An even more complex situation is when a person is confronted by an information retrieval system where (s)he can choose between a variety of routes to reach a 'destination' or set of 'destinations' (e.g. abstracts, references, videotex end-pages, word processing 'tracks' or 'files'). Some limited experimental work has been done on Prestel (British Telecom's videotex service) which is relevant to this.

Bush and Williams (1978) report an experiment in which 24 people each searched for information. None had used Prestel before. For the purposes of the study 20 Prestel pages were selected as 'targets'. They belonged to level 4 of the Prestel tree (containing 950 pages in total at the time of the experiment).

Each person searched for information in 10 of the 20 target pages; five searched via one tree structure and five via another. The order in which the structures were searched was alternated and the order in which questions were asked was varied.

This experiment was useful for showing that the structure derived from an analysis of the way people naturally group Prestel pages (see Bush, 1977) was more effective than that based on an arbitrary though 'sensible' approach. The 'derived' structure resulted in 79 per cent success (56 per cent with no backtracking) compared with only 59 per cent (43 per cent with no backtracking) for the 'arbitrary' structure. The experiment therefore shows that research in this area can have tangible practical benefits. It was limited, however, because: (a) it gives little indication of *why* one structure was better than the other, and so does not help much in developing structures that might be better than 79 per cent effective; and (b) it was based on searches involving well-defined targets which were known to exist, whereas many real searches are for ill-defined targets which are not known definitely to exist in the database.

These simple examples are interesting but fail to bring out the complexity of what is involved in broader contexts. The studies which follow help to do this.

SOME MORE COMPLEX EXAMPLES

Harwood's Study

People can seek information in different ways. These may or may not involve Type B communication (face-to-file) and an understanding of the variety of options which are available is important for understanding the behavioural context in which face-to-file communication occurs.

Berlyne (1960) suggested there might be three main classes of information seeking: Consultation; observation; and thinking. Harwood (1973) conducted a study of secondary school students to see if these three classes could be distinguished empirically. He also hypothesized that he would be able to detect reading as a separate category, and that some finer distinctions could be made. In all, he hypothesized seven main categories of information seeking, as follows:

- reading;
- consultation, personal contact with authority;
- consultation, personal contact with non-authority;
- thinking, rigorous;
- thinking, intuitive;
- observation, systematic;
- observation, casual.

As an initial step, he asked 'several hundred' students to list the ways they went about securing information. Two judges then placed the items elicited in the seven categories, and selected the best ten in each category—'best' in terms of general applicability and common usage of terms. The resulting 70 items were listed in random order in the form of a questionnaire where each item started 'to get information I like to . . .' and the respondent was to rate each item on a scale from 1 (lowest possible desirability) to 5 (highest possible desirability).

The questionnaire was completed by 180 males and 179 females, and the responses were factor analysed with the sex of the respondent included as a variable. An orthogonal rotation (varimax criterion) was done, yielding six main factors (plus one uninterpreted 'residual' factor), as follows:

- reading (e.g. go to libraries);
- consultation, personal contact with authority (e.g. put questions to skilled people);
- consultation, personal contact with non-authority (e.g. talk to people);
- consultation, dependence upon well-defined statements (e.g. get instructions);
- thinking (e.g. contemplate possible solutions);
- observation (e.g. test for accuracy).

These factors clearly overlap substantially with those hypothesized, but there are differences. The 'consultation, dependence upon well-defined statements' factor had not been expected; the distinction between rigorous and systematic thinking does not appear; and the distinction between systematic and casual observation does not appear.

In terms of our own theoretical framework, we can regard the reading factor as an example of Type B communication, and all the consultation factors as examples of Type A (unless done by letter, in which case they would be examples of Type B). The study therefore is of interest in supporting and illustrating this basic distinction, and in describing part of the behavioural context in which Types A and B communication occur, namely thinking and observation.

It is of passing interest to note that Harwood went on to show in a further sample of students that firstborns showed significantly stronger preferences for reading (Type B communication) than did those born second or later. There were no other birth-order effects.

Graney's Study

Graney (1975) conducted another study of interest in describing the behavioural context for Type B communication. This study was concerned with elderly persons rather than young students, and was seen by Graney as an attempt to classify 'social communication activities' (e.g. visiting friends and relatives, telephone use, television viewing, reading).

Sixty women, aged 52–89, were interviewed, and 46 of them were interviewed again four years later. The interviews provided data on nine activities of the type indicated above. Cluster analysis was performed to place activities representing dissimilar behaviours in different categories, and three clusters emerged, as follows (with the labels given by Graney), for the original set of interviews only:
primary associations:

- frequency of attendance at religious services;
- frequency of visiting friends and relatives;
- number of telephone calls made and received each day;

secondary associations:

- number of memberships held in voluntary associations;
- frequency of attendance at meetings of voluntary associations;
- frequency of visiting with neighbours;

tertiary associations:

- number of hours spent watching television;
- hours spent reading;
- hours spent listening to the radio.

The analysis of the second interviews yielded a similar set of clusters, the three main differences being: telephone use appeared in the second cluster; visiting neighbours moved to the first cluster; and reading just missed the criterion for being included in the main clusters at all. Although these differences are small, they may indicate that a larger sample might yield slightly different results.

The study is interesting if only for the conspicuous absence of any Type B communication except for reading, which appears in the main clusters only for the first analysis. Actually the absence is more apparent than real since many of the activities listed normally would involve Type B communication to varying degrees, especially activities associated with voluntary associations. One might expect Type B communication to become more important in this context with the advent of home information systems such as Prestel. It is difficult to get a feeling for just how important such systems could be for the elderly in this context without knowing more about the reasons involved in visiting neighbours, joining voluntary associations, and so forth. It is not clear from Graney's study to what extent these activities reflect information seeking, if at all, compared with satisfying other needs.

Wolek's Study

Just as the students in Harwood's study displayed preferences for ways of obtaining information, so one might expect other groups to do likewise. Wolek (1972) examined the information-seeking strategies of scientists and engineers. He was particularly interested in their behaviour when they needed to enrich their understanding of a technical subject prior to an interpersonal (face-to-face) communication.

The study was based on interviews with thirty scientists and engineers from three different establishments. The interviews were concerned with a detailed analysis of the most recent incident in which the person concerned had searched for and obtained useful information through interpersonal channels. The 'critical incident' method was adopted to tease out information about all the relevant events leading up to the actual interpersonal exchange.

Three methods of information seeking were identified, as follows:

The first—'piggybacking'—involved deliberately delaying the search for information in the hope that between the time of realizing the need and the time when action would be required (the time of the interpersonal exchange) the information required would become available through the normal course of events, e.g. routine information gathering, chance encounters with colleagues, and so forth. The need for information was 'piggybacked' on routine activities.

The second—'friendly consultation'—involved contacting friends for references to likely sources of information. The interviewees preferred to go to friends first even when an expert was available who was an acquaintance. It seemed to serve three main functions: Reducing the possibility of embarrassment by asking an uninformed question; improving the precision of the questions that needed to be asked so as to avoid ambiguities or misunderstandings; keeping friends in touch with the work being done.

The third method—professional peripheration—was a deliberate attempt to learn about areas of work peripheral to the person's special field of expertise. It usually involved reading research abstracts, review articles, and similar materials. Even more than the other two methods, this reflected the assumption the interviewees seemed to make that it was their responsibility to educate themselves sufficiently to be able to ask appropriate questions and understand the replies.

The choice of method used seemed to depend on three main factors. First, a person would tend to 'piggyback'—i.e. effectively give the information search a low priority—if there were higher priority demands on his or her time (the 'opportunity cost of time'). Secondly, a person would be guided by previous experiences, especially in regard to selecting appropriate sources of information ('experience with similar needs'). Finally, professional peripheration tended to be used when an understanding of the context of the question or problem was necessary ('context appreciation').

Whitley and Frost's Study

Wolek's study suggests one mechanism—'friendly consultation'—whereby the seeking and exchange of information might help to establish or maintain informal networks of communication between scientists. Whitley and Frost (1974) looked at the question further, particularly in regard to the role of scientific tasks in hindering or facilitating the flow of information within and between research organizations.

The division studied was responsible for the operation of a major technological facility (M.F.T.), also assisting scientists from outside who had access to the M.F.T., and for modifying and improving the facility. Other scientists in the division used the facility for research, and a small group were engaged in research only remotely related to the facility.

Four task categories were defined for the purposes of the study, based on how scientific tasks were selected and problems defined. Forty-eight scientists were interviewed and, on the basis of these interviews, allocated to the various task groups: 12 on 'responsibility tasks'; 13 on 'extension'; 5 on 'new development'; and 16 on 'research'.

Information flow was studied by asking the scientists to complete a questionnaire indicating information sources which had provided useful information of direct relevance to their current work on the day the questionnaire was circulated. Fourteen different days' worth of questionnaire data were collected from 45 of the scientists over a period of 15 days.

Two main findings emerged. First, task type was at least as important as level of educational experience in influencing the scientists' use of external information sources. Secondly, differences between scientists in terms of their task type tended to coincide with boundaries of information transfer, especially where the differences in task type followed formal organizational boundaries. Scientists who combined different task types in their work were especially important as gatekeepers, providing other scientists with access to useful information and generally facilitating the transfer of information within the organization.

Holland's Study

Holland (1972) studied special communicators such as the 'gatekeepers' of Whitley and Frost's study in more depth. He hypothesized that special communicators would be regarded by their colleagues as having especially high value as information sources and in turn would have exposure to both a greater number of and a greater diversity of information sources.

Questionnaires were distributed to 219 professional researchers in three different organizations. Of these, 143 were returned. The perceived value of the researchers—their 'information potential'—was defined as the number of times they were cited by other researchers as likely sources of technical information. Level of information exposure was measured by questions regarding information-seeking behaviour, such as the number of journals read and meetings attended.

With regard to external information, the results indicated that researchers with high information potential:

- either contacted an unusually large number of acquaintances or read an unusually large number of journals and reports;
- tended to contact a more diverse set of information sources;
- in contacting personal sources, tended to prefer face-to-face and telephone communication rather than written communication.

With regard to internal information, the results indicated that researchers with high information potential:

- were more frequent users of personal contacts;
- read only about the same number of internal reports as the low information potential researchers (except in one of the three organizations, where they read more);
- tended (in two of the organizations) to contact a more diverse set of information sources;
- perhaps surprisingly, tended to prefer telephone communication rather than face-to-face communication for internal technical communication.

The two variables studied, information potential and information exposure, were treated as though a simple dependency existed between them. However, Holland was careful to point out in discussing his results that the relationship between these two variables is usually very complex. In particular, many variables—such as location, status, experience, telephone and travel budgets—will affect both information potential and information exposure.

White's Study

White (1970) conducted a study of the information sources used by crop farmers in Ontario, to see which sources were the most important.

Ten sources were compared, ranging from daily newspapers to government extension personnel. A modification of the paired-comparisons technique, called the 'most important source instrument' was used. In this technique, items within a logical group (e.g. radio, television) are compared and the one judged the more useful compared with the more useful from another group (e.g. daily newspapers, weekly newspapers), and so on until an overall rank order is established. In White's study, the rank order based on 106 crop farmers was as follows (from most important to least important):

- company field men;
- neighbours;
- merchants and mill operators;
- government extension personnel;
- government pamphlets and bulletins;
- weekly newspapers;
- farm magazines;
- radio;
- daily newspapers;
- television.

It is not known from White's study to what extent the people sources mentioned (e.g. company field men) used Type B communication in their contacts with the farmers but it seems likely they relied mainly or entirely on Type A (face-to-face). On this assumption, we can say the farmers seem to have regarded the 'Type A sources', such as company field men and neighbours, as more important than 'Type B sources', such as pamphlets, newspapers and magazines.

Rosenberg's Study

Rosenberg's (1967) study is particularly interesting in the present context, both in terms of its methodology and its results. Rosenberg was able to demonstrate that the expected amount of information available from a source can be less important than ease of use in determining whether it is selected.

In Rosenberg's study, 96 professional personnel in industry and Government (52 in research, 44 not) ranked eight methods according to their preference in hypothetical situations. The methods were:

- search your personal library;
- search material in the same building where you work, excluding your personal library;
- visit a knowledgeable person 20 miles away or more;
- use a library that is not within your organization;
- consult a reference librarian;
- visit a knowledgeable person nearby (within your organization);
- write a letter requesting information from a knowledgeable person 20 miles away or more;
- telephone a knowledgeable person who may be of help.

The hypothetical situations were:

- you are working on a design for a procedure or experiment and wish to know if similar work has been done;
- you are preparing a proposal for a new project either to the management of your organization or to an outside agency. You wish to substantiate the proposal with a thorough bibliography. The proposal involves approximately $60 000;
- you wish to gather information in order to write an article in your area of specialization for a trade or research journal.

The subjects used 7-point scales to rate: (a) ease of use, and (b) amount of information expected. A statistically significant correlation was found between order of preference (averaged over the three situations) and ease of use (Spearman rank correlation coefficient greater than 0.86 for both groups) but not between preference and amount of information expected (coefficients of −0.17 and −0.11 for the 'research' and 'non-research' groups).

This experiment is interesting both for its results and for its methodology. Its results are particularly interesting because an important effect that networked information services (e.g. EURONET), videotex systems, communicating word processors, and related technological developments are likely to have is to reduce the differences in the ease of using different information sources. Rosenberg's results suggest that this could have significant effects on the pattern of use of information sources. It also suggests that information providers will have to pay increasingly closer attention to the real value of the information to consumers (and not just its accessibility) if they are to maintain their place in the market.

The experiment is particularly interesting on methodological grounds because it was based on subjects' judgements of their probable behaviour in hypothetical situations. This approach has been used in other related contexts, including factors affecting: The choice of communications media (e.g. Christie and Kingan, 1977) and the use of public transport (e.g. Norman, 1977). In all of these contexts it has provided internally consistent, interesting results which in many cases seem to agree with findings obtained by other methods. This suggests it is a potentially fruitful methodology for research in this area and work along these lines could usefully be developed further.

A variant of the method is to ask people about sources they have actually used in the past. This has the advantage of greater 'face validity' in that it is apparently more 'realistic', but there is no convincing evidence that the 'realism' improves validity in any absolute sense. There are reasons for suspecting it might not, for example: Random, irrelevant factors affecting behaviour which are not present in the 'hypothetical' situation; reliance on subjects recalling accurately what they did, and why, or—if behaviour is observed as it happens—possible effects of the researcher being present; difficulty of sampling behaviour over the whole range of interesting situations; and so forth. The variant is also more expensive. Despite these possible weaknesses, using different variants of a methodology can only improve the convergent validity of the findings obtained and should be encouraged.

RECENT PACTEL RESEARCH

Information-Seeking In The Home

Rosenberg's study was concerned with scientific and technical information seeking in industry and Government. A recent study conducted by the author and his colleagues at PACTEL, and based on Rosenberg's method, looked at information seeking in the home environment. The study was conducted as part of a larger, international assignment conducted by PACTEL for The Commission of The European Communities, and was concerned with videotex.

An important function of videotex in the home, as in other contexts, is information retrieval. The purpose of the experiment was to examine the relative importance of several factors that might be expected to influence the use of videotex for information retrieval in the home, compared with other methods of acquiring information, for several different kinds of situations where information is needed. This kind of information is helpful in understanding the likely uses which might be made of videotex systems in the future.

In view of Rosenberg's findings, it was hypothesized that in the home environment ease of using a particular method for acquiring information would be more important than the expected effectiveness of the method. The experiment was designed to test this hypothesis and the relative influence of several other factors.

The subjects were twenty UK women volunteers, from early thirties to late fifties in age. They were run as a group.

Following a demonstration of Prestel (the UK public videotex service), each subject was given a set of five sheets, in random order. At the top of each sheet was typed one of the following five situations requiring information:

- the children need new clothes. You want to find out the best place to go to get some;
- you are thinking of buying a car. You are not sure what sort. You need information;
- you want to catch up on the national news;
- a pipe has just started to leak badly. You need a plumber urgently;
- you are bored cooking the same old things. You want to try something new. You need to get an interesting recipe that you will feel confident attempting.

Down the side of each sheet were listed 9 methods of acquiring information:

- Prestel (= videotex);
- turn on the TV or radio;
- make one or more telephone calls;
- visit somewhere (e.g. a shop, Post Office or an Agency) to make enquiries;
- go and see a neighbour about it;

- look in a newspaper, magazine or directory (e.g. yellow pages);
- look in some other kind of book or magazine you already have;
- get a book or magazine from the library or a shop;
- other (please describe briefly).

The order of the first eight methods was reversed for half the subjects.

The subjects were asked to work through the sheets in the order in which they appeared and for each situation to rate the eight or nine methods on the following scales:

- how likely it is you would use this method;
- what you think it would probably cost you, taking everything into account;
- how convenient you think it would be;
- how speedy you think it would be;
- how good or bad for you in very general terms (taking all the above factors into account and any others felt relevant).

All six rating scales ran from 0 (e.g. 'extremely unlikely') to 5 (e.g. 'extremely likely').

Subjects were asked to assume that the year was 1980 and that they had a 26-inch colour television set capable of receiving Prestel in their lounge. They were asked to assume the cost of using Prestel to be twice the cost of a normal telephone call, including both page charges and call charges.

Fifteen minutes were allowed for the experiment after which time subjects were asked to complete the sheet on which they were working, and the packs were then collected.

The median ratings given the various methods of acquiring information are presented in Figure 11.1. The number of subjects on which the medians are based varies because the subjects were only able to complete two or three sheets in the time available and which sheets were completed by which subjects was a matter of chance.

The product–moment correlations between the median ratings of likelihood and the median ratings on the other scales are shown in Figure 11.2. These are based on 40 cases (5 situations × 8 methods, the 'other' method being ignored in this analysis because so few subjects ever thought of any other method they might use). The product–moment correlations between the median ratings of 'how good' and the other scales are also presented for comparison. All the correlations are significant at the 5 per cent level.

The correlations in Figure 11.2 reflect variance due to situations and variance due to methods. To allow for the effects of individual differences in perceptions of cost, convenience, and so forth to show, product–moment correlations were also calculated based on the 8 or 9 methods × n subjects for each situation. These are presented in Figure 11.3.

The hypothesis that convenience would be more important than effectiveness in influencing the likelihood of a method being used is not supported.

Figure 11.1. Median ratings.

(a) How likely?

	P	TV	Phone	Visit	Method Neigh.	Paper	Book	Library	
News	5	4	0	0	0	4	0	0	n = 5
Recipe	3	0	0	0	1	0	5	0	n = 5
Car	4.5	0	3	2	0	2.5	2	1.5	n = 8
Clothes	2	0	3	4	0	0.5	0.5	1	n = 8
Plumber	1	0	3.5	0	1	3	0	0	n = 6

(b) How convenient?

	P	TV	Phone	Visit	Method Neigh.	Paper	Book	Library
	5	5	2	0	1	4	2	0
	3	0	0	0	1	1	5	0
	3	0	3	2.5	0	2	2.5	1.5
	2.5	1.5	2.5	2	0.5	2	2.5	0.5
	4	0	4.5	0	4	4	0.5	0

(c) What cost?

	P	TV	Phone	Visit	Method Neigh.	Paper	Book	Library
	2	1	0	0	0	1	1	1
	3	0	0	0	1	0.5	5	0
	4.5	0	3	2	0	2.5	2	1.5
	2	0	0	4	0	0.5	0.5	1
	1	0	3.5	0	1	3	0	0

(d) How effective?

	P	TV	Phone	Visit	Method Neigh.	Paper	Book	Library
	5	4	0	0	0	4	0	0
	2	0	0	0	2	1	4	1
	3.5	0	2	2	0	2.5	2	2
	2	0.5	2	3.5	1.5	2	1	1
	2	0	4.5	0	1	3	0	0

(e) How speedy?

	P	TV	Phone	Visit	Method Neigh.	Paper	Book	Library
	5	4	2	0	0	3	0	3
	3	0	0	0	1	1	4	0
	4	2	2	2	0.5	2.5	1.5	1
	3.5	1.5	2	2	0.5	2	1	0
	2.5	0	3.5	0	1	3.5	0	0

(f) How good?

	P	TV	Phone	Visit	Method Neigh.	Paper	Book	Library
	4	4	1	0	0	4	0	0
	2	0.5	0	0	1	1	4	2
	4	0	2	2	0.5	3	2	2
	2	0	1.5	3.5	0.5	2	1	0.5

Figure 11.2. Correlations between the median ratings.

	'How likely?' with:	'How good?' with:
What cost?	0.84	0.71
How convenient?	0.81	0.79
How effective?	0.89	0.84
How speedy?	0.83	0.82
How good?	0.90	1.00

Critical r at the 5% level = 0.26
for a unidirectional test.

The correlations, whether based on the median ratings or on the individual ratings, show that the expected effectiveness of a method of acquiring information, at least for this group of subjects, is at least as important as its convenience. This is particularly evident in Figure 11.3, where it can be seen that in considering methods of acquiring information about children's clothes, the perceived effectiveness of the method predicts the judged likelihood of its use to a high degree ($r = 0.81$), whereas the perceived convenience of the method does not ($r = 0.25$). Clearly, the subjects in our sample were all 'good mothers', willing to tolerate some inconvenience in order to get the information needed to make 'good buys'.

The home environment therefore seems to differ from the research and development environment studied by Rosenberg (1967), and one must conclude that the relative importance of factors influencing information seeking is dependent upon the situation.

An alternative explanation for the difference between this study and Rosenberg's

Figure 11.3. Correlations between the individual ratings.

(a) How *likely* with:

n		Cost	Convenience	Effective	Speedy	Good
42	News	0.12	0.77	0.91	0.72	0.88
42	Recipe	0.18	0.83	0.81	0.75	0.73
67	Car	0.65	0.61	0.59	0.51	0.53
67	Clothes	0.26	0.25	0.81	0.39	0.79
50	Plumber	0.40	0.72	0.82	0.75	0.80

(b) How *good* with:

n		Cost	Convenience	Effective	Speedy
42	News	−0.13	0.79	0.90	0.81
42	Recipe	0.16	0.86	0.87	0.83
67	Car	0.40	0.54	0.71	0.70
67	Clothes	0.43	0.46	0.88	0.55
50	Plumber	0.25	0.82	0.93	0.87

is that 'effectiveness' (used in this study) and 'amount of information' (used in Rosenberg's study) are not the same, and are not highly correlated. This would be consistent with the difficulty of defining effectiveness unambiguously. Even if this is so, context still seems to be important. Evidence for this is provided by Figure 11.3 where it can be seen that even in the home environment the correlations vary between situations; for example, convenience seems to be much more important when looking for a recipe than when looking for information about children's clothes or even a new car.

If people in the home environment are willing to sacrifice convenience to some degree to achieve effectiveness, at least in some situations, this may be even more true of cost. The correlations between the judged likelihood of using a method and its perceived cost are almost all positive, i.e. the greater the cost the greater the likelihood of use. This suggests that the methods which are perceived to be the more costly are also perceived to be the more effective. This is illustrated by reference to Figure 11.1, where it can be seen, for example, that Prestel was judged the most costly method of acquiring information about new cars but was also judged the most effective method.

CONCLUSIONS

Information seeking is important in a variety of contexts and the particular form it takes depends on the interactions between many different factors. The studies reviewed illustrate the range of methods that have been used to map out some of the complexity involved. They show that this type of behaviour can be studied systematically. Much further analysis is needed and it is hoped that this brief review will encourage researchers to take up the challenge. As we move into the 'information society' of the 1980s and beyond, this surely must be an area where psychologists could contribute a great deal to the scientific description and understanding of human behaviour in an information-oriented environment.

PART 4
Attitudes

Chapter 12

Managers' attitudes toward the office of tomorrow

Attitudes are of vital importance in shaping the influence of new technology. The reason we use voice telephones today and not picture telephones (videophones) is not because the necessary technology has not been developed—the technology has been available since the early 1960s—it is because of people's attitudes toward the technology. Similarly, word processors are used primarily for power typing (the production of documents) rather than the communication of information from one place to another because of attitudes not technology—the technology is already available.

It is surprising that so little scientific research has been done on attitudes toward the electronic technology that promises (or threatens) to have such an impact on our lives. What work has been done has been confined largely to *ad hoc* 'user needs' surveys which generally have failed to add systematically to knowledge in this field. This is hardly surprising in view of their extreme emphasis on the 'practicalities' of particular situations at the expense of being able to draw fundamental conclusions that can be generalized to a great many situations.

A scientific approach to the study of attitudes in this area is both feasible and necessary if the human factors governing evolution toward the electronic or other future are to be properly understood and controlled.

Some useful work has already been done. This suggests that at least some of the factors involved in attitudes toward Type A communication systems, e.g. teleconferencing, are common to attitudes toward Type B. The two most important of these factors are:

- general evaluation;
- social presence.

The general evaluation factor requires little explanation. It is an index of general attitude 'for or against' a concept relating to, in the present context, Type A or Type B communication. It is 'attitude' in the narrow, Thurstonian sense, representing, if you will, a resolution of other, more specific factors, including social presence. Social presence requires more explanation and is dealt with below.

THE SOCIAL PRESENCE FACTOR

The social presence factor was discovered in work on Type A communication at the Communications Studies Group of University College London during the early 1970s (see Short, Williams, and Christie, 1976). Its presence had been suspected on the basis of earlier work by other researchers, especially Douglas, and Morley and Stephenson.

Douglas (1957) distinguished between two aspects of interpersonal communication which he called 'interparty' and 'interpersonal'. The 'interparty' aspect reflects the concern which people have in acting out their assigned roles in order to achieve a particular kind of outcome; it is relatively 'task-oriented'. The 'interpersonal' aspect reflects the concern for maintaining the personal relationship which is involved.

Morley and Stephenson (1969, 1970) proposed that the balance between these two aspects of communication could be affected by the medium of communication used—that, for example, use of the telephone rather than face-to-face communication would lead to relatively greater emphasis on the inter-party aspect of the communication.

Short, Williams, and Christie (1976), related this to the relative availability or non-availability of certain non-verbal, especially visual cues. They proposed, however, that the relative availability of non-verbal cues did not affect the communication directly but only through the perceived 'social presence' of the medium. Use of a medium perceived by its users to be relatively low on social presence would lead to relatively high emphasis on the 'inter-party' aspects of the communication.

We can propose a simple scheme for relating the type of task to be done to the perceived social presence of the communications medium, as in Figure 12.1. In this scheme it is proposed that a medium which is low on social presence, e.g. the telephone, is not very suitable for person-oriented tasks, e.g. recruiting a new manager or more generally getting to know someone. On the other hand, the telephone or other medium low on social presence is, according to this scheme, suitable for task-oriented activities such as a simple exchange of information, placing of an order, and so forth.

Figure 12.1. Hypothesized relationship between suitability of a communications medium and type of task.

		Social presence of the communication medium	
		low	high
Type of task (meeting or conversation)	Person-oriented	not suitable	suitable
	task-oriented	suitable	suitable

Social presence is conceived of as a single dimension representing a cognitive synthesis of a variety of more specific factors as they are perceived by the person concerned to be present in the medium. The capacity to transmit information about facial expression, direction of looking, posture, dress and non-verbal vocal cues, all contribute to the social presence of a communications medium. How they contribute, the weights given to all these factors, is determined by the person, because social presence is actually an attitudinal dimension of the person, a 'mental set' toward the communications medium.

The relative importance of a person's perceptions of a situation compared with what is objectively the case is illustrated by a very early experiment by Dashiell (1935). Dashiell showed that it was possible to influence a person's performance on a task simply by informing the person concerned that others were working on the same task in another room, whether or not that was actually the case. Similarly, it is postulated that it is a person's perception of a communications medium with regard to social presence that is of prime importance in influencing behaviour, not the objective features of the medium *per se*.

Social Presence In Relationship To Other Psychological Concepts

The concept of social presence is related to both 'intimacy' (Argyle and Dean, 1965), and 'immediacy' (Wiener and Mehrabian, 1968), but is distinguishable from both of these. Argyle and Dean (1965) proposed that people communicating with one another will try to adjust whatever factors they can, including seating arrangement, to establish an equilibrium of approach and avoidance forces relating to intimacy. For example, they might avoid eye contact, move further apart, and change the topic of conversation to a less personal one if intimacy becomes too high. Short, Williams, and Christie (1976), propose that the social presence of the communications medium is one of the factors that contributes to intimacy. For example, use of a videophone in preference to a voice telephone is likely to make the conversation more intimate in the sense described above, other things being equal.

The postulated connection between social presence and intimacy suggests people might sometimes prefer to use a medium low on social presence when extremely personal matters are to be discussed. For example, someone wishing to call the 'Samaritans' for help might be less inclined to do so, or might terminate the call prematurely, if a videophone rather than a voice telephone were all that was available—or, perhaps more likely, might cover the camera during the call. As far as the author is aware, this particular prediction has not been tested experimentally. The possibility of such an effect suggests, however, that the 'suitable' entry in the top-right cell of Figure 12.1 (high social presence for person-oriented tasks) may need to be qualified when very high levels of intimacy are likely to be involved.

Immediacy is related to social presence in a different way. Wiener and Mehrabian (1968) conceived of immediacy as a measure of the psychological distance which a person communicating puts between himself or herself and the person being addressed, the topic of conversation or the message itself. A person can express high immediacy by saying 'let us . . .' or 'we . . .' rather than 'I . . .' or 'You . . .'. Physical proximity, formality of dress, facial expression, and other nonverbal cues, can also convey immediacy.

Heilbronn and Libby (1973) have suggested that the use of one communications medium rather than another can also convey immediacy. Use of media such as a videophone, which transmits a lot of information, suggests more immediacy than use of media such as the voice telephone, which transmits less information. Heilbronn and Libby refer to their concept as 'technological immediacy' and the more traditional concept as 'social immediacy'.

Technological immediacy is different from social presence. This can be seen by considering the case of a person who uses a telephone to speak to someone in an adjacent office when it would be just as convenient to go and see the person concerned. An impression of low immediacy is likely to be created. No such impression is likely to be created if one person is in England and the other in Australia. The level of social presence afforded by the telephone, however, is the same (or slightly higher in the former case because of the better audio quality associated with very short distances). Of course, in some cases immediacy and social presence may vary together. For example, if a person has both a videophone and a voice telephone available, both immediacy and social presence will be greater if (s)he chooses to use the videophone.

Measuring Social Presence

Research on attitudes toward Type A communications media (see Short, Williams, and Christie, 1976) indicates that the social presence factor is marked by the following semantic differential scales:

$$\begin{array}{r}
\text{impersonal} \dots \dots \text{personal} \\
\text{unsociable} \dots \dots \text{sociable} \\
\text{insensitive} \dots \dots \text{sensitive} \\
\text{cold} \dots \dots \text{warm}
\end{array}$$

Media having a high degree of social presence are rated as personal, sociable, sensitive and warm.

In the classic semantic differential technique (Osgood, Suci, and Tannenbaum, 1957), subjects are asked to rate a variety of concepts on a wide range of different bipolar scales. It has usually been found that only about three factors are needed to account for most of the variance in the ratings. These are: evaluation (good/bad); potency (strong/weak); and activity (active/passive). However, this 'E-P-A' structure is most commonly found when both the concepts and scales are heterogeneous (Miron, 1969). When the concepts to be judged are more homogeneous, e.g. all are communications media, then different structures can emerge.

Champness (1973) showed that other types of questionnaire items could be used to measure social presence, including degree of agreement or disagreement with the following statements (amongst others):

- one does not get a good enough idea of how people at the other end are reacting;
- one gets no real impression of personal contact with the people at the other end of the link;
- one can easily assess the other people's reactions to what has been said;
- it provides a great sense of realism.

In Champness' study, each of the eight highest loading items on this factor of his questionnaire correlated significantly with semantic differential ratings on the scale personal–impersonal.

The semantic differential remains the prime technique for measuring social presence because it is readily applicable to a wide variety of different situations and provides data which can be used to compare widely different media.

SOCIAL PRESENCE IN RELATION TO TYPE B COMMUNICATIONS MEDIA

Type B Media Compared With Type A

Relatively little work has been done comparing Type B and Type A communication media with respect to social presence, but Short, Williams, and Christie (1976), present a bar chart based on two experiments by the author, which gives some clues.

The chart is reproduced in Figure 12.2. It is based on averaging the factor scores obtained from two experiments in which businessmen and civil servants rated a range of communications media on semantic differential scales.

The chart shows an intuitively reasonable ordering of the media from face-to-face communication at the 'high' end to the 'business letter' at the 'low' end. Short, Williams, and Christie are careful to caution their readers against reading too much into the chart, based as it is on very limited results. Nevertheless, the chart suggests that, whilst Type A media vary over a wide range of social presence, Type B media seem to be lowest of all on this factor. All the telecommunications media are judged lower than face-to-face communication and this may help to explain why managers seem to feel the office of tomorrow will be lower on social presence than the office today, as we discuss below.

Katzer's Study

We said above that social presence is a factor in attitudes toward Type B media as well as toward Type A. Most of the evidence for this comes from the PACTEL work considered below. Prior to that work, very little systematic research had been

176

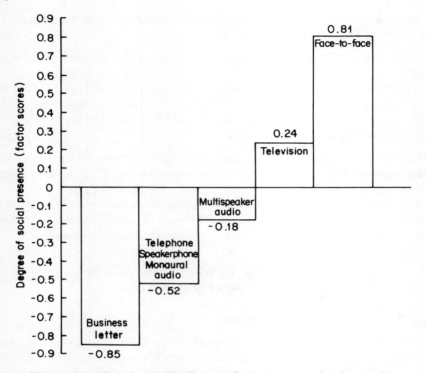

Figure 12.2.   Relative social presence of several communications media.

done—in fact, the author could find only one study, done by Katzer (1972). Katzer used the semantic differential technique but the study fails to provide any support for the social presence hypothesis. In view of its status as the only relevant study identified prior to the PACTEL work, it is important to examine the study and consider possible reasons why a social presence factor failed to emerge.

Katzer measured the attitudes of students and staff toward SUPARS (Syracuse University Psychological Abstracts Retrieval Service). The 71 respondents (of 90 who were asked) rated 20 concepts on 19 scales. Most of the respondents were library science students, about half of whom had completed at least one SUPARS search and half of whom had not. The concepts rated included, for example:

- 'psychological abstracts';
- 'PA UNDEFINED' (an error message);
- 'computer';
- 'TOO MANY USERS—TRY AGAIN SOON';

and so forth, including default messages as well as more general concepts.

A factor analysis of the 19 scales over the 71 × 20 cases resulted in three factors which were labeled: 'evaluative specific'; 'desirability'; and 'enormity'. The solution differs from the 'traditional' evaluation–potency–activity solution reported by Osgood, Suci, and Tannenbaum, and also from the solutions reported by Short, Williams, and Christie in connection with attitudes toward person-to-person media. Katzer acknowledges the desirability of replicating the study before coming to definite conclusions about the stability of the factor solution.

It is possible that the unusual factor solution obtained by Katzer might be attributable in part to the somewhat unusual nature of the set of concepts he used. Being directly concerned with SUPARS, the concepts spanned a much more limited range than those used in the original Osgood, Suci, and Tannenbaum studies, which included concepts as diverse as, for example: 'quicksand'; 'methodology'; 'white rose buds'; and 'sleep'. On the other hand, Katzer's concepts were very much more heterogeneous in terms of mixing levels of generality (e.g. 'computer' on the one hand, a specific error message on the other) than were the concepts typically rated in the studies reviewed by Short, Williams, and Christie (which tended to be labels given to different media, e.g., 'face-to-face contact', 'video', and so forth).

Two alternatives to Katzer's approach might be worth considering for future research. The first is to ask subjects to rate just a single concept (e.g. SUPARS, or some other particular system of interest) and base the analysis on the correlations between the rating scales over the different subjects who do the rating. The second is similar to Katzer's approach but would use concepts at a similar level of generality, perhaps selected to span the range of current technological developments, for example:

- 'stand-alone word processors';
- 'shared-logic word processors';
- 'videotex systems';
- 'personal computers';
- 'networked information services';
- and so forth.

A further methodological point worth pursuing in future research might be the scales used. Katzer based his on the original Osgood, Suci, and Tannenbaum studies, but it may be worth considering modifying this set to include descriptors subjects tend to use in connection with information–communication systems, and to test hypotheses—such as the identifiability of a 'social presence' factor—suggested by the studies on Type A media.

ATTITUDES TOWARD THE OFFICE OF TOMORROW

We saw above that telecommunications media generally are judged lower on social presence than face-to-face contact, and Type B media are judged lower still. In view of this, it is perhaps not surprising to find that managers expect the office of tomorrow to be low on social presence—after all, telecommunications media for both Type A and Type B communication are expected to be a significant feature of tomorrow's office.

The study to be described was done by the author and his colleagues recently and is reported here for the first time. It provides evidence not only for the low expectations managers seem to have for the office of tomorrow in regard to social presence, it also provides further evidence for the functional independence of the social presence and general evaluation factors.

Middle and senior managers from 54 organizations covering a wide range of different types gave their impressions of the office of tomorrow compared with the office of today. They did so by rating the two concepts on the seventeen 7-point bipolar scales shown in Figure 12.3. This also shows the factors the scales were intended to measure. The general evaluation, potency, and activity factors are the standard semantic differential factors. The remaining factors, including the social presence factor, were suggested by the earlier research on attitudes toward Type A telecommunication systems.

The managers, who participated on a voluntary basis, were allocated randomly to one of two groups. Group I (29 males) were asked to think about their own offices and offices in general today and rate "the office today", then listen to a presentation (with visual aids) on the Office of Tomorrow (lasting about ten minutes), and finally rate the Office of Tomorrow. Group II (25 males) listened to the presentation first, then rated the Office of Tomorrow, then participated in a seminar lasting about two hours, and finally rated the Office of Tomorrow for a second time. The scheme is shown diagrammatically in Figure 12.4. This design allowed for a test of the effect of a lengthy discussion on attitudes toward the office of tomorrow. The discussion focussed on the introduction of electronic systems for the typing of documents and

Figure 12.3. Scales used in a study of managers' attitudes toward the office of tomorrow.

Scale	Hypothesized factor
bad–good harmful–beneficial negative–positive	General evaluation
weak–strong yielding–unyielding flexible–rigid	Potency
passive–active slow–fast static–dynamic	Activity
impersonal–personal dehumanizing–humanizing	Social presence
colourless–colourful ugly–beautiful unaesthetic–aesthetic	Aesthetic appeal
simple–complex boring–interesting	Interestingness
not secure–secure (not private) (private)	Privacy

Element	Group I	Group II

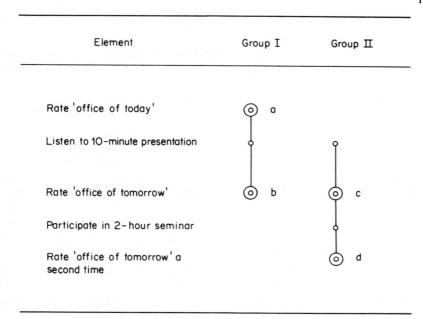

Figure 12.4.   Basic experimental design of a study of attitudes toward the office of tomorrow.

other papers, the electronic manipulation of information, and the communication of documents electronically from office to office. The design also allowed the effects of completing the rating scales twice to be controlled. In Figure 12.4, a and c compare the office of tomorrow with the office of today, where the respondents in each case are completing the scales for the first time. Also, b and d compare ratings made before and after a two-hour seminar, where the respondents in each case are completing the scales for a second time.

Another feature of the experimental design was the use of two forms of the rating scales: 'random' and 'grouped'. The purpose of this was to check on the robustness of the factor structure, that is the extent to which the way the subjects interpreted and used the rating scales was influenced by the order in which the scales were presented. In the 'random' version, the rating scales were presented in a standard random sequence on a single sheet. In the 'grouped' version, they were grouped according to the factors they were intended to measure. In both versions the polarity of the scales (e.g. good–bad or bad–good) was random. In Group I, 14 managers were given the 'random' form and 15 the 'grouped'; in Group II, 11 were given the 'random' form and 14 the 'grouped'.

The subjects were run in groups of between 4 and 10 which included other managers who, for various reasons (mainly pressure of time in running the seminars, which were held for other purposes as well) only completed the rating scales once.

In all, 62 sets of ratings (manager–concept combinations) were obtained for the 'random' version, and 65 for the 'grouped'.

The product–moment intercorrelations between the rating scales were computed separately for the 'random' and 'grouped' versions, to check on whether the grouping of scales had a significant influence on their interpretation. Of the $n(n - 1)/2 =$ 136 correlations, 14 differed by 0.36 or more. This is the value required for significance at the 5 per cent level (non-directional test) when comparing just two correlations. In the present case, the correlations 'overlap'—if the interpretation of a single scale shifts, it will create changes in the correlations with all the other scales—so the number of shifts in interpretation may be much less than the differences in the correlations might suggest at first glance. Nevertheless, the differences were felt sufficient to require two separate factor analyses to be done: one for the 'grouped' version, and one for the 'random'.

The factor analyses were done by the SAS computer package, with the following steps: principal components analysis; rotation of eigenvectors with eigenvalues greater than unity to varimax orthogonal simple structure; rotation to promax oblique simple structure. The factor-loading patterns are presented in Figures 12.5 and 12.6, and the inter-factor correlations in Figure 12.7.

Factor scores were computed on all factors and differences between the concepts

Figure 12.5.   Factor loading pattern (random scales).

			Factor			
	Social presence	Activity	Aesthetic appeal	Com- plexity	Privacy	General evalua- tion
Rating scale	I	II	III	IV	V	VI
impersonal–personal	−0.95	0.12	0.01	−0.10	−0.14	−0.14
humanizing–dehumanizing	0.88	0.09	−0.16	−0.09	0.18	0.03
active–passive	0.25	−0.92	0.25	0.04	−0.09	0.00
positive–negative	−0.10	−0.89	−0.01	−0.37	−0.03	−0.04
aesthetic–unaesthetic	−0.15	0.32	−0.89	−0.01	−0.05	−0.07
boring–interesting	−0.27	0.17	0.75	−0.06	0.08	−0.21
colourful–colourless	0.39	−0.05	−0.70	−0.29	−0.06	0.08
ugly–beautiful	−0.05	0.04	0.57	−0.09	0.01	0.46
complex–simple	0.03	0.18	0.06	0.95	0.00	0.10
secure (private)–not	0.23	0.09	0.19	−0.04	0.91	−0.16
harmful–beneficial	0.08	0.02	−0.15	0.16	−0.17	0.81
good–bad	−0.02	−0.21	−0.21	0.42	0.52	0.05
weak–strong	0.42	0.41	0.24	0.05	−0.18	0.06
unyielding–yielding	−0.55	−0.05	0.12	0.14	−0.04	0.59
flexible–rigid	0.57	−0.05	0.04	0.25	−0.28	−0.39
slow–fast	0.43	0.42	0.05	−0.13	−0.07	0.09
dynamic–static	−0.15	−0.31	−0.20	0.23	−0.10	−0.46

Figure 12.6. Factor loading pattern (grouped scales).

Rating scale	General evaluation I	Aesthetic appeal II	Social presence III	'Residual' factor IV
positive–negative	−0.87	−0.23	−0.10	0.01
weak–strong	0.77	0.03	−0.12	0.22
harmful–beneficial	0.75	−0.13	0.11	−0.32
good–bad	−0.73	−0.03	0.07	−0.22
slow–fast	0.69	−0.04	−0.37	0.16
active–passive	−0.62	0.03	0.04	−0.39
dynamic–static	−0.53	0.12	0.14	−0.44
boring–interesting	0.49	−0.30	0.37	0.07
aesthetic–unaesthetic	0.14	0.87	−0.12	0.15
ugly–beautiful	−0.02	−0.71	0.00	0.24
complex–simple	−0.11	−0.69	−0.23	0.38
colourful–colourless	−0.31	0.57	−0.35	0.11
impersonal–personal	−0.09	0.02	0.93	0.29
humanizing–dehumanizing	0.08	0.11	−0.82	−0.16
unyielding–yielding	−0.04	−0.16	0.14	0.86
flexible–rigid	−0.09	−0.19	−0.40	−0.81
secure (private)–not	−0.29	0.03	−0.12	−0.45

(the a/c and b/d comparisons) were tested using the t-test for uncorrelated observations. The results are presented in Figures 12.8 and 12.9. Attitudes before and after the two-hour seminar were compared in a similar way and the results are presented in Figures 12.10 and 12.11. In making these comparisons, analysis was restricted to those subjects who had completed the rating scales twice, to avoid possible artefacts that might have been introduced by mixing such subjects with others who had completed the scales only once.

The main conclusion to be drawn from this experiment is that managers do indeed seem to believe the office of tomorrow is likely to differ from the office of today. The most reliable difference seems to be in terms of social presence. This difference emerged from both analyses at a level that is statistically reliable.

Inspection of the factor patterns given in Figures 12.5 and 12.6—especially Figure 12.5—suggests the following interpretation of the social presence effect: compared with the office of today, the managers in this experiment believed the office of tomorrow is likely to be more impersonal, dehumanizing, rigid, unyielding, fast, strong, colourless and boring.

This is not a very pleasant picture of the office of tomorrow, and one might have expected that to be reflected in the general evaluation factor. In fact, this factor showed a significant difference only in the analysis based on the grouped scales. This analysis showed that the managers concerned believed the office of tomorrow is likely to be better, not worse than the office of today. This effect must be due to

Figure 12.7. Inter-factor correlations.

(a) Random scales

	I	II	III	IV	V	VI
I Social presence (−)		0.038	−0.031	−0.254	−0.220	−0.030
II Activity			0.337	−0.179	−0.159	0.358
III Aesthetic appeal (−)				−0.122	−0.090	0.323
IV Complexity (−)					−0.077	−0.199
V Privacy (−)						0.062
VI General evaluation						

(b) Grouped scales

	I	II	III	IV
I General evaluation		−0.319	−0.066	0.366
II Aesthetic appeal			0.157	−0.141
III Social presence				−0.182
IV Residual				

beliefs about the office of tomorrow which do not emerge so clearly from the rating scales, probably beliefs related to the efficiency of the office. This hypothesis receives some support from the judgements given (above) of the 'office of tomorrow' as being relatively 'fast' compared with that of today. This finding is reminiscent of the work on teleconferencing reported elsewhere (Short, Williams, and Christie, 1976). There it was found that teleconferencing systems tend to be judged lower than face-to-face contact on social presence, but often seem to have the advantage of making meetings more business-like.

The general picture that emerges therefore is of an office which is more impersonal and more dehumanizing, but possibly more efficient than the office today.

Figure 12.8. The office of tomorrow compared with the office today (random scales).

	$n =$	14 a today		11 c tomorrow		t
Factor			Mean factor scores (and standard deviations)			
I Social presence (−)		−0.97	(0.55)	0.05	(0.81)	3.59*
II Activity		−0.07	(0.05)	−0.42	(1.11)	0.81
III Aesthetic appeal (−)		−0.20	(1.08)	−0.31	(0.93)	0.26
IV Complexity (−)		0.37	(0.91)	0.33	(0.93)	0.10
V Privacy (−)		0.25	(0.94)	0.31	(0.72)	0.17
VI General Evaluation		−0.33	(0.60)	0.13	(0.87)	1.50

* $p <0.05$ or better; critical t at 5% level (2-sided test) for $N_1 + N_2 - 2 = 23 df = 2.07$.

Figure 12.9.   The office of tomorrow compared with the office today (grouped scales).

Mean factor scores
(and standard deviations)

		$n =$ 15		14		
		a		c		
	Factor	today		tomorrow		t
I	General evaluation	−0.66	(1.21)	0.22	(0.80)	2.21*
II	Aesthetic appeal	0.05	(0.86)	−0.21	(0.96)	0.74
III	Social presence	0.73	(0.80)	−0.04	(0.87)	2.40*
IV	Residual	0.04	(1.03)	0.32	(0.79)	0.79

* $P <0.05$ or better; critical t at 5% level (2-sided test) for $N_1 + N_2 − 2 = 27 df = 2.05$.

A second general conclusion from the experiment is that attitudes toward the office of tomorrow do not seem particularly easy to modify. In the present experiment, a two-hour seminar failed to produce a shift on any of the attitude factors identified.

It must be said, however, that the seminar was structured around an 'objective'

Figure 12.10.   Attitudes toward the office of tomorrow before and after a two-hour seminar (random scales).

A.   Random

Mean factor scores
(and standard deviations)

		$n =$ 14		11		
		b		d		
	Factor	before		after		t
I	Social presence (−)	0.24	(0.82)	0.63	(0.82)	1.25
II	Activity	0.35	(0.83)	0.16	(0.89)	0.53
III	Aesthetic appeal (−)	0.33	(0.87)	0.07	(0.72)	0.77
IV	Complexity (−)	0.14	(0.88)	0.41	(0.74)	1.59
V	Privacy (−)	−0.09	(0.95)	0.02	(1.10)	0.16
VI	General evaluation	0.45	(1.03)	0.45	(0.89)	0.00

Figure 12.11.   Attitudes toward the office of tomorrow before and after a two-hour seminar (grouped scales).

B.   Grouped

Mean factor scores
(and standard deviations)

		$n =$ 15		14		
		b		d		
	Factor	before		after		t
I	General evaluation	0.22	(0.92)	0.34	(0.66)	0.39
II	Aesthetic appeal	0.37	(1.12)	−0.11	(1.05)	1.15
III	Social presence	−0.25	(1.02)	−0.53	(0.79)	0.79
IV	Residual	−0.43	(1.13)	0.17	(0.95)	1.49

analysis of the 'office of tomorrow'. There was no deliberate attempt to influence the attitudes of the managers who participated; the emphasis was on explanation of technological innovations, without evaluation, to see if a better understanding of the technology involved would lead to different attitudes. It did not. Of course, it is difficult to explain something as complex as the office of tomorrow without any evaluative bias at all. If there was any such bias, it was probably in the direction of presenting the office of tomorrow as more efficient. If so, this appears to have had no significant effect on the managers' attitudes.

A third conclusion is that the social presence factor is important in this context as in previous research (Short, Williams, and Christie, 1976). It is functionally independent of the general evaluation factor and, at least in this experiment, distinguishes the office of tomorrow from the office of today more reliably.

These conclusions appear especially warranted in view of the relatively good agreement between the two separate analyses conducted.

CONCLUSIONS

Attitudes are of vital importance in shaping the influence of new technology. In view of this it is surprising that relatively little scientific research has been done on attitudes toward the electronic technology that promises, or threatens, to have such an impact on our lives. In this chapter, we have looked at some of the broad factors—including social presence—that are involved in managers' attitudes toward the general concept of the office of tomorrow. Our findings suggest that managers may view the office of tomorrow with mixed feelings. The office of tomorrow may be faster and more efficient, but some managers at least see possibilities of its being more impersonal and dehumanizing. Ways of avoiding or minimizing such negative aspects of automation in the office are discussed in a later chapter. In the next chapter we examine in more detail attitudes toward the kinds of information systems that can be found in the office environment.

Chapter 13

Attitudes toward information systems

We saw in the previous chapter how a group of managers drawn from a variety of different organizations expressed mixed feelings about the office of tomorrow, how some of them expected it to be faster but more impersonal and more dehumanizing. How this pattern of reactions develops during the 1980s will depend in part on how people regard the new kinds of information systems that will be introduced. This may vary somewhat from one organization to another, depending to a large extent on the sorts of organizational and personal factors that we examine in Chapters 15 and 16. In this chapter we shall examine some of the key approaches to the study of attitudes toward information systems, and identify some of the key factors that are involved. Like most of the work in this area, the findings should be regarded as tentative; their main value lies in encouraging other researchers to extend the work done in this important area, and to provide a broad framework to help guide that work productively.

A SEMANTIC DIFFERENTIAL APPROACH

The author and his colleagues at PACTEL recently completed a study of attitudes toward a variety of information systems, based on the semantic differential technique and designed to illuminate the broad structure of attitudes toward information systems.

It is surprising in view of the widespread use of the semantic differential that it does not appear to have been used before as a basis for a systematic study of attitudes toward information systems. In a recent review (Christie, 1979) the author was able to find only one strictly relevant study. This was the study by Katzer (1972) described in the previous chapter in relation to the 'social presence' factor. We saw there that the study had some unusual methodological features which make its findings difficult to interpret. Primarily, a rather peculiar range of concepts was chosen for study, ranging across concepts as diverse as: 'psychological abstracts'; 'PA UNDEFINED' (an error message); 'myself and computers'; 'EXEC PA'; 'Keyword'; and so forth. Also, the study used the semantic differential scales used in the original Osgood, Suci, and Tannenbaum studies, rather than making any attempt to test hypotheses based on previous research in the information–communication area or any attempt to select scales particularly relevant to that area.

The study described below did not suffer from these weaknesses. It compared different information systems within a broad range including 'manual' systems such as libraries and personal files as well as computer-based systems. And it made the comparisons in terms of semantic differential scales selected for their relevance to the domain in question and their suitability for testing hypotheses based on relevant previous research.

Method

The study was conducted as part of a larger assignment for the Commission of the European Communities, parts of which have been described in previous chapters. Its purpose was to establish the broad factors involved in officials' attitudes toward the information systems designed to serve their needs, and to draw comparisons between different systems and different parts of the Commission. This account of the study will concern itself only with a description of the main attitude factors involved, i.e. the structure of attitudes toward the information systems, and very general comments about differences and similarities between the main types of systems.

Self-completion semantic differential forms with instructions were distributed to 1000 officials. There were 113 usable returns, an overall response rate of just over 11 per cent. (A questionnaire was regarded as usable if no more than two of the 42 scales had been missed.) Both French and English versions were distributed and respondents chose which to use. Translation was achieved by translating from English into French, back-translating (by a different translator) from French into English, and resolving the few areas of difficulty by consensus after discussion with a key Commission official.

Each respondent was asked to complete the standard set of 42 seven-point bipolar rating scales to give his or her impressions of one of the following eight sources of information used in the Commission, the source being named at the top of the rating form:

- central records department of your DG;
- divisional filing system;
- files kept in your own office or by your secretary;
- CELEX (a computerized system);
- ECDOC (a computerized system);
- SCAD (a document-request system);
- the libraries in the Commission;
- Agence Europe (a publication giving recent news).

These sources had been identified in pilot work as being representative of the main information sources used by officials.

The 42 scales were presented in a standard random sequence of 23 marker scales and 19 additional scales (intermixed). The 23 marker scales were included to provide estimates of six factors found in previous research, as follows:

- general evaluation (E) and social presence discussed in Chapter 12;
- aesthetic appeal and privacy (Security), found to be important in relation to Type A communication (see Short, Williams, and Christie, 1976);
- potency (P) and activity (A), being the remaining two of the 'standard' three semantic differential factors (evaluation–potency–activity, or E–P–A).

The 19 additional scales were based on words used by 57 officials interviewed in a preliminary study, and were included to ensure comprehensive coverage of the main attitude factors involved.

The order and polarity of the scales was determined by a quasi-random number generator and was as follows:

1	neglected–cared for	
2	not confused–confused	
3	convenient–inconvenient	
4	rigid–flexible	(P)
5	responsive–unresponsive	(soc pres)
6	weak–strong	(P)
7	boring–interesting	(aesth)
8	not secure (not private)–secure (private)	(priv)
9	useful–useless	(E)
10	incomplete–complete	
11	good–bad	(E)
12	human–mechanical	(soc pres)
13	slow–fast	(A)
14	complex–simple	(aesth)
15	unfriendly–friendly	(soc pres)
16	closed–open	(priv)
17	not pragmatic–pragmatic	
18	comprehensive–not comprehensive	
19	ineffective–effective	
20	well-kept–poorly kept	
21	underworked–overworked	
22	efficient–inefficient	
23	dynamic–static	(A)
24	unhelpful–helpful	
25	warm–cold	(soc pres)
26	amateur–professional	
27	tidy–untidy	
28	beneficial–harmful	(E)
29	active–passive	(A)
30	unreliable–reliable	
31	limited–unlimited	
32	poorly conceived–well-conceived	

33	small–large	(P)
34	colourless–colourful	(aesth)
35	sensitive–insensitive	(soc pres)
36	backlog–no backlog	
37	easy-to-use–difficult-to-use	
38	unsociable–sociable	(soc pres)
39	personal–impersonal	(soc pres)
40	well-structured–poorly structured	
41	aesthetic–unaesthetic	(aesth)
42	constricted–spacious	(P)

First-order Factor Analysis

Of the $42 \times (42 - 1)/2 = 861$ product–moment correlations between the rating scales, a total of 597 (about 70 per cent) were significant at the 5 per cent level. This indicated there was an underlying psychological structure that could be found by analysis of the correlations.

The factor analysis was conducted using the SAS computer package. The number of factors was determined by conducting a principal components analysis with unities in the diagonals and rejecting all components (factors) with eigenvalues less than unity, i.e. all factors which contributed less than the average variable to the total variance. This gave 11 first-order factors. These were rotated to oblique simple structure using the Promax criterion. The factor loadings are given in the factor pattern matrix in Figure 13.1. These loadings show to what extent the factors 'explain' or 'predict' the individual ratings—the higher the loading, the more important the contribution made by the factor concerned.

The first-order factors show the fundamental ways in which the officials in the study judged their information environment. As a result of the care taken in designing the semantic differential forms used to ensure broad coverage of the range of attitudinal responses involved, it seems likely that most of the comments officials might make about information systems would be interpretable to a large extent in terms of the eleven factors identified. In this connection it may be of interest to note that there is plenty of room for varied comments: Even assuming just three levels per factor, e.g. high, medium, low, eleven factors give enough space for up to 177, 147 comments to be fitted—all with slightly different meanings; similarly, up to 177, 147 different profiles describing different information systems can be generated. The factors therefore provide a basis for a fundamental understanding of how people, at least in the organization studied, perceive their information environment. The factors may be interpreted as follows:

1. *General evaluation.* This factor accounts for a large proportion of the variance in people's responses in many different contexts. It was postulated on the basis of previous research (e.g. Short, Williams, and Christie, 1976). It can be regarded as a measure of general attitude 'for or against' a concept—in this study, an in-

189

					FACTORS						
	I	II	III	IV	V	VI	VII	VIII	IX	X	XI
9. useless	.91	-.00	-.08	.02	.03	-.08	.12	.08	-.04	.03	-.10
24. helpful	-.74	-.08	-.01	-.02	.10	-.09	-.04	.04	.02	.06	-.06
28. harmful	.57	.09	.06	-.06	-.09	.03	-.28	-.13	-.04	-.18	.05
19. effective	-.54	.03	-.18	.23	.11	.17	-.10	.13	.01	.11	.01
11. bad	.54	-.01	.19	-.02	.12	-.01	-.04	-.29	.16	-.12	-.13
17. pragmatic	-.44	.01	-.07	-.13	-.01	.08	-.09	.41	.12	.31	-.13
22. inefficient	.43	-.01	.33	-.11	-.01	.02	-.10	.03	.26	-.11	.10
4. flexible	-.07	-.72	.08	.07	.09	-.06	.01	.22	.04	.04	-.13
23. static	.18	.46	.12	-.08	-.02	.08	-.03	-.05	.45	.07	.13
1. cared for	-.00	.04	-.89	-.17	-.05	.11	.06	-.02	-.17	-.02	.04
2. confused	-.06	.13	.74	.06	-.00	.28	-.07	-.15	-.04	.16	-.15
6. strong	-.19	-.14	-.66	-.01	.02	-.12	-.10	.01	.15	-.20	.23
3. inconvenient	-.10	.21	.61	.04	-.03	-.05	.14	-.17	.01	-.17	.04
20. poorly kept	.06	-.19	.57	.13	-.05	.10	.05	.12	.16	-.24	.06
36. no backlog	-.14	.09	.52	.36	-.12	.27	-.12	-.08	-.06	-.03	-.25
27. untidy	.26	-.20	.51	.09	.06	.27	-.09	.28	.19	-.10	.05
30. reliable	-.21	.01	-.47	.03	-.02	-.40	.14	-.08	.20	.28	-.07
31. unlimited	.22	-.13	.19	.78	.02	-.24	.14	-.01	-.39	.06	.02
18. not compreh.	.19	-.09	-.15	.71	-.01	-.07	-.00	-.13	.06	-.19	-.11
21. overworked	-.27	-.34	.04	.62	-.20	-.06	-.07	-.26	.09	-.20	.03
42. spacious	.13	-.10	-.14	-.11	.80	.19	.03	.03	-.35	-.08	-.01
33. large	.24	-.03	.18	.01	.78	-.15	.05	-.06	.12	-.07	.12
32. well-conc'vd	.29	.08	-.22	.38	.05	-.69	-.23	.09	.14	.15	-.01
25. cold	-.05	.40	-.02	.07	.07	.62	.01	.00	.17	-.09	.10
39. impersonal	.29	.04	-.19	.21	.11	.54	.44	-.15	.14	.16	.23
38. sociable	.02	-.06	-.00	.06	.05	-.53	-.16	-.06	-.26	.33	.10
12. mechanical	.06	-.04	.00	-.01	.06	.23	.88	.11	.03	.07	.07
13. fast	-.05	-.23	.04	.00	-.05	-.08	.12	.83	-.00	.22	-.03
41. unaesthetic	-.13	-.07	.07	-.15	-.06	.08	-.03	.03	.85	.22	-.02
34. colourful	.11	-.35	-.01	-.06	-.05	-.08	-.01	.02	-.58	-.09	-.46
35. insensitive	.21	.00	-.24	-.07	-.26	.03	.27	.10	.56	-.20	-.11
7. interesting	-.22	-.21	-.26	.11	-.13	.18	-.01	.18	-.50	.07	.24
14. simple	-.05	.01	.07	.10	-.20	-.18	.14	.25	.15	.83	.01
16. open	-.27	-.18	-.03	.07	.12	.01	-.15	-.13	.22	.65	-.06
37. dif.-to-use	.05	-.02	.04	-.09	-.04	.17	-.01	-.13	.07	-.56	.11
15. friendly	-.22	-.25	-.01	-.17	-.09	-.32	-.02	.04	-.06	.48	.16
10. complete	-.29	-.04	-.22	.13	.25	-.20	-.00	.36	.04	-.41	.04
8. secure (prv)	.00	.10	-.09	.06	.08	.13	.06	-.06	-.05	-.06	.76
26. professional	-.07	.22	-.13	-.01	-.07	-.20	-.03	.15	-.44	.03	.45
40. poorly strc.	.11	-.12	.27	-.15	-.06	.31	.04	-.25	.14	-.13	.21
29. passive	.18	.36	.19	.02	-.22	.27	-.14	.11	.05	-.22	.05
5. unresponsive	-.26	.38	.38	.04	-.03	.11	.43	-.01	-.01	.22	-.15

Figure 13.1.   First-order factor pattern.

formation system. It is 'attitude' in the narrow, Thurstonian sense, representing a resolution of other, more specific factors, including social presence.

2. *Flexibility.* This factor may reflect the degree to which the officials regarded their information sources as amenable to change, new ideas, able to cope with unusual requests, and so forth.

3. *Maintenance.* High scores on this factor indicated that the information sources

concerned were seen to be relatively well cared for, not confused, convenient, well kept, tidy and reliable.

4. *Comprehensiveness.* A concern for the completeness and comprehensiveness of information emerged qualitatively from interviews with the officials, and this factor seems to represent the same concern.

5. *Spaciousness.* This factor is difficult to interpret. It seems to be related to the physical domain covered, but in a rather nebulous way, e.g. SCAD—concerned with routing documents from anywhere in the Commission to officials anywhere in the Commission—was rated fairly high on this factor.

6. *Social presence.* The nature of this factor has been discussed in the previous chapter. It is interesting in view of its psychological significance that it did not discriminate significantly between the information systems.

7. *Humanness.* This factor distinguished the more 'human' information sources from the more 'mechanical'. It is important to remember that high scores on this factor do not necessarily mean 'better'; the correlation between 'humanness' and 'general evaluation' was only 0.11. Although there is an obvious conceptual link with the 'social presence' factor, the two are different and this is reflected in the low correlation (only −0.086) between them.

8. *Speed of response.* As the name implies, this factor is concerned with how fast the information systems deliver information, and how 'pragmatic' they are. Interestingly, officials' own files were judged somewhat better in this regard than some of the computerized systems.

9. *Aesthetic appeal.* This factor was identified in work on Type A communication (see Short, Williams, and Christie, 1976). High scores reflect judgements that the information source is relatively aesthetic, colourful, sensitive, interesting and dynamic. Interestingly, this factor also makes a small contribution (roughly about 20 per cent of variance) to judgements on the scale 'amateur-professional', the more 'professional' sources being a little less colourful and dynamic than the more 'amateur'.

10. *Simplicity.* Information systems scoring high on this factor were judged relatively simple, open, easy to use, and friendly, although possibly incomplete.

11. *Security.* This factor was postulated on the basis of previous research on Type A communication (see Short, Williams, and Christie, 1976). The libraries were judged relatively secure, and officials' own files—not surprisingly—somewhat less secure than some of the other systems.

Of the six factors postulated, four were actually identified in the factor analysis summarized above. These were:

- general evaluation;
- social presence;
- aesthetic appeal;
- privacy (security).

All of these have been identified as being of particular importance in relation to Type A communication. The two factors which were postulated but did not emerge from the analysis were postulated on the basis of general semantic differential research rather than research specifically concerned with the information-communication area. These were 'potency' and 'activity'.

This illustrates the importance in research of this sort of tailoring techniques to the particular area being studied, consistent with being able to develop principles of sufficiently interesting generality. The point is further emphasized by the fact that seven of the factors to emerge from the analysis had not been postulated on the basis of previous work. Further research is needed to establish the reliability of these factors and to develop an understanding of them in greater detail.

Second-order Factor Analysis

The correlations between the first-order factors, shown in Figure 13.2, were considered sufficiently high to warrant further analysis. This was done by applying the factor-analysis program to the correlations in the same way as to the primary correlation matrix. This resulted in five second-order factors, describing more general dimensions than the first-order factors. The second-order factor pattern (the loadings of the first-order factors on the second-order factors) is presented in Figure 13.3 and the inter-factor correlations in Figure 13.4. The factors may be interpreted as follows.

I. *Comprehensiveness*. This second-order factor contributed most to the first order factors 'comprehensiveness' and 'spaciousness'. It reflects the concern for comprehensive information expressed by officials in personal interviews as well as in the semantic differential.

II. *General appeal*. This is the main second-order factor underlying the first-order factors: 'aesthetic appeal', 'simplicity' and 'maintenance'. Although this factor emerged as a general dimension of officials' perceptions, none of the information systems judged was rated above average in all aspects of this factor, i.e. no source was judged more than averagely aesthetically appealing, easy and simple to use, and well maintained. This may be a general criterion that designers of information systems might wish to strive for.

III. *Sympathetic responsiveness*. This may be a factor peculiar to the particular

		I	II	III	IV	V	VI	VII	VIII	IX	X	XI
I	evaluation		.201	.441	-.234	-.192	.332	.106	-.236	.209	-.397	.081
II	flexibility			.067	.025	-.032	.038	.194	.089	.146	-.193	-.047
III	maintenance				-.255	-.213	.223	.142	-.304	.336	-.421	.042
IV	comprehensiveness					.222	-.041	-.035	.158	.044	.027	-.162
V	spaciousness						-.238	-.111	.129	-.113	.173	-.015
VI	social presence							-.086	-.180	.207	-.173	.033
VII	humanness								-.119	.147	-.192	.004
VIII	speed of response									-.190	.127	-.008
IX	aesthetic appeal										-.416	.073
X	simplicity											-.154
XI	security											

Figure 13.2.   Correlations between the first-order factors.

organization studied but this is a question for future research to decide. It is a particularly interesting factor as—rather unexpectedly—it influenced social presence and humanness in opposite directions. Put simply, there seems to have been an element in the officials' feelings about their information sources which said that the more human sources had a tendency to be relatively cold and impersonal. It should be noted that this is a psychological factor which was relatively 'well covered', first by a series of first-order factors and then by 'surface behaviour' (e.g. the individual ratings made in the questionnaire), so one would not expect it necessarily to be very obvious in discussions with officials—they may not even be aware of it themselves. In this sense it can be regarded as a subconscious influence on the

		S1 compre-hensiv-eness	S2 general appeal	S3 sympathet-ic respon-siveness	S4 secur-ity	S5 rigid respons-iveness
IV	comprehensiveness	-.82	.26	.12	-.29	.09
V	spaciousness	-.67	.05	-.08	.16	-.08
I	evaluation	.46	.44	.14	.06	.13
IX	aesthetic appeal	-.28	.85	-.01	.06	-.09
X	simplicity	.03	-.80	.06	-.23	-.13
III	maintenance	.31	.56	-.06	.03	-.20
VII	humanness	.08	.22	-.78	-.13	.08
VI	social presence	.26	.33	.65	-.14	.01
XI	security	.03	.27	.05	.93	.01
II	flexibility	.14	.19	-.20	-.13	.76
VIII	speed of response	-.15	-.33	.33	.19	.67

Figure 13.3. Second-order factor pattern.

officials' behaviour in relation to the information systems. Further research could usefully be directed at establishing the generalizability of the factor and how it contributes to the differential use made of information systems of different types. It seems reasonable to suppose that users are happiest with an information system that does not simply respond to their requests, but responds sympathetically. This may be especially true of 'manual' systems. People may not expect machines—or electronic information systems?—to respond sympathetically to their needs, because

	S1	S2	S3	S4	S5
S1 comprehensiveness		.347	-.036	-.040	-.104
S2 general appeal			-.020	-.197	.053
S3 sympathteic responsiv.				-.037	.002
S4 security					-.049
S5 rigid responsiveness					

Figure 13.4. Correlations between the second-order factors.

sympathy is a human quality. But they are likely to expect a sympathetic response from systems run entirely or largely by humans, i.e. 'manual' systems.

IV. *Security*. This is the second order equivalent of the first-order security factor and no further explanation is required except to point out its relative importance as a general influence, even at the second order level.

V. *Rigid responsiveness*. This factor is marked by the two first-order factors: speed and flexibility, in the direction that speed and pragmatism coupled with a relative lack of flexibility indicate rigid responsiveness. A system characterized by high scores on this factor would cope well with routine requests but would have difficulty in dealing with less routine needs.

General Comments

The semantic differential factors discussed above provide a systematic and fairly detailed framework for the understanding of attitudes toward information systems. To the extent that they represent significant dimensions of users' response to systems they should also have predictive value. Their value in this respect is illustrated in Figure 13.5. This shows the Spearman rank order correlations between the rank orders of the eight information sources included in the study on each of the eleven first-order factors and their rank order in terms of how familiar officials judged themselves to be with the sources (on a scale from 0 to 5), which agreed with how frequently they reported using them. The data were obtained from a questionnaire attached to the semantic differential.

The r_s value indicates the rank order correlation between a source's position on the particular semantic differential factor concerned and its position with respect

Figure 13.5. Usage and familiarity with sources in relation to their standing on the first-order semantic differential factors.

Factor	Rank order correlation (r_s)
Humanness	0.86*
General evaluation	0.74*
Social presence	0.69
Flexibility	0.60
Speed of response	0.31
Maintenance	0.21
Spaciousness	−0.21
Comprehensiveness	0.14
Simplicity	−0.07
Aesthetic appeal	−0.07
Security	−0.01

* $P < 0.05$.

to familiarity and usage. It is interesting to note that the factor with highest predictive value in this respect is not general evaluation, as one might have expected (although that, too, has high predictive value) but humanness. The most highly used sources were those perceived to be the most human. The social presence factor is not far behind in this regard, either, with the 'cold', 'impersonal' sources being used relatively little compared with the 'warmer', more 'personal' sources.

A REPERTORY GRID APPROACH

Another fairly widely used technique of attitude measurement is the repertory grid. Peace and Easterby (1973) discuss its use in connection with computer-based management systems.

The technique is based on 'elements' and 'constructs' which are roughly analogous to the 'concepts' and 'scales' of the semantic differential. The elements are usually elicited by interviewing individual respondents about the domain of interest. Peace and Easterby give an example in which respondents were asked questions relating to the use of computers in relation to their work, for example: 'If you had a job here that could be done by computer, which particular aspect would be most difficult to actually get the job done?' 'What is the most satisfying task in your job?' In their example, 24 questions were asked and 21 elements elicited. These included, for example (in summary form): 'understanding errors on computer runs'; 'numerical control'; 'cyclic strain hardening experiments'; and so forth.

The constructs are elicited by presenting respondents with selected triads of elements (e.g. A, B and C), and asking them to indicate the odd one out (e.g. B). They then indicate the way in which the two similar elements are similar (e.g. A and C might both be jobs) and how they differ from the odd one out (e.g. B might not be a job). In Peace and Easterby's experiment, 14 constructs were elicited, for example: 'machine-man'; 'useful–not useful'; 'practical-intellectual'; and 'experimental-nonexperimental'.

The third stage is for each respondent to rate each of the elements according to the various constructs, and for the correlations between the constructs to be factor analysed to yield 'superordinate constructs' which are roughly analogous to the factors of the semantic differential technique.

The parallels with the semantic differential technique are clear but the repertory grid approach has some unique weaknesses. Typically, a separate grid (of elements against constructs) is developed for each respondent. This is very time consuming and therefore expensive, but it also creates several more serious problems. First, the researcher must be very skilled to avoid influencing the elements elicited by imposing his or her own construct system on the respondent through the particular questions asked and the way they are phrased.

Secondly, the possible number of triads that can be created from a set of elements, although finite, is large, and Peace and Easterby recommend just using triads the researcher judges useful. Here again there is clearly a danger of the researcher unwittingly selecting triads that seem useful in terms only of his or her own construct system. Thirdly, since each factor solution is unique to a particular grid, and therefore a particular respondent, it is difficult to assess the reliability of the factor solutions obtained. Fourthly, in many practical cases, individual differences are of less interest than general characteristics of a group or groups of people. Because of the emphasis on individual testing in repertory grid work and the difficulty of comparing the factor solutions of different respondents, it can be difficult to identify general trends.

Despite these weaknesses, the repertory grid technique may be useful in some instances, especially where one wishes to take a more 'clinical' or 'personal' approach—perhaps as an aid in discussing possible impacts of new systems with individual managers, for example. It also illustrates a fundamental point, discussed in a later chapter—that people differ in their needs and capabilities, and systems need to be designed accordingly.

AN EXPERIMENTAL APPROACH

The semantic differential and repertory grid studies considered above are similar in their emphasis on understanding the structure of users' responses, with relatively less emphasis on the specific design features or other factors influencing those responses. The experimental approach, as the term is used here, differs in its relatively greater emphasis on the factors influencing the response. The response, however, is still attitudinal in the sense of being a verbal evaluation or description of the system rather than, say, a measure of performance.

The experimental approach will be illustrated by two experiments conducted by the author and his colleagues at PACTEL, concerned with the design of videotex systems so as to maximize user acceptance. They are concerned with:

• colour versus monochrome displays;
• features of frame design.

Colour versus Monochrome Displays

An interesting feature about videotex is its capacity to display a variety of colours. This represents something of a break with tradition, at least in office systems where displays typically have been monochrome (black on white, white on black, green on black, and so forth). The value of a colour display has been a contentious issue, some people claiming that it is of little value in the office environment and that as long as the information can be read the display is acceptable. A related claim is that the quality of the display, in terms of the detail it can present, is much more important.

A recent experiment conducted by the author and his colleagues as part of a larger assignment for the Commission of the European Communities in Luxemburg was designed to test the following hypotheses:

(a) Both quality and colour affect the acceptability of videotex displays.
(b) The effect of quality depends upon whether the display is in colour or monochrome.
(c) Colour has greater effect than quality.
(d) Both colour and quality are more important in the home than in the office.
(e) There are some differences between countries.
(f) The type of display affects what is considered a reasonable price for a set.
(g) The type of display affects how much people expect they would use videotex.

Subjects. There were 126 subjects in all (66 managers, 44 householders, 16 educationists), run in group sessions held in France, Germany, the UK and Holland.

Displays. Seven sets of four slides were prepared. The four slides in each set contained the same information. The seven sets were designed to span a range of different types of display and were (in arbitrary order):

- text plus secondary heading (a job advertisement);
- text plus main heading;
- tabular text (bandwidths of different telecommunications systems);
- bar chart (bandwidths);
- cartography (map of PA offices in London);
- pictogram (including a tree and a chemical flask);
- photograph (of a mansion used as a management training centre).

In each set, one slide was made by photographing a Prestel (1976) colour display and a second was made by making a colour photograph of a display simulated assuming no bandwidth or other constraints, e.g. an actual colour photograph of the management training centre. These two types of display are referred to here as 'Prestel' and 'video' quality. Black and white versions of the slides were also prepared.

Procedure. The subjects were run in groups. The slides were presented in a standard block random order, for ten seconds each with a blank screen between each block of four slides. The subjects were asked to work individually and rate each slide as it was shown by writing a number from 0 (completely unacceptable) to 100 (completely acceptable) on rating forms provided. They were asked to imagine themselves using videotex in their office (home, or classroom) and rate the slides according to how acceptable the displays would be in that situation. In two sessions, the order of the slides was reversed to see if this made any marked difference but appears not to have done though detailed statistical checks were not considered warranted.

Results. The seven sets of slides, based on the seven different types of information, were treated similarly as replications of the four basic combinations of quality and colour.

No analysis of possible differences between the seven types of information was attempted. The median ratings for the four experimental conditions are presented in Figure 13.6.

The overall effect of quality was tested separately for each session in the following way. In each of the seven blocks of four slides ($7 \times 4 = 28$ slides), the ratings given the two low quality slides were added and the result subtracted from the sum of the ratings for the two high-quality slides. The median of the seven different scores was taken as a measure of the effect of quality. This was done for each person. A similar procedure was used to test for the effect of colour. The results are presented in Figure 13.7.

The hypothesis that quality and colour would not be equally important was tested by subtracting the 'colour' scores from the 'quality' scores. This was done for each block of four slides, the median of the seven blocks being the score for the person. The overall medians (over all people within a given session) are presented in Figure 13.7. They differ from what might be expected by simply taking the difference of the first two columns in Figure 13.7 because of the method of calculation.

To test for an interaction between the effects of quality and colour, the effect of quality was tested separately for the colour displays and for the monochrome. The results are presented in Figure 13.8.

The hypothesis that colour and quality would be more important for the homes sessions than the business/government ones was tested by comparing the overall 'quality' and 'colour' scores. The results are presented in Figure 13.9.

Figure 13.6.   Median ratings.

	Colour		Black/white			
	Prestel	Video	Prestel	Video		
Business/ government						
France 1	52.5	85	27.5	55	$n =$	12
France 2	37.5	77.5	20	55	$n =$	12
Germany 1	50	70	20	50	$n =$	11
Germany 2	50	80	30	50	$n =$	13
UK 1	50	60	40	20	$n =$	9
UK 2	55	50	40	40	$n =$	9
Netherlands	50	50	30	45	$n =$	11
Homes						
France 3	40	80	20	40	$n =$	11
Germany 3	50	80	30	40	$n =$	13
UK 3	45	50	30	30	$n =$	20
Education						
UK 4	33	50	19	20	$n =$	16
Medians	50	65	30	40	$n =$	126

Figure 13.7. Overall effects of display quality and whether in colour or monochrome.

	Overall effects of		Significance of difference (two-tailed tests)
	quality (a)	colour (b)	
	(one-tailed tests)		
Business/ government			
France 1	30*	23*	ns
France 2	15*	18*	ns
Germany 1	20*	15*	ns
Germany 2	20*	20*	ns
UK 1	0 ns	25*	*
UK 2	0 ns	8*	ns
Netherlands	10*	13*	ns
Homes			
France 3	20*	30*	ns
Germany 3	20*	25*	ns
UK 3	0 ns	10*	*
Education			
UK 4	9†	15*	ns
Medians	15	18	

* $P < 0.01$, (Wilcoxon T.).
† $P < 0.05$.
ns = not significant.

Additional results for business/government sessions. After rating the slides from 0 to 100, subjects in the business/government sessions (but not the homes or education sessions) were told there were four main types of display (Prestel or 'other', and each in monochrome or colour), and were asked individually to rank order these from 1 (most preferred) to 4 (least preferred). The overall rankings are shown in Figure 13.10.

The order of the Prestel/colour and the video/monochrome is arbitrary (does not deviate from a chance or random result) except for the German session, and only then when the subjects considered videotex in the home.

Subjects were then asked, separately for the office and home: for every 30 minutes you would spend using a set giving your *most* preferred display, how many minutes would you spend using a set giving your less preferred displays? The medians are presented in Figure 13.11.

They were also asked: for every £10 you would spend to buy or rent a set giving your *most* preferred display, how much would you spend to buy or rent other sets? The medians are presented in Figure 13.12.

Discussion. The hypothesis that both quality and colour will affect the acceptability of videotex displays is only partially supported. Figure 13.7 shows that colour had a statistically reliable effect on the ratings in all eleven sessions, but quality had

	Effects of quality for		Significance of difference (two-tailed tests)
	monochrome (a)	colour (b)	
	(one-tailed tests)		
Business/ government			
France 1	15*	17*	ns
France 2	10*	12*	ns
Germany 1	5*	10*	ns
Germany 2	10*	10*	† (1)
UK 1	−5 ns	5 ns	†
UK 2	1 ns	0 ns	ns
Netherlands	5*	5†	ns
Homes			
France 3	10*	15*	ns
Germany 3	10*	10*	ns
UK 3	3 ns	0 ns	ns
Education			
UK 4	0 ns	5*	†

Figure 13.8. Effects of quality for monochrome and colour displays.

* P <0.01, (Wilcoxon T.).
† P <0.05.
ns = not significant.
(1) Although not reflected in the overall medians, because of skewed distribution, there was a significant tendency in this group for quality to have a greater effect for the colour than for the monochrome displays.

an effect that exceeded what might be expected by chance in only eight sessions; furthermore, the effect of colour was significantly greater than that of quality in two of the sessions.

These results suggest that quality as we have defined it is almost but probably not quite as important as colour in determining the acceptability of videotex displays. Figure 13.8 shows that the effects of these two variables are additive, in the sense that providing colour improves acceptability but it can be improved still further by adding high quality. Further research should examine which particular aspects of quality are the more important.

The hypothesis that colour affects the acceptability of displays in the home more than in the office is barely supported. The French results suggest this (see Figure 13.9) but the German and UK results do not. The hypothesis that quality affects acceptability more in the home than in the office is not supported at all.

Concerning country differences, there is some evidence from Figure 13.7 that quality may be less important in the UK than in the other countries but the reasons for this are not clear. One possibility is that the UK participants felt somehow obliged to give the Prestel displays comparatively good ratings because Prestel is British, but there are many other possibilities including the possibility that people in the UK really are less concerned with quality as we have defined it above.

(a)   Colour

Figure 13.9.   Similarities between home and business.

	Home		Business		Significance of difference
France	$n = 11$	30	$n = 24$	20	*
Germany	$n = 13$	25	$n = 24$	20	ns
UK	$n = 20$	10	$n = 18$	15	ns

(b)   Quality

	Home		Business		Significance of difference
France	$n = 11$	20	$n = 24$	30	ns
Germany	$n = 13$	20	$n = 24$	20	ns
UK	$n = 20$	0	$n = 18$	0	ns

* $P < 0.01$, one-tailed text (Mann-Whitney U.).
ns = not significant.

Turning to the other two measures of acceptability, expected amount of use and perceptions of an acceptable price for a set, display type affects both of these. The subjects' judgements—which seem remarkably consistent across different countries—suggest the effects could be quite large, e.g. poor displays could reduce usage by 85 per cent. Whether such large effects could be expected in all possible groups of subjects is debatable, but it is likely that the trend at least is general.

Conclusions. Quality and colour affected the acceptability of videotex displays about equally, over the range of quality and colour examined, though there is some indication colour was the more important. There was little or no difference between the home and office in this respect. There were few if any important differences between countries, though there is some indication that the quality of the display may have been less important in the UK than elsewhere.

Colour and quality of displays seem likely to affect both what is perceived to be an acceptable price for a videotex set and how much a person will use videotex. Our present sample of potential users believed that poor displays (Prestel quality in monochrome) could reduce usage by as much as 85 per cent compared with their expected usage of their most preferred type of set (video quality in colour).

Frame Design

Whatever the 'technological quality' of a videotex system—e.g. whether it is in black and white or in colour—the author of information in the system can influence the overall acceptability of the system by designing frames well or poorly ('author quality').

In a recent experiment by the author and his colleagues, the relative effects of four factors involved in frame design were measured:

Figure 13.10. Participants' preference for the four types of display (averaged over all participants; business/government sessions only).

(a) Office

	Monochrome		Colour			
	Prestel (a)	Video (b)	Prestel (c)	Video (d)	b/c difference	
France	4	2	3	1	$n = 24$	ns
Germany	4	3	2	1	$n = 20$	ns
UK	4	3	2	1	$n = 18$	ns
Netherlands	4	2	3	1	$n = 11$	ns
Overall	4	3	2	1	$n = 73$	ns

(b) Home

	Monochrome		Colour			
	Prestel (a)	Video (b)	Prestel (c)	Video (d)	b/c difference	
France	4	2	3	1	$n = 19$	ns
Germany	4	2	3	1	$n = 19$	*
UK	4	3	2	1	$n = 18$	ns
Netherlands	4	2	3	1	$n = 11$	ns
Overall	4	2	3	1	$n = 67$	*

* $P < 0.05$ (two-tailed sign test).
ns = not statistically significant.

- margin width (affecting the shape of the area actually used);
- use of colour;
- line spacing;
- use of the 'flash' facility.

Subjects. Twenty-one telecommunications managers from a variety of different companies who were attending a seminar by the author on the role of videotex in the office of tomorrow participated on a voluntary basis.

Procedure. Sixteen versions of a single frame of text were written varying the following factors: margin (wide or narrow); colour (green throughout or alternate paragraphs in green and purple); line spacing (single or double); and 'flash' (no flash or one key sentence flashing on and off). These were recorded in random order on an audio cassette and played back to the group through a Prestel 1976 26-inch set. Each frame was presented for ten seconds. As each frame appeared, the subjects individually marked it from 0 to 10 according to their judgements of how well it was designed. Prior to the ratings being made, the group was shown the last four frames in the series to give an idea of the variety they would be asked to judge. Subjects kept one copy of their responses and returned one copy to the experimenter.

Figure 13.11.   Expected effect of display type on usage: Amount of time participants indicated they would use videotex given sets with various types of display, relative to every 30 min spent using a set with the most preferred type of display (percentages to nearest 5%) (business/Government sessions only).

	(most) (pref.)	Type of display next to most pref.	next to least pref.	least pref.
(a) Office				
France	(30)	30	20	10
Germany	(30)	30	20	10
UK	(30)	28	15	10
Netherlands	(30)	20	20	10
Overall	(30)	30	20	10
	(100%)	(100%)	(70%)	(35%)
(b) Home				
France	(30)	20	15	8
Germany	(30)	20	10	5
UK	(30)	25	10	6
Netherlands	(30)	20	10	5
Overall	(30)	20	10	5
	(100%)	(70%)	(35%)	(15%)

Results. Nineteen usable response sheets were returned. The analysis of these is summarized in Figure 13.13. The P-values are based on Wilcoxon matched pairs signed ranks tests.

Discussion. Two factors stand out clearly as being important: margin width and

Figure 13.12.   Effect of display type on acceptable price: Amount participants indicated they would be willing to pay for videotex sets giving displays of various kinds, as a proportion of what they would pay for sets giving their most preferred type of display (business/Government sessions only).

	(most) (pref.)	Type of display next to most pref.	next to least pref.	least pref.
(a) Office				
France	(100%)	80	50	23
Germany	(100%)	80	30	20
UK	(100%)	88	50	20
Netherlands	(100%)	80	50	20
Overall	(100%)	80	50	20
(b) Home				
France	(100%)	80	40	20
Germany	(100%)	30	20	10
UK	(100%)	85	40	20
Netherlands	(100%)	70	40	10
Overall	(100%)	80	40	20

Figure 13.13.   Some factors influencing the acceptability of videotex frames ('author quality' factors).

Factor		Medians (interquartile ranges)			Two-tailed P
* Flash	yes:	33.0 (26–36)	no:	39.0 (32–44)	0.01
† Margin	narrow:	31.5 (29–43)	wide:	37.0 (35–42)	0.05
Colour	double:	32.0 (30–43)	single:	38.0 (33–42)	0.06
Line space	single:	33.5 (30–41)	double:	35.0 (33–42)	0.23

use of the flash. The effect of margin width is consistent with the hypothesis that a display shaped approximately like a page in a book (wide margins) is likely to be more acceptable than one which is wider than it is tall (narrow margins).

This is not very surprising when one considers that the shape of the written or printed page has evolved over hundreds of years. In view of this it is interesting that many information providers to Prestel use the less acceptable, narrow-margin format, perhaps to economize on the number of frames required. If the reason is economy, it could be false economy if it reduces the likelihood of people reading the information. Similarly, many information providers use the 'flash' a great deal whereas our results suggest this may often reduce the acceptability of the display rather than improve it.

The effect of colour is interesting. The use of two colours helps one to fix on a particular line or paragraph when reading from a distance but may not be very pleasing aesthetically, depending partly on the colour combination used. The author is given to understand that users of Ceefax and Oracle prefer text to be in a single colour (personal communication), which is consistent with the results above.

There is no evidence from this experiment that line spacing is important.

One needs to be cautious in generalizing from these results as much more work needs to be done. The present results are based on varying a few factors in designing a frame containing only text, using upper and lower case letters but no headings of any kind or graphics. Other factors which need to be considered in further research include, for example:

- effect of particular colour combinations;
- different ways of using the flash;
- effect of headings and sub-headings;
- other ways of mixing colours;
- various ways of designing graphics;
- and so forth.

It is surprising and disappointing that at the time of writing, there appear to be no useful guidelines for information providers based on human-factors research of the kind illustrated here. What guidelines do exist appear to be based largely on intuition and generalization from other media, especially print.

EXPECTANCY-VALUE THEORY

Fishbein (e.g. Fishbein and Ajzen, 1975) has developed a model of attitude based on expectancy-value theory which emphasises overt behaviour, especially the choices made by people. This model was introduced in Chapter 3 in our discussion of types of information. The model can be applied well to the concept of the 'behaviour tree' introduced in Chapter 10. We saw in that chapter how a person can be thought of as moving continuously from one decision node to another. At any particular point in time his or her choice depends upon an awareness of the options available and information available about those options. These statements can be expressed more formally in terms of the basic Fishbein equation, as follows:

$$BI = W_1 \cdot A_{\text{act}} + W_2 \cdot NB$$

In this equation, BI represents the strength of the behavioural intention to choose a particular option. It is assumed that the actual choice made will normally be whichever option is associated with the greatest behavioural intention, although sometimes unforeseen events or other factors outside the control of the person concerned may intervene to block the option that normally would be chosen. The term A_{act} (attitude toward the act) represents the sum of the weighted costs and benefits of the option concerned, where the weightings reflect the degree to which the person believes the costs and benefits to apply. The term NB reflects the person's beliefs about what significant other people expect him or her to do (normative belief). The weights W_1 and W_2 need to be determined empirically for particular cases or classes of situations.

This formulation brings attitudes much closer to observable behaviour than the formulations implicit in the approaches discussed above. This does not make research based on the semantic differential or other approaches valueless; rather, we can see a hierarchical analysis of behaviour and attitude in which each approach has something to offer at its own particular level in the hierarchy, as described below.

A HIERARCHICAL MODEL OF ATTITUDE

The model envisaged is summarized in Figure 13.14. At the highest level (nearest to overt behavioural choice) we are concerned with behavioural intention. For example, we may be interested in whether a certain kind of person, e.g. senior executive, is likely to use a monochrome desk-top videotex system to find out when the next train leaves for a place (s)he has to visit urgently, or whether (s)he will prefer to ask his or her secretary for the information. According to the Fishbein model,

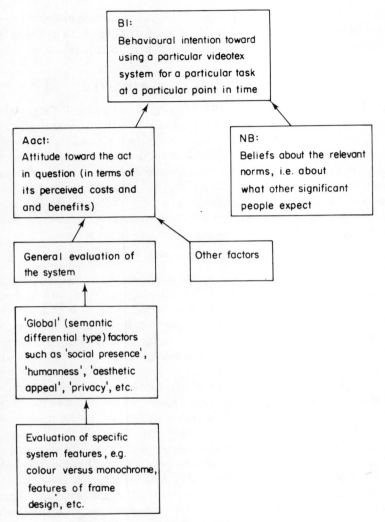

Figure 13.14.   A hierarchical model of attitude.

the choice will depend on the two terms, A_{act} and NB, explained above. We can postulate that A_{act} will be influenced by the person's general evaluation of the system, as measured perhaps by the semantic differential. That is, a person who judges a system favourably is more likely to use it than one who judges it less favourably. This is just a special case of the first law of attitude, discussed in Chapter 9. General evaluation of the system in turn is likely to depend on other factors such as social presence, aesthetic appeal, privacy, and so forth, as discussed above in relation to the semantic differential approach to studying attitudes in this area.

Finally, these factors will themselves be influenced by specific features of the system, such as whether it has a monochrome or colour display, in ways that can be examined experimentally.

This hierarchical model of attitude really adds no new elements to what has already been discussed above and in earlier chapters, but it does serve to synthesize these and demonstrate their interdependence. It also serves to show diagrammatically how far from 'actual behaviour' evaluation of specific system features really is. We should not be too surprised, for example, to find that in some situations a system incorporating a relatively 'poor' design feature (e.g. monochrome display) is used a great deal.

Certainly system designers and managers should take care to evaluate the specific features of systems individually and in combination, but it is also important to take account of more general factors, including the organizational factors considered in the next two chapters.

CONCLUSIONS

General evaluation and social presence are among a number of distinguishable factors that need to be considered in assessing attitudes toward information systems. These can be identified using various methods including the semantic differential and repertory grid. Analysis of the main dimensions involved needs to be complemented by an experimental approach concerned with assessing the relative importance of various design features, e.g. colour compared with monochrome displays, in influencing attitudes. The relationships between some of the elements involved in attitudes and behaviour are explained by expectancy-value theory. This in turn can be considered to form part of a more general, hierarchical model of attitude.

PART 5
Managing Change

Chapter 14

Forecasting change

We have assumed in previous chapters that the world is changing. What we shall try to do in this chapter is indicate some of the factors that need to be taken into account in order to forecast the rate and extent of change so that appropriate inputs can be made to planning processes, both at the organizational and national level. We shall not attempt to do any actual quantification. Our more modest aim will be to go some way towards developing a basis for a model which could be used for such quantification.

We shall take the telecommunications impact model as our starting point and elaborate around it as necessary.

THE TELECOMMUNICATIONS IMPACT MODEL (TIM)

The telecommunications impact model was devised by Reid (1971) to help assess the impact of electronic systems, especially teleconferencing, on Type A communication, especially with regard to office location. The model is summarized in Figure 14.1.

There are four main stages in the model. At the first stage, 'amount', the amount of communication is quantified. In practice this was mainly the frequency of all different types of meetings, both formal and informal, in which all levels of management engage.

At the second stage, 'type allocation', the different types of meetings were allocated to various types of electronic systems, ranging from the telephone to sophisticated audio–video systems of the 'Confravision' and other types. The allocation was made largely on the basis that an electronic system could 'substitute' for a face-to-face meeting only if it did not result in a decrease in effectiveness. The allocations made reflected the results of experiments on the relative effectiveness of different types of systems for various tasks. At the third stage, 'mode allocation', it was assumed that the type allocations in practice would be modified by people's attitudes which in turn would be influenced by a variety of other factors such as costs in time and money, relevant norms, novelty effects, aesthetic appeal, and so forth. The 'social presence' afforded by the systems turned out to be an important factor. Finally, at the fourth stage, 'impact', conclusions were drawn about the relative impacts different types of systems could have on the feasibility of relocating offices.

211

212

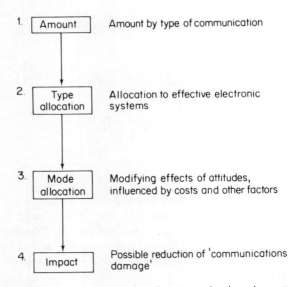

Figure 14.1. The basic telecommunications impact
model.

For a more detailed discussion of this model the reader is referred to Short,
Williams, and Christie (1976). The most important point to make here is that the
model was concerned primarily with a fairly well-defined problem. This concerned
the concept of 'communications damage' discussed in the Hardman (1973) report
on the dispersal of government work from London. It was felt that an important
disincentive for such dispersal would be the possible 'communications damage' done
by 'stretching' the communications links between the offices that would relocate
and those that would remain. The telecommunications impact model was concerned
primarily with the extent to which electronic systems for Type A communication
could minimize this 'communications damage'.

BEYOND TIM

The experiments, case studies, and field surveys undertaken by psychologists and
sociologists at the Communications Studies Group and elsewhere demonstrated
fairly convincingly that the 'substitution' logic of the basic TIM was necessary but
not sufficient to forecast more general impacts of the electronic systems.

Much of this work has been summarized by Short, Williams, and Christie (1976),
and Christie and Elton (1979). Essentially, it became clear that the electronic
systems would be used for some 'meetings' which would never have taken place at
all before the systems were introduced. This meant there were two main effects:

- substitution: some communications (meetings) previously conducted face-to-face
  would be conducted electronically;

• generation: in addition, there would be some new types of communications.

The implications of this are shown in Figure 14.2 which also makes a distinction between 'specific' and 'diversive' communication. Whether or not this distinction is useful in the case of Type A communication is debatable but it certainly would seem to be for Type B. Berlyne (e.g. 1960) has argued that in exploring their environment (including looking at pictures, reading, and so forth), people do not always seek out a specific item or piece of knowledge. When they do, this is specific exploration. It includes, for example, looking in a telephone directory for a friend's telephone number, or in a dictionary for the spelling of a particular word. Very often, people explore without having a particular target. This is diversive exploration. It includes general browsing.

Figure 14.2 presents the hypothesis that electronic systems will have substitution and generation effects on both specific and diversive communication. For example, people may use Prestel to get the time of a train rather than telephone the station (specific) and may browse through new information instead of spending quite so much time browsing through a newspaper (diversive).

The distinction between specific and diversive activity has usually been applied to the 'information seeking' side of our source–store–sink model but our hypothesis predicts similar effects on the 'commitment' side, that is that electronic systems will affect the amount of 'diversive commitment'.

We do not know if such a phenomenon actually exists but some examples which come to mind as possible candidates include: whistling or humming to oneself; talking to oneself; some of the utterances of simple schizophrenics; doodling; and

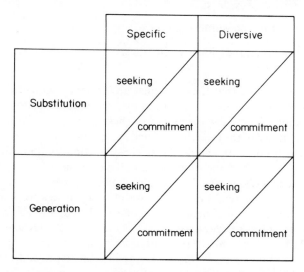

Figure 14.2. Specific and diversive Type B communications.

generating 'Snoopy' pictures on a computer. Berlyne has argued that diversive activity serves an important function in helping a person to maintain an optimal level of cortical arousal. Is it possible that part of the 'information' produced as a normal part of business activity reflects this same phenomenon? If so, we would expect that electronic systems, by reducing the amount of effort needed to produce a document, would result in more documents being produced (to compensate for the reduction in effort). There is anecdotal evidence at least that word-processing systems sometimes have just this effect.

ACQUISITION VERSUS USE

The substitution and generation effects of electronic systems will only occur if organizations and individuals actually acquire such systems. Much previous work has concentrated on forecasting the usage of particular types of systems assuming the systems to be available. It may sometimes be reasonable to assume that systems which are both effective and acceptable will be acquired, but this is not always so. Price is only one factor which may work against system acquisition. In general, we may assume there are two main aspects to the acquisition problem:

- the behaviour of suppliers, including:

  - computer manufacturers;
  - the PTT;
  - the information service (e.g. videotex) providers;
  - the information providers;

- the behaviour of the consumers, either:

  - organizations, e.g. individual companies; or
  - individual people.

We may further assume that these parties can influence each other's behaviour. They can also influence and be influenced by government policy.

The factors influencing the behaviour of these parties are likely to extend far beyond considerations of the effectiveness and acceptability of systems for particular tasks or particular contexts, though these considerations will play a role.

The situation, both from the suppliers' and the consumers' point of view, can be modelled by the behaviour tree discussed earlier. At any level of the tree, limited options are available. Each option has a set of more or less likely consequences associated with it, and each of these may be more or less desirable. Each option also has a set of more or less relevant norms. For example, at the present point in time, consumers, PTTs, other computer manufacturers, all expect any given computer manufacturer to think seriously about moving into the 'electronic office' or 'office of tomorrow'. This is a norm. Similarly, the same parties expect any given company to think seriously about moving into the 'office of tomorrow'. This is a norm which may influence consumers, though it may be a less powerful norm than that concerning manufacturers' behaviour.*

In forecasting the behaviour of suppliers and consumers, it will be necessary, implicitly or preferably explicitly, to map out a behaviour tree which:

- identifies the options available at each level of the tree;
- identifies the consequences, their likelihoods and their desirabilities, associated with each option; and
- identifies the norms relating to the options.

Having done this, it will be possible to identify the few most likely routes that suppliers and consumers will take. As they actually move down the tree from one level to the next, more reliable information about the next levels will become available. In this way the forecasts can be continuously updated, always looking a few steps ahead of the current situation. A generalized behaviour tree for suppliers, with a few hypothetical examples of 1980 options, is shown in Figure 14.3.

In thinking about the consumers' behaviour tree, especially where the consumer is an individual person rather than an organization, we may expect a particularly important set of option consequences to be related to the concept of discretionary budgets, though it is not clear which is the more important in practice:

- the amount of money left over after a person has paid for all items (s)he considers 'essential'; and
- the amount of time left over after (s)he has done all those things considered 'essential'.

We may hypothesize that the money budget will have the greater influence on the acquisition of systems; the time budget will be more important in connection with the amount the systems are used. To the extent that these budgets are important in practice, forecasting them over the period of any behaviour tree will help in assessing the likelihoods associated with the options at the various levels of the tree, and thus the most likely routes through the tree.

THE DEMAND AND SUPPLY MATRIX

Figure 14.4 shows a generalized demand and supply matrix which is relevant to both system acquisition and system usage, in the following ways.

The matrix shows the most likely dates that particular systems features will be commercially available, and the particular types of Type B communication that the features can support.

In this way, the matrix shows which types of Type B communications (e.g. continuously updated news headlines; 'scrapbook' facilities; maps; messages) are likely to be available at any given date. The communications can be grouped according to, for example:

* Even the phrase 'office of tomorrow' implies a norm since we must assume if we are to be practical that tomorrow is inevitable.

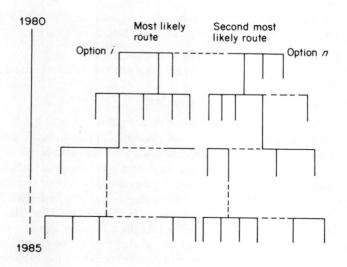

Examples of 1980 options:

- concentrate on small, stand-alone word processors;
- offer a range of 'office of tomorrow' products;
- concentrate on very large, shared-logic systems;
- wait to see what trends emerge before changing or upgrading current product lines.

Figure 14.3.   A generalized behaviour tree for suppliers.

- whether they represent 'substitution' or 'generation'; and
- their importance for the feasibility of particular patterns of working, e.g. working from home 60 per cent of total working time; working from home 80 per cent of total working time; and so forth.

The matrix also shows the potential amount of each type of communication ('demand') at each date. It may be very likely that a set of systems features will be available by a particular date but that the demand for the communications supported by those features may be quite low; conversely, the features needed to support communications for which there is high demand may not be likely to be available for some time.*

The matrix helps in forecasting acquisition only to the extent that the kinds of

* These are just hypothetical possibilities to illustrate how the matrix can be used.

Systems features required	e.g. required for working from home		most likely date available
	substitution	generation	
	specific types of type B communication		
	e.g. letters	e.g. electronic time sheets	
e.g.:			
colour	no	no	1980
hard-copy	yes	no	1981
local intelligence	no	no	1982
1980	estimates of demand (specific + diversive) by type of communication		
1990			

Figure 14.4.   The demand and supply matrix.

communications supported by a system influence the acquisition decision. As we have already noted, other consequences of acquiring or not acquiring a particular system (including the effect on one's discretionary money budget), as well as relevant norms, may be more important and certainly need to be taken into account. An analogy may be drawn with pocket calculators. People do not always buy the calculator with the greatest variety of functions. It is reasonable to suppose, however, that the functional capabilities of a system will influence the acquisition decision to some extent, and the matrix is useful in this regard.

The matrix also helps in forecasting the usage that will be made of systems with particular combinations of features, once such systems have been acquired, and the particular mix of communications that will be observed at any given date, assuming particular availability–acquisition conversions. Absolute levels of communications will depend, once again, on the consequences and norms involved. A norm toward higher reading of news than obtains at present will, other things being equal, result in a generally higher level for this type of communication, by any medium. A change in norms toward less interest in news will have the opposite ef-

218

fect. On the consequences side, use of a given system depends not only on whether it will meet a particular demand (e.g. for news) but on other things as well (such as its effect on the discretionary money budget, which depends partly on the prices charged for accessing the information).

CONCLUSIONS

What we have done here is outline what we see as being some of the more important concepts that need to be taken into account in developing a model for forecasting the development of electronic Type B communication and its impact on such things as patterns of working. We have also set out several hypotheses which we believe warrant research, such as those relating to the concept of discretionary budgets. We have indicated in general terms the kinds of variables that need to be estimated for forecasting purposes, but it is important to appreciate that we have not discussed how the estimates can be made. They will depend upon data of one sort or another, whether, for example, 'expert judgement' or observations of actual behaviour, but the kind of data collection methods employed will reflect considerations such as desired level of reliability, resources available for the work, and so on, at least as much as the model. For this reason we have chosen not to discuss methods of data collection but to concentrate on the bases for a model. It must be the task of others to propose alternatives so that areas of agreement can be identified, competing hypotheses can be tested, and a workable, practical model developed.

In the next chapter we shall consider the 'other side of the coin'—not the factors we need to consider to forecast what is likely if we act as passive observers, but what we can do actively to support and promote change in an effective way.

Chapter 15

Promoting change

Most of the literature on organizational change that is significantly relevant to the introduction of new technology or to information systems in particular can be classified very roughly into three groups, concerned with:

- the effects of new technology, e.g. Taylor (1971);
- techniques of 'organizational development', e.g. Fordyce and Weil (1979);
- documentation of significant events and processes in particular instances where technology has been introduced (case studies), e.g. Sletten and Ulett (1972), Ulett (1974), and others summarized below.

In this chapter we shall consider each of these briefly and then examine the extent to which it may be possible to draw out general principles and develop a conceptual framework that can both guide research and meet the needs of the manager who has to deal with the very practical task of introducing new information systems as effectively as possible.

STUDIES OF EFFECTS

A study reported by Taylor (1971) serves to illustrate this approach. The purpose of the study was to test several hypotheses suggested by previous work concerning the effects of 'sophisticated technology', including in particular the following three hypotheses:

- that sophisticated technology in and of itself is associated with more autonomous and participative group process;
- that sophisticated technology will facilitate planned change efforts directed toward increasing participative group process;
- that the change toward participative group process will be more permanent when the change is facilitated by technology than when it is not.

'Sophistication of technology' was assessed for each of the work groups studied in terms of sophistication of input (e.g. standardization of materials used), of throughput (e.g. the proportion of routine operations handled by machines) and output control (e.g. nature of supervisor feedback).

The study was conducted in a large petroleum refinery. A total of 1000 people

219

in 140 non-supervisory work groups participated. Respondents completed questionnaires dealing with supervisory and peer leadership, work group behaviour, job satisfaction, and related areas. The questionnaires were completed on three occasions over a period of 12 months. A planned change programme aimed at more participative management was introduced following the initial survey.

Taylor presents the results of the study in some detail. They will not be rehearsed here because, whilst of interest in a general sense, they do not contribute much to an understanding of what this type of study has to offer our present area of inquiry. The broad conclusions were as follows.

Technological sophistication in the refinery did have a measurable association with democratic and autonomous group process. Taylor felt the technology probably had a causal role in this, although he acknowledged other possibilities. It also seems that the social-change programme was facilitated in the groups with the more sophisticated technology, and appeared to be somewhat more stable. Taylor concluded on the basis of the results that 'disruptive inputs from the organizational environment, in the service of social change, would more likely be technological than social in nature' and that, rather than attempting to change attitudes in an organization directly, 'attitude change is better approached indirectly via more impersonal and compelling changes in behaviour.'

Some other studies have been more directly concerned with information systems or closely related technology, as follows.

Edwards (1978) presents the results of a questionnaire study of 100 users of a prototype 'Office of the Future' system developed at Stanford Research Institute. The users surveyed were dispersed among thirteen organizations and had been using the system for a year and a half. They included managers, researchers and support staff. The system, referred to as NLS, supported a number of office functions, including communications features, numeric and text manipulation, retrieval, and database management. In this respect it was similar to the shared-logic word-processing type of system described in Chapter 5, though perhaps somewhat more limited in terms of its capabilities than some of the systems we might expect to see over the next few years.

The primary impacts of the system seemed to be in terms of:

- new tasks, particularly new modes of document production and communication; and
- reduction of routine tasks relating to typing, filing, handwriting, and so forth.

Secondary impacts included, amongst others:

- increased productivity;
- decreased privacy;
- increased accessibility to others' work, and so forth.

Tertiary impacts included:

- less dependence on secretaries;
- remote management;

• decreased use of telephone and conventional mail.

As well as these impacts on what Edwards termed the 'mode' of working, she noted various impacts on what she called 'portability of office', specifically:

Primary:

• more flexible hours;
• more flexible work location.

Secondary:

• reduction in 'line of sight' management;
• flexibility in work schedule;
• working from home;
• increased productivity and related benefits.

Tertiary:

• extended working day.

Johansen, De Grasse, and Wilson, (1978) present the results of a study of the effects of computer conferencing on working patterns. Their conclusions are based on an analysis of questionnaire responses from approximately 230 participants in 12 different groups. The period of time each group had used computer conferencing varied from one month to one year and nine months. Most had used it for several months. In all cases, the computer system had been used for real work throughout the period of the study. The groups involved included, for example:

• NASA Communications Technology Satellite Experimenters;
• Kettering Foundation Colorado Plateau Research Project;
• Energy Research and Development Administration National Coal Assessment;
• Energy Research and Development Administration Inter-laboratory Working Group for Data Exchange.

The main findings are summarized in Figure 15.1. Some caution is needed in interpreting this table. Not all the groups behaved in the same way. The researchers were able in some cases to identify likely extraneous influences causing anomalies in the data, and the summary in Figure 15.1 reflects a good deal of interpretation. Nevertheless it seems clear that computer conferencing can affect when, where, how and with whom people work.

The variety of possible effects the introduction of new information systems or related technology might have appears to be very wide. Harkness (1978) suggests they may be classifiable in terms of four successively more complex levels of impact, as follows:

• task substitution, mainly concerned with eliminating routine and nuisance activities;
• automation of well-structured office processes;

222

Figure 15.1. Effects of computer conferencing on patterns of working suggested by the Johansen *et al.* study (From Johansen, DeGrasse, & Wilson, 1978)

	Range of options	Documented effects	Possible effects
With whom people work	Nearby colleagues Distantly located colleagues Persons from varied disciplines Persons of varied quality	More communication with distantly located researchers Expedites communication among those interested in communicating (requires high communication need)	More international communication More geographically separated working groups Information overload
When people work	Office hours Evenings Weekends Simultaneously with others Irregular times	Often used outside office hours (25–40% of the time) Participants continue to work outside office hours, apparently assisted by access to computer conferencing Participants can 'meet' without being present simultaneously	More flexibility in working hours Longer working hours
Where people work	Office Home While traveling Neighborhood office centre Remote retreat	Work at home is common when terminals are available Researchers can stay in touch while travelling, moving, or homebound	More variations in where researchers live and work Less office-based research
How people work	Face-to-face Mail Telephone Video teleconferencing Audio teleconferencing Computer-based teleconferencing	Computer conferencing is perceived as more productive in some instances than mail or telephone Can be used for joint authorship, information exchange, scheduling, planning, and follow-ups for face-to-face, as a bridge to other computer resources	Substitute for some mail usage Substitute for some telephone usage, but could also add new uses for telephone Could even *increase* travel

- optimization of the office worker's interactions with the knowledge base and extension of intellectual capability to conceptualize, structure and process information; and,
- the facilitation of qualitatively and quantitatively different structures or processes.

The last point in particular emphasizes the facilitating function of new systems, and Harkness suggests the following possibilities regarding new structures or processes that might be facilitated:

- working from home or neighbourhood work centres;
- flexible reorganization of people into new and changing project teams without having to transfer them physically;
- the creation of national consulting networks in which a large number of freelance engineers, scientists, managers, and other professionals communicate with each other and with clients through electronic systems.

The possibilities seem endless, and without knowing what the basic pressures and incentives on organizations are it probably is not possible to forecast accurately which particular changes will occur if they are facilitated, a point discussed later.

The approach exemplified by these studies takes the technology as 'given', and is then concerned with what effects the technology produces directly and how the technology moderates the effects of other variables, e.g. introducing a social-change programme. This is certainly of general interest to organizational theorists. It may also have some value to organizations in helping them to evaluate likely impacts of new systems without actually having to implement them in order to find out. What this approach does not do very well is help the manager concerned with introducing new technology to go about doing so in the most effective way possible. Similarly, it does not provide much guidance to the researcher concerned with identifying those factors involved in the implementation process that influence the success or otherwise of the changes being promoted.

TECHNIQUES OF ORGANIZATIONAL DEVELOPMENT

A handbook of organizational development methods written by Fordyce and Weil (1979) illustrates this approach well. The handbook is divided into three main parts. The first sets the scene by pointing out some of the difficulties with 'traditional' organizations, some of the advantages of new forms of organization, and the need for help from third parties—in particular, specialists in organizational development (OD).

The second part presents a series of five case studies to give a flavour of what OD is all about, benefits it offers, and factors that require attention if it is to succeed (e.g. 'Be sure that use of OD methods is voluntary.' p. 67). The final part presents a series of specific techniques (or 'methods') under the following main headings:

- meetings to bring about change, e.g.

- the manager's diagnostic team meeting series
- the confrontation goal-setting meeting
- and others;
- methods for finding out what's going on, e.g.
  - questionnaires
  - interviewing
  - and others;
- methods for better meetings, e.g.
  - making deals
  - building communication skills
  - and others;
- methods for changing the quality of relationships, e.g.
  - positive feedback
  - hearing
  - and others.

The strength of this approach lies in the way it translates general principles of organizational psychology into specific techniques that can be learned and communicated easily and used in a wide variety of specific contexts. For our present purposes, however, this generality is its weakness. The general goals of OD are not entirely clear, but seem to have more to do with general shifts in the style of organizational communication than with the effective introduction of new systems. The lack of clarity is illustrated well in the following statement (Fordyce and Weil, 1979, p. 16):

'In this book we emphasize two aspects of organization development (OD): (1) as a way of *managing change*, and (2) as a way of *focusing human energy toward specific desired outcomes*. Our approach rests on a fundamental belief that in any organization setting the individual members must have the opportunity to grow if an ailing organization is to revive or a vital one is to maintain its health.' (Original italics.)

These general aims are laudable but operational definitions for many of the terms, e.g. 'human energy', 'ailing', or 'health', are not immediately obvious and the practical relevance to the introduction of new information systems even less so.

The OD approach therefore has more to offer than the kind of study reviewed above in terms of techniques that can be used to modify the style of communication within an organization and perhaps create a climate more favourable for the introduction of new systems. The generality of the approach means, however, that it needs to be complemented by the more specific kind of information provided by the approach above, and even more by the information provided by case studies.

CASE STUDIES

Case studies specifically concerned with the introduction of new information systems are a valuable source of hypotheses, 'rules of thumb', and 'things to watch out for', as the following examples illustrate.

Sletten and Ulett (1972) report on the implementation of an automated information system in a state psychiatric system (specifically, the Missouri Division of Mental Health). They say the following difficulties were encountered:

- cost: costs initially outweighed benefits, though it was felt this could be justified by a longer-term view;
- resistance to change: it was felt that a strong central administrative backing is needed to get a programme such as this going. Clinicians provided only a part of the resistance, but an interesting comment was that some clinicians expressed concern that the computers might end up actually making decisions;
- technology: numerous technical difficulties were encountered which were frustrating and costly;
- qualified staff: it was difficult to find computer experts and psychiatric professional staff with the necessary technical and clinical knowledge and experience;
- outcome data: it was difficult to collect information needed to improve the service offered by the new system.

Ulett (1974) gives additional information about the Missouri system. He reports that the following were important prerequisites to initiating the programme:

- ensuring financial support;
- familiarizing key decision-making personnel with computer ideology;
- developing the proper administrative structure.

Another medical example is provided by Abrams (1975). Three of seven general practitioners in a group practice at Harlow, Essex, used a real-time on-line computer system in their surgeries. They had used it for about a year before Abram's report. The system catered for 3000 of the group's 19 000 patients and was based on the creation of a patient-integrated medical record. The records were accessed by the doctors, for either retrieval or recording, using a visual display unit during their consultations.

The records consisted in essence of a birth to death compilation of all the patients' contacts with health care services of every sort. The main difficulty encountered was having to keep a manual system going as well as the computer system, as—for reasons unspecified by Abrams—the computer system could not be operated permanently; this meant substantial extra paperwork during the period of the study. Several other difficulties arose as well, especially:

- due to the long period between starting the project and 'going live', the practice administrative staff felt uninvolved;

- as well as the extra paperwork involved, the computer-printed summaries had to be filed separately from the manual records;
- as only 3000 patients had computer records, and only three of the doctors had a terminal, it was necessary for 'computerized' patients sometimes to be seen by 'non-computerized' doctors and vice versa;
- due to shortage of space, the staff had to manage without a common room; this meant their receptionists had to remain in the reception area during their lunch break which in turn meant effectively they had no break.

In a different context, Cook (1970) describes work on the implementation of an experimental on-line retrieval system for 'psychological abstracts' at Syracuse University (SUPARS). He reports that the concept of searching abstracts by computer was new to most of the user community and it was felt important to go out to potential users and 'sell' the idea. Emphasis was on how the computer could augment the normal searching for information, rather than replace it. The methods used included:

- presenting mixed media lectures and 'hands on' demonstrations;
- development of a user's guide going from simple to complex searches;
- setting up a telephone service whereby users could telephone for help or advice;
- an advertising campaign, including campus newspaper advertisements, posters, and letters to students and faculty.

In connection with office systems, Uhlig (1977) makes several points based on anecdotal evidence and general observations:

- the enthusiasm shown by managers can make it easier to tackle the hesitance that secretaries may have in using a computer system for the first time;
- commitment to use a system can be improved by requiring that the people concerned have to provide their share of the cost out of their own budgets;
- it helps if training is done on site.

Computer conferencing is a special example of office systems, and Johansen, De-Grasse, and Wilson, (1978) summarize their conclusions about the prerequisites for organizational acceptance, based on a number of field studies and related research:

- there must be a perceived need to communicate;
- the system must be highly accessible to users, and it must be reliable;
- adequate introductions to the system must be provided, and appropriate training in concepts and techniques;
- there must be an 'openess' to use the terminal (to type, in the case of computer conferencing);
- there must be minimal conflicting needs or demands on users, e.g. those who really enjoy a lot of travelling will be unlikely to use alternative means of communication;

- there must be an 'advocate' within each key organization who encourages use of the system.

Dordick and Goldman (1978) suggest a number of other factors which they feel are likely to influence acceptance of a system, especially:

- the perceived reliability of the system;
- sterotypes about different kinds of systems;
- the ease or difficulty of trying the system out before making a major commitment;
- the perceived complexity of the system, simpler systems generally being favoured;
- whether or not potential users can see demonstrations of the system;
- the amount of organizational change required to implement the system;
- the likelihood of constraints in the form of 'red tape';
- the perceived need for the applications the system does well;
- compatibility with existing values and past experiences.

To these lists we could add compatibility of the system with equipment already installed, availability of funds, suitable staff to operate the system if specialists are needed, and a host of other items. Systematic research is needed to test out the many hypotheses which have emerged and to develop a proper understanding of the relationships between the many factors involved.

A Field Experiment

A field experiment can be regarded as a special type of case study or as an improvement over the 'case study' as such. A study by O'Keefe, Kernaghan, and Rubenstein, (1975) is included here as an example of this type of study. There was systematic collection of data, testing of hypotheses, and comparisons were made between groups using appropriate statistical methods. It could be argued that the study does not quite qualify for the term 'experiment' as subjects were not randomly assigned to conditions; certainly, future research could go further in this direction.

The study was concerned with some of the behavioural factors, especially group cohesiveness, influencing the adoption of an experimental information system by medical researchers and clinicians in six hospitals in the Chicago area of the US. The study was divided into three main phases. First, an extensive questionnaire was given to 110 medical researchers and clinicians (of whom 99 completed all three phases of the study). This asked about their educational backgrounds, organizational structures, work habits, and preferences for new types of information services.

Secondly, an experimental information retrieval system was introduced and use of the system was monitored. The system was operated for seven weeks. Finally, six months after the service was discontinued the participants were asked to evaluate the system and their evaluations were compared with their actual use of the system. Three main behavioural factors were identified which influenced use of the system:

- the information-seeking and using patterns of the potential users, e.g. some users had formed predominantly verbal styles of seeking information whilst others were more print oriented;
- the structure of the user's work group, e.g. the research groups were more highly cohesive than the clinical groups and group cohesiveness was positively correlated with the amount of usage (in each type of group); and
- the people acting as 'gatekeepers' were important in relation to how much they encouraged their colleagues to use the new system.

Future research could usefully build upon this approach, including appropriate control groups in the experimental design wherever possible.

GENERAL PRINCIPLES

The approaches considered above provide a wealth of information that needs to be integrated in terms of a set of general principles if one is to avoid merely compiling a catalogue of interesting facts, with the attendant risk of such a catalogue soon becoming unmanageable. The very complexity of what is involved leads one to reject the idea that everything of interest can be derived from some such simple notion as a generalized 'resistance to change', and yet this concept needs to be discussed because it is widely used as an 'explanation' for difficulties in introducing new systems, and we cannot make much progress until we clear this notion out of our way.

Resistance to Change

Katz and Kahn (1978) identify six important sources of resistance to change, as follows:

1. *Enduring systems are overdetermined.* Specifically, personnel are selected, trained, and rewarded in accordance with criteria associated with the system. Attempts to create change normally require modifications to be made at all these levels.

2. *Local changes affect the whole system.* Conversely, the organization as a whole can nullify changes made at a local level.

3. *Individual and group inertia.* Established procedures are well learned; new procedures usually require some effort to learn. Even if one person or a group does change, it may be all to no avail if others fail to modify their behaviour so as to mesh in properly.

4. *Special expertise may be threatened.* Job enlargement for one group may be perceived as a threat by others. For example, head operators of complex, multilevel office systems in the near future may be making many administrative decisions—concerning who receives which reports, the form of the reports, and to some extent even their contents—formerly made by first-line management.

5. *Power relationships can be threatened.* Depending on the nature of the decision-making that moves downward in the organization, some managers may feel concerned that their previous authority in some areas seems to be weakened.

6. *Reallocation of resources.and rewards.* Complex office systems are particularly likely to create changes in the way resources are allocated. More people will be required to use support staff (especially word-processing staff) on a shared basis, and information which they previously may have kept in their own files will more often be kept in a common electronic storage system, more easily accessible by more people.

This complexity in the possible sources of resistance suggests that the concept of resistance as a generalized reaction against change, or even as being inevitable, is probably naive.

Mumford (1965a), who has been concerned with the introduction of computer systems into organizations for many years, has commented on the concept of a general resistance to change as follows.

It has often been regarded as a natural and universal human condition, reflecting, perhaps, a desire for security and stability, both at the individual and the organizational levels. It has sometimes been linked to irrational fears or lack of understanding. These assumptions seem to lead to the idea that the resistance can be overcome if change is sufficiently 'sold' to those involved.

Mumford herself rejects the idea that resistance is always due to irrational fears or lack of understanding, at least understanding of the purposes of management. She argues that what may seem 'irrational' from one point of view may often be entirely 'rational' from another and, similarly, 'lack of understanding' implies there is a unitary conceptual framework to be understood. She argues that:

> 'An alternative and more realistic approach would seem to be to consider change in terms of its effect on individual, group and organizational goals. It can then be suggested that change is not always automatically resisted, but that it may be sought and welcomed providing it is seen as leading to important benefits. If, on the contrary, change is seen as preventing the attainment of desired objectives, then there will be a rational and well-founded opposition to it.'

The fundamental conclusion she draws from this is that when an organization

230

sees innovation as essential to the attainment of its economic goals, it is not sufficient merely to adopt public relations techniques of 'selling'. It is necessary to:

- understand the social relationships within the organization;
- identify the goals and norms of all the various groups involved; and
- develop a plan which will show how the innovation will further as many individual and group goals as possible.

> 'In order to handle change in this way a firm needs to understand itself as a social system and to recognise such variables as the degree of conflict between one occupational group and another, and the likely effect of change on the power structure.'

The Sociotechnical Approach

The sort of plan suggested by Mumford's approach is likely to be complex in many practical situations, and is likely to involve cooperation and compromise. It would seem to be entirely consistent with what Katz and Kahn (1978) call the sociotechnical approach.

The sociotechnical approach is concerned with the goodness of fit between the social and the technical aspects of organizations, including the fit between technical aspects and the needs and abilities of the people involved. This goodness of fit can be improved by changing any element, either social or technical. Also, the changes can be made at any of three main levels: The job, the work group, or the organization as a whole. Katz and Kahn propose a simple classification, shown in Figure 15.2.

Katz and Kahn report that early experiments based on the sociotechnical approach usually concentrated on the social aspects, for example changing the structure of the work group whilst leaving the technology unchanged (cell c in Figure 15.2). Later experiments, however, attempted to make improvements in both aspects.

The sociotechnical approach seems particularly appropriate in the case of complex office systems. Manufacturers appear to be increasingly aware of the need for both

- *modularity*—the design of an office system in terms of modules which can be interconnected in various different combinations, and

Figure 15.2   Main possibilities for change
(based on a classification by Katz & Kahn, 1978).

| Organizational level | System aspects | |
	Social	Technical
Job (role)	(a)	(b)
Work group	(c)	(d)
Organization	(e)	(f)

- *granularity*—the design of the modules to be small rather than large, so that a working system is made of many modules rather than few, thus adding to the flexibility of the modular approach.

Such an approach allows the user organization to develop system configurations that are tailored to its own particular requirements rather than being suited only for the 'average' organization. Despite the high level of flexibility being offered by manufacturers, it would be a mistake if user organizations were to forget the 'social' side of the sociotechnical approach. Flexibility in the technical design of a system is important, but changes will certainly be required on the people side as well if the result is to be of maximum benefit. These changes are discussed in the next chapter.

In the following sections we shall develop a theoretical framework that acknowledges the importance of some of the key concepts referred to above, especially:

- individual, group and organizational goals;
- degree of conflict or harmony between the parties involved.

Expectancy-value Theory

Expectancy-value theory, in particular Fishbein's formulation of it (e.g. Fishbein and Ajzen, 1975), was introduced in Chapter 3 in our discussion of types of information and we used it again in considering attitudes toward information systems. It provides a useful model for clarifying the similarities and differences between individual, group and organizational goals. The basic equation is:

$$BI = W_1, A_{act} + W_2. NB$$

where
BI = the strength of behavioural intention toward a particular act, which strongly influences the probability of that act occurring;
A_{act} = 'attitude toward the act', being the sum of weighted costs and benefits to the person concerned, as explained below;
NB = 'normative belief', being the person's understanding of what significant other people expect him or her to do.

In this theory, the equation above governs what people decide to do in any given situation. The same equation applies equally well to all the parties involved in the introduction of new systems into an organization, be they senior management, middle management, trade-union representatives, system operators, or anybody else. The equation therefore represents an area of very strong similarity between all the people involved, and it is important to bear this in mind in deciding how best to manage the introduction of a new information system.

The central equation above does more than indicate an area of similarity— similarity in regard to the 'rules' governing the behaviour of the parties involved—it also points to a number of specific areas where differences in attitude and behaviour might arise and so helps us to consider these systematically. In doing so, we can see that it is relatively straightforward in principle to see things that might be done to maximize cooperation, as follows.

1. *The specific behaviours (BI's) involved are not the same for all the parties concerned.* There are usually at least three different kinds of behaviour involved:

- voting to buy and install the system concerned;
- making use of it, e.g. a manager choosing to have a report compiled on a word processor rather than being typed conventionally;
- operating the system, e.g. doing the actual keying-in and other operations involved in word processing.

Variations around this general pattern will depend on the particular organization concerned. The important point here is that the factors encouraging a favourable buying decision may be quite irrelevant or may even have a negative effect in relation to the operator's decision about whether to operate such a system or not. For example, the buying decision may be based on an argument that costs will be reduced or performance improved—the detailed design of the work station may not be a very salient consideration at this level, but it may be crucial in deciding the operator's attitude and behaviour.

The likelihood of cooperation by all parties can be improved by ensuring that the logically early decisions, e.g. whether to buy the system, take due account of the factors that are likely to influence the logically later kinds of decision, e.g. whether to use it and whether to operate it. At the very least those responsible for the buying decision should ensure the supplier provides information based on adequate research (e.g. controlled human-factors experiments, case studies, and so forth). Preferably, such information should be supplemented by a survey of the attitudes of the parties concerned in the buying organization itself. If this seems too much of an effort and not normal practice one must be prepared to face difficulties later and possibly end up with hundreds of thousands of pounds worth of equipment standing idle, as has happened in some British companies and elsewhere.

In this connection it is worth pointing out that the term 'user' is often used in a somewhat misleading sense in market research and consultancy circles. Evaluations of systems based on interviews with 'users' are often more precisely described as being based on interviews with 'buyers'.

The information provided by the 'buyers' concerning the attitudes of the 'users' and 'operators' (in the sense indicated above) is second-hand. This is not itself a criticism of such work, but it does serve to indicate that more could be done to ensure a more thorough and precise understanding of the factors involved at *all* levels of a system's success or failure.

2. *Different parties may not perceive the same set of options.* Let us suppose an organization is thinking of automating some of its office functions and a difference of attitude has emerged between management and staff representatives.

There are several possible reasons for such a difference but it might be that the options available—the range of BIs—as understood by the staff representative are not precisely the same as those understood by management. One party might tend to equate 'automation' in this context with microform systems whereas the other understands there is a range of options within 'automation' including word processing, videotex and other systems as well as microform.

What is needed here is a sharing of information. It is unwise to assume the other parties have the same level of understanding of possible options as oneself, or that one cannot learn something from the others. Misunderstandings at this early stage can be avoided relatively easily but if they are not they can be compounded by further misunderstandings or differences of opinion later on, until the differences become so large that they may appear to be irreconcilable.

3. *There may be differences in attitude toward the act (A_{act}) based on differences in salient beliefs.* In Fishbein's model, attitude toward the act (A_{act}) is the sum of weighted salient beliefs about the consequences of the act, i.e.:

$$A_{act} \sum_{i}^{n} B_i \cdot e_i$$

where,

> B_i = the strength of the person's belief that the ith possible outcome of performing the act in question will actually occur;
> e_i = the extent to which the person judges the ith possible outcome as being good or bad for the person himself or herself.

It appears that only the seven or so most salient beliefs contribute significantly to A_{act} (see Fishbein and Ajzen, 1975). In many situations this gives plenty of room for the set of salient beliefs about the same or similar act to vary markedly from one person to another. For example, possible cost savings may be highly salient for managers thinking of installing an automated system whereas possible changes in the skills required may be more salient for the staff representatives.

4. *There may be differences in attitude toward the act (A_{act}) based on differences in the strengths of beliefs (B_is).* Even if the parties concerned share exactly the same set of salient beliefs, they may vary in the strengths of those beliefs. For example, managers may consider cost savings to be almost certain but staff representatives may not be convinced, and staff representatives may feel sure that very different skills would be needed whereas managers may doubt whether the changes would be as radical as might appear.

5. *There may be differences in attitude toward the act* (A_{act}) *based on differences in the way possible outcomes are evaluated* $(e_i s)$. Continuing the example above, managers and staff representatives may agree in broad terms that there may be cost savings, but the staff representatives may not judge this to be so important (relative to other factors involved) as perhaps the managers do, and may consider a radical shift in skills required as being extremely bad, whereas the managers may not have quite such an unfavourable opinion of this. (Note that we have used the term 'important' for ease of exposition but it is actually the extent to which the outcome is judged 'good' or 'bad' that is measured; this point is discussed in detail by Fishbein and Ajzen, 1975.)

Differences arising as a result of points (3)–(5) above can all be dealt with to some extent by a sharing of information between the parties involved, and by adequate research. For example, questions of cost savings and a need for new skills are essentially empirical in nature. Case studies, controlled experiments and pilot trials can do a lot to provide sound information on which intelligent debate can be based. Even so, differences will remain as a result of the relative credence given to certain points of fact, and—of greater importance—the way the facts are evaluated (especially point 5 above). This is inevitable and in a democratic society is to be encouraged. The resolution of this type of difference must always depend on the more general value system of the organization concerned and of society.

6. *There may be differences in normative belief* (NB). Whenever any kind of 'us–them' situation is allowed to develop, differences in normative belief are likely to be marked. In management–union confrontations, the managers are likely to look to the norms they believe to be set by other managers whom they respect, and the union representatives will look to the norms they believe to be set by other union people. This is an unhealthy, positive feedback situation which exacerbates whatever more fundamental differences there may be.

It is important to avoid an 'us–them' situation developing and this is best achieved by ensuring a good level of consultation from the very start of projects of this sort.

Representatives of all relevant parties should be involved as far as is practicable in all stages of the planning process, so that there is only one 'team'—the organization—not several different factions with possibly different understandings of what is going on, different degrees of influence, and different norms.

7. *There may be differences in the relative weighting of* A_{act} *and NB*. Even in the very unlikely case where all the factors above are identical for all the parties concerned significant differences in BI may arise because some people are guided mostly by what they understand to be the relevant norms whereas others are influenced more by A_{act}.

It is difficult to see how this situation can be avoided in practice, or why we should try to avoid it. It may be better to regard it as another example of the 'checks and balances' operating in a democratic society.

*General comments.*Expectancy-value theory provides a systematic framework for analysing the similarities and differences between the various parties involved in the introduction of information systems into an organization. The model considered postulates that the same 'rules' govern the attitudes and behaviour of all the people involved but there is room for much variation within this general framework. Several different areas where differences can arise have been identified above. The analysis offers a way of understanding the 'individual, group and organizational goals' referred to by Mumford (see above) and some aspects of possible conflicts that can arise, in terms of understandings and evaluations. In the section below, we shall examine the question of conflict further.

Figure 15.3 presents a hypothetical example of how differences in behavioural intention might arise, in this case in relation to voting for the installation of a private viewdata system as part of a company's internal information system. All the salient beliefs indicated are of a rather general, impersonal nature.

In some instances, more personal factors may come in at this stage to influence behaviour. For example, Person A's behavioural intention would be likely to become stronger if (s)he felt that voting for the system would be likely to improve his or her chances of promotion. Such a belief could become salient if (s)he were to learn that (s)he was being considered for promotion and that the managing director of the company was very interested in being seen to be supporting the new technology. Other personal factors might be found that could influence Person B's behavioural intention.

The Conflict–Harmony Model

The conflict–harmony model was introduced in Chapter 6 as a derivative of the information sphere. It provides a more general framework than expectancy-value theory for understanding the various sorts of conflicts that can arise in an organization, for example in setting up a new information system. Expectancy-value theory can be considered as a model that provides a detailed analysis of Level 3 of the conflict–harmony model (specific attitudes) but it clearly relates to some of the other levels as well, as we shall now see.

We saw in chapter 6 that the conflict–harmony model postulates seven main levels at which conflict of one sort or another can arise. Figure 15.4 presents a hypothetical example relating to the example used above and in Figure 15.3. The

Figure 15.3. Hypothetical example of differences in behavioural intention.
Option: Vote to install a private viewdata system as part of the Company's internal information system.

	Person (or party) A				Person (or party) B			
BI	+30				+20			
A_{act}	$= W_1 A_{act} + W_2 NB$ $= 1.0 \times 20 + 1.0 \times 10$				$= W_1 A_{act} + W_2 NB$ $= 1.0 \times 12 + 1.0 \times 8$			
	abbreviated salient belief	B	e	$B \times e$	abbreviated salient belief	B	e	$B \times e$
	reduce costs	2	2	4	new skills	2	-2	-4
	improve performance	1	2	2	redundancies	1	-4	-4
	faster response	2	1	2	reduce costs	2	2	4
	up to date information	4	2	8	faster response	2	2	4
	good image	2	2	4	job enlargement	2	2	4
					up to date information	4	1	4
					higher productivity	1	4	4
				20				12

(All values are in arbitrary units.)

Figure 15.4.   The conflict–harmony model applied to the question of installing a private viewdata system.

Level of sphere	Representative of department X	Representative of department Y	Result
1. Items of information	roughly in view-data format	difficult to fit into viewdata format	conflict
2. Information systems	has viewdata-compatible terminals	does not	conflict
3. Specific attitudes	go for viewdata	go for another option	conflict
4. General attitudes	automate	automate	harmony
5..Personality	$A+$, $I-$	$A-$, $I+$	conflict
6. Sentiments	High Ca (career)	High Ca (career)	harmony
7. Ergs	High Pg (Pugnacity)	High Pg (Pugnacity)	conflict

example shows conflicts at several levels. At the first three levels, these relate to:

- information-   whether the items involved could be put into a form suitable for viewdata without too much difficulty;
- technology   whether existing technology is compatible with viewdata or not;
- attitudes   whether favourable or unfavourable toward viewdata as an option for automation.

Expectancy-value theory provides an analysis of the third level, 'attitudes' (e.g. as in Figure 15.3). An important element in that analysis, as we have seen above, is the 'salient belief'.

One thing the conflict–harmony model does is bring out two classes of factors (and beliefs relating to these) that are likely to be salient when information systems are considered, relating to: information and technology. Whether or not beliefs relating to these are in fact salient for any of the people involved, these factors still need to be considered in an 'objective' assessment of the situation. The conflict–harmony model therefore provides an 'objective' framework in which expectancy-value theory—dealing with the subjective realities influencing people's attitudes and behaviour—can be fitted.

The reasons for the conflicts and harmony at levels 5–7 in the example have been discussed in Chapter 6 and will not be rehearsed here. They do, however, bring out the point that real people are involved, with real personalities and real needs—a point discussed in more detail in the next chapter.

GUIDELINES

We can see from the discussion so far that introducing a new information system

238

into an organization is a complex business both at a practical and at a theoretical level. It may help to cut through this complexity by setting out some principal guidelines, as follows. These are just *guide*lines and do not substitute for careful research and theoretical analysis, but they may help to summarize in a convenient form some of the main points to which attention needs to be given.

1. *Ensure commitment at the highest level in the organization at the very start.* This is important for gaining the more specific kinds of support required, including financial and administrative support. Information systems have impacts on all areas of an organization's activities, and so are an appropriate subject for the attention of the most senior people.

At this level in the organization, it may be more appropriate to evaluate the benefits of new systems in terms of where the organization is going rather than where it is at the moment. The point is not so much whether the information system will produce improvements relative to the current situation but whether it will put the organization in a better position at some specified point in the future relative to where it would be otherwise. This point of view is compatible with the 'orientation' activities of senior management. The point is made clearer in Figure 15.5.

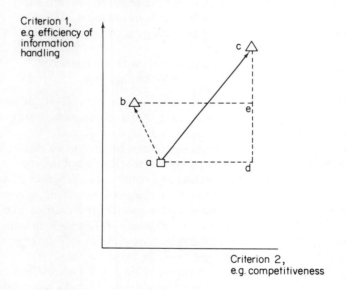

Figure 15.5   A 'dynamic' approach to evaluating the benefits of an information system.

Figure 15.5 shows the organization concerned to be currently at location a—moderately competitive and with a moderately efficient information system. Upgrading the information system by an amount equal to e − d might appear quite beneficial in terms of costs and some other criteria but the diagram shows that by a specified time in the future, say five years, this would take the organization to position b, i.e. actually *less* competitive despite the improved information system. This is simply because (hypothetically) other organizations will have upgraded their information systems even more. To achieve an improvement in competitiveness by an amount equal to d − a would mean upgrading the information system by an amount equal to c − d, i.e. almost twice as much.

The diagram is designed to make just one simple point: We need to compare future situations, not a future situation with a current one.

The diagram is deliberately simplified. For example, only two criteria are shown, whereas many criteria would normally need to be considered. Another complication is that competitiveness is influenced by many other factors apart from the nature of the organization's information systems, so each position on the diagram (except the current position, which is the only certain one) should have a probability associated with it. This is not the place to go into these and other complications in detail.

2. *Ensure adequate financial and administrative support.* This is essential if the project is not to founder before it has had a chance to 'get off the ground'. The introduction of a new system needs to go smoothly and effectively. Users will quickly become disenchanted and withdraw their support if their belief system shifts in the direction of:

> 'It's easier to go to the library and look it up there.' 'The information is often out of date or unreliable.' 'The terminal is always being used by someone else when I want it—except when it's not working.'

This kind of situation is certain to reduce attitude toward the act of using the new system, perhaps to the extent that attitude toward the act of using conventional systems is more positive. It therefore is unwise to attempt a 'pilot' trial which is actually simply a poorly funded, poorly supported system. Sufficient funds and administrative support must be made available to allow a service to be provided that is better (even if in pilot areas) than that provided currently by conventional systems. This may involve recruiting people with special skills that are required; it is not adequate to 'muddle through' until the system 'takes off' and the greater investment is 'justified'—with such a policy it may never be justified, because the system may never 'take off'.

3. *Involve all key parties at the earliest possible stage.* We have seen in our discussion of expectancy-value theory how important it is for all the parties involved

in the possible introduction of new systems to share information so that as far as possible they share a common appreciation of:

- the options available;
- the likely outcomes of the various options;

and feel part of a single team, with common norms.

An advocate for the option to be adopted should be identified for each part of the organization and each rank within the organization as soon as possible. The advocates will provide information and set norms that will be important in influencing the success of the system. From the case studies considered earlier it would seem that the organization's information 'gatekeepers' may be good advocates if their support can be gained.

4. *Maximize awareness*. In addition to involving all the key parties and identifying advocates, it is important to maximize awareness throughout the organization of:

- the general system concept;
- The particular applications for which it is being used;
- how the system is being implemented.

This could involve a programme of structured discussions, demonstrations, and training sessions.

5. *Monitor and evaluate the system's impacts*. We have seen from the studies of the effects of introducing new systems that the effects can be varied and complex, and perhaps not always entirely predictable. No matter what care is taken in the initial planning, it is always wise to accept the possibility in principle of a gradual evolution, even to encourage such an evolution, to an even more effective system. Systematic monitoring and evaluation over a period of time can facilitate this as well as providing an important 'de-bugging' function by allowing difficulties to be identified early on and corrected before they cause real problems.

6. *Attend to 'global' system factors*. The notion of 'global' system factors was introduced in Chapter 13 in relation to our hierarchical model of attitudes toward information systems. They include such factors as convenience and reliability, which have emerged from some of the case studies, and factors such as humanness, social presence and others that can be measured by the semantic differential.

The importance of these global factors is illustrated by a series of experiments reported by Chapanis (1971).

The experiments were conducted by Kinkade and colleagues and involved a specialized information-retrieval system set up in cooperation with The Federation of American Societies for Experimental Biology. In one study fifty university researchers in biology could telephone requests for information to a central office where the requests were recorded. Requests were always tape recorded but in one condition of the experiment this was done automatically, whereas in another condition a biologically trained receptionist also discussed the request with the person concerned. The 'social presence' hypothesis discussed in Chapter 12 would predict that the system with the receptionist would be judged 'warmer', 'more personal', and so forth, and would be used more than the one without. We would also expect this in terms of the 'humanness' factor we identified in Chapter 13. Chapanis does not indicate whether any ratings of the systems were made but certainly the system with the receptionist was used more. Both systems were used increasingly over the first twenty days of operation, but by the end of that time the system with the receptionist was being used about twice as much as the one without. This supports the 'social presence' hypothesis but it must also be said that the effect could have been due to other factors, e.g. help given by the receptionist in the 'fine tuning' of the requests. More research is needed if this ambiguity is to be resolved. In any case, it seems clear that 'global' factors of this sort can have a very significant effect on the success or otherwise of a new system.

7. *Attend to specific system features*. We saw in Chapter 13 that the specific design features of a system are important in influencing the attitudes and behaviour of users toward the system. Some design criteria which have been suggested for the interface between the system and the user are shown in Figure 15.6. Thompson (1971) argues that a system which orders files hierarchically (as with videotex pages) and presents the user with a visual representation of the tree goes a long way towards meeting these criteria. He cites several systems using this principle, including one at the Biotechnology Laboratory of Stanford University which he describes in some detail. In practice, design features should reflect the needs of particular groups of users and operators as far as possible.

8. *Attend to the needs of different user groups*. A particular difficulty in designing information systems is that users vary in their needs and capabilities. There are two main aspects to the problem. First, some groups of people may simply show lower general acceptance of a system than other groups. Secondly, assuming some minimal level of acceptance, some groups may need different kinds of interfaces with the system than other groups.

Borman and Mittman (1972) addressed themselves to the first aspect of the problem in a study of the acceptance of an on-line interactive bibliographic retrieval system in an academic environment. They found a marked difference between university research workers and students. The research workers typically expressed very little interest in continuing to use the system even after careful preparation and individual help, and preferred to use more traditional methods. The students, on the other hand, were enthusiastic about the system. The researchers concluded that a continuing 'marketing' and 'hand-holding' approach would be needed to gain acceptance by the research workers. They interpreted their findings as indicating

Figure 15.6.   Some criteria suggested for retrieval system interface design.

1.	•	simplicity, (1), especially
	•	minimum operator action to initiate interaction (2)
2.	•	prompt reaction (1) by
	•	stacking commands (2) or by
	•	executing commands as assembled (3)
3.	•	special reference (1) perhaps by
	•	visual display of the search tree (3) and/or
	•	rapid display of 'neighbour' or 'surround' terms (2)
4.	•	appropriate order of file arrangement (1) perhaps by
	•	hierarchical arrangement (3)
5.	•	completeness (1)
6.	•	association among information terms (1) perhaps with
	•	rapid display of 'neighbour' or 'surround' terms (2) and
	•	many search terms for a single search (2) and
	•	'mixed mode' operation—combining terms from different categories of unit record (2) and
	•	use of partially specified (incomplete) search terms
7.	•	Convenient access (1)
8.	•	manageability (1) including
	•	program interaction control by user with interrupt (2)
9.	•	versatility in means and modes of access (1) including
	•	'mixed mode' operation (2) and
	•	unrestricted use of Boolean AND, OR and NOT (2) (or visual display of the search tree (3))
10.	•	compatibility in multichannel communication (1)
11.	•	reliability (1) including
	•	systems safeguards to prevent the user 'bombing' the system (2)
12.	•	assistance on demand (1) including
	•	extensive, specific error messages (2) or
	•	not allowing the user to input an erroneous request (3)
13.	•	pacing queues avoiding distraction (e.g., turning off the display during the 300–700 ms need to search the file) (2)

1: Treu, cited by Thompson (1971)
2: Katter, cited by Thompson (1971)
3: Thompson (1971)

that it is easier to introduce new kinds of systems to groups, e.g. students, who have not already learned other approaches.

The second aspect of the problem, concerned with interface design, has been discussed by several researchers. Eason (1976), for example, emphasizes the special needs of the 'naïve user'. Typically, such users:

- need a computer only for specific tasks;
- do not have a deep knowledge of computer technology;
- wish to minimize the time and effort involved in learning and operating the system;
- can experience errors as 'traumatic' especially if they find themselves without an 'escape route'.

For such people, the interface has to be both a link (with required facilities) and a barrier (protecting the user from other aspects of the system).

Acceptance of a complex system will reflect an interaction between the type of user and the kind of thing the user is trying to do. Eason reports the conclusions from a survey which indicated that managers experienced a sharp increase in difficulty with operating procedures as the complexity of their task increased from 'data input and predefined outputs only' to 'high level language programming', whereas specialists experienced a much more gradual increase. There was also a difference between levels of seniority. The more senior people were particularly likely to:

- stop using the system;
- use only a few, familiar routines; or
- introduce a 'human interface', i.e. someone more skilled in operating the system.

These findings have been interpreted to suggest there may be a need to provide alternative interfaces to a system.

Naïve users may require a much more 'helpful' interface than those who have had considerable experience with the system. This general notion is reflected in, for example:

- some word-processing systems where various levels of 'helping' and 'promoting' by means of 'menus' (annotated lists of options) and other devices are available according to individual user needs;
- Prestel, where:
  - the user is given explicit instructions and options at every stage;
  - invalid entries are not accepted but the options available are always made clear along with any instructions that are necessary;
  - various 'escape routes' are provided; and
  - an on-line explanatory introduction to the system is available if required; and
- some personal computers in which programmes are available which train the naïve user how to use the system.

These guidelines may be helpful in providing a general framework within which to proceed but they cannot substitute for a thorough understanding of the more general principles reviewed in this chapter.

CONCLUSIONS

Studies of the effects of new technologies, the techniques of organizational development, and case studies documenting the factors involved in the success or failure of new information systems, all indicate in different ways that a wide variety of specific factors need to be considered in managing the successful introduction of a new information system.

The concept of a generalized 'resistance to change' is too simplistic but we do need a general theoretical framework if we are to avoid simply amassing specific facts. Expectancy-value theory provides such a framework and can be fitted into the more general conflict–harmony model introduced in Chapter 6. The model and broader theory associated with it, combined with the practical experience from case studies, form a basis for a set of guidelines that may have some pragmatic use in providing a broad framework within which to proceed in managing the introduction of a new information system.

Chapter 16

The manager of tomorrow

The organizational factors considered in the previous chapter are really only half the story. An organization is an organization of people, and in this chapter we shall consider some of the characteristics of people as individual human beings that are relevant to the information environment of tomorrow, and we shall focus our attention on the manager of tomorrow. What sort of characteristics will the successful manager of tomorrow need? We shall consider them under four main headings:

- skills;
- personality;
- motivational structure;
- ability to cope with stress.

SKILLS

We saw in Chapter 3 that the work done in the office environment can be divided into three broad categories, concerned with:

- orientation activities—enabling an organization to adjust to changes in the environment; they are often novel, unstructured, complex, and involve information about new markets, new products, new competitors, changes in legislation, and so forth;
- planning activities—taking the findings and policies based on orientation activities and implementing them by setting up new projects, new departments, new companies, or in some other way, establishing programmed activities;
- programmed activities—routine, repetitive and standardized, involving information in the form of routine reports done to a consistent format, standard letters, contracts, invoices, and so forth.

These distinctions are very broad and it may be difficult to separate some of the activities in practice. For example, orientation activity may require programmed activity in the form of routine scanning of parts of the Prestel database, routine commissioning of market research, and similar activities. The distinctions are useful to make despite the close connection between the various activities involved, for the following reasons: Automation in the office will shift the mix of activities on which a manager spends time away from programmed activities towards planning

246

and orientation activities. This is simply because the kinds of automated information systems we have been discussing, especially in Chapter 5, enable routine activities to be accomplished more effectively in less time. For example, the potentially huge amount of information available through Prestel 'at the touch of a button' means the environment (i.e. company information, share prices, competitors' offerings, information on new legislation, and so on) can be scanned very rapidly to give up to the minute information on a routine basis. To take another example, reports can be compiled on word-processing systems in a fraction of the time taken conventionally—especially when they are largely recompilations of material already stored in electronic form. The manager will therefore be able more and more to off-load the routine aspects of his or her work on to automated systems and the office personnel responsible for running them, leaving him or her with more time for thinking, discussing, and making decisions.

The shift in managers' activities away from the routine collection, use/processing, and origination of items of information is reflected in another, related area: the increasing use of computers for performing analyses on data locally and on-line.

The advent of the microcomputer has brought prices down to such an extent that £1000 or so can purchase more computer power than was available for hundreds of thousands of pounds when computers first appeared on the market. The manager in a modern office environment can perform far more sophisticated analyses than ever before, and in a fraction of the time.

The extra time made available by electronic systems taking the burden of routine information handling of all sorts will mean the manager of tomorrow will be able to spend more time with people and less with pieces of paper or their electronic equivalents. The kinds of activities alluded to above—thinking, discussing, making decisions—will put much greater emphasis on Type A communication than on Type B. This means that in addition to the specialist technical skills needed for particular areas of responsibility managers generally will need a higher level of competence in 'people skills'. This is important because organizations essentially are groups of people working together within a common framework and organizational effectiveness ultimately must depend upon the extent to which the people involved can cooperate to work together productively.

Behavioural Demands of Contacts With People

The level and nature of demands put on a person by his or her contacts with other people depend on the nature of the job. Stewart (1976) reports the results of her empirical research on this point. Her main findings are illustrated in Figure 16.1. Her research concentrated on jobs in industry and commerce but the illustration shows that her findings can be applied to a wide range of occupations, e.g. police inspector, hospital administrator, bank manager, and store (chain) manager. The table summarizes how the four jobs shown compare in the behavioural demands studied. The high, medium and low ratings shown are a simplification.

Job Title	Police Inspector	Hospital administrator	Bank manager	Store (chain) manager
Type of job contact	Hub 1	Hub 1	Apex	Man management O
Type of work pattern	2b	4	2b	1
Behavioural demands made:				
By subordinates	☒	☒	☐	☒
By peers and other seniors	☒	■	☐	☐
By boss(es) dependence	☐	■	☐	☐
By external contacts	■	☒	■	☐
By short-term contacts	■	☒	■	☐
By conflicting demands	■	■		
On private life	■	☐	☒	☐
By exposure	■	☒	■	☒
Totals	13	10	9	3

Key   ■ High   ☒ Medium   ☐ Low

Scoring: 2 for high, 1 for medium; Exceptions: exposure = 4 for high and 2 for medium; conflicting demands = 1 for high (more conflicts than usual) and 0 for medium.

Figure 16.1.   Behavioural demands of four jobs (from Stewart, 1976).

The 'type of job contact' refers to one of the two typologies Stewart developed in her research, which identified twelve contact types according to the nature of contacts that a job requires. There are four main groups in the job contact typology, as follows:

- hub—the most common type of managerial job, which has contacts radiating outwards (up, down, sideways, within and outside the manager's own unit);
- peer-dependent—mainly staff jobs, where more time is spent with people at the same level than with one's own subordinates or boss;
- man-management—where the contacts are with subordinates and boss;
- solo—where the emphasis is on Type B communication.

The 'type of work pattern' classifies jobs into four main types, as follows:

- Type 1—fragmented activities, recurrent work, and frequent trouble-shooting;
- Type 2(a)—recurrent work that has to meet deadlines, where the precise nature of the work can be predicted fairly well;
- Type 2(b)—as above but where the precise nature of the work is difficult to predict;
- Type 3—work that needs sustained attention, a longer time-scale, and involves more self-generated activities;

- Type 4—no dominant characteristics because the person concerned has more choice in the extent to which the work is self-generated or arises in response to other people or problems.

The table shows that the behavioural demands made on the people concerned vary considerably according to the type of job. The research helps to redress the emphasis that has often been put on the similarities in managerial work whilst at the same time clearly illustrating the range of behavioural demands put on managers by their contacts with other people.

The successful manager of tomorrow will need to have better and more formal training in how to work effectively with people, including such areas as:

- interpersonal skills;
- group processes;
- personality;
- motivational structure;
- and many related topics.

Perhaps the most significant difference between the manager of tomorrow and the manager of yesterday will be not in their relative technical expertise—although the manager of tomorrow will generally be more knowledgeable in specialist areas—but in this: the manager of tomorrow will not be able to afford to rely on common sense and intuition in dealing with other people. Common sense and intuition will remain important qualities but the successful manager of tomorrow will be able to back these up with a thorough understanding of the relevant parts of the science of psychology—rather than the art of psychology. For those who are sceptical whether there is any 'science of psychology', all we can say is: wait until you meet the successful manager of tomorrow, then you will see. We can add, perhaps, as an extra hint that much of what seems 'common sense' and 'intuitively obvious' today did not necessarily appear so yesterday but has become 'common' sense by filtering into general management circles from the research world of psychology and other disciplines.

PERSONALITY*

It has become 'common sense' and 'intuitively obvious' that 'the fittest survive'. Which characteristics make a person the fittest depend, of course, on the nature of the environment.

As we move into the 1980s and beyond, the office environment is changing markedly under the impact of the new information technology, and some characteristics are becoming much more important than ever before. Some of these have to do with skills and knowledge, as discussed above, but others have to do with our

* This and the next section have been written bearing in mind that some readers are likely to have little background in psychology. Psychologists are asked to forgive what is a deliberately simplified account of what is involved.

temperament. The manager of tomorrow will need some personality traits that may not have been so important yesterday, and will certainly need to understand himself or herself better so as to capitalize on those traits that will help and perhaps keep others in check.

Some non-psychologists may feel repulsed by the idea that people can be compared in terms of traits, and may feel obliged to point to the obvious individual differences between people and to the equally clear fact that each of us is unique and special. Actually, the notion that we are each unique and the notion that people can be described in terms of common personality traits are not at all incompatible. Just as we are each unique psychologically, so we are each unique physically; yet, if we go to a tailor to have a suit measured, does (s)he throw up his or her hands in despair at the complexity of the situation? Of course not, (s)he makes measurements along standard dimensions and then produces a garment that is uniquely suited to us. Thus it is with personality traits—the dimensions themselves are common to us all, just as we all have arms, legs, a head, and so forth, but there is so much flexibility in terms of our positions along those dimensions that each of us is unique.

We are each unique but we can fairly readily distinguish between those of us who are physically strong and those of us who are less so. The physically strong are better able to cope with physically arduous tasks. Similarly, the manager of tomorrow will need certain psychological characteristics to be able to deal as effectively as possible with the new office environment.

We use words and phrases all the time to distinguish between people in terms of their psychological characteristics, e.g. 'lively', 'extrovert', 'depressing', 'narrow-minded', and so forth. There are a large number of such terms. Allport and Odbert (1936) identified about 4500 in the English language. These overlap considerably in what they mean. Extensive research based on factor-analytic methods by Cattell and his colleagues has indicated that about 16 main dimensions, called personality 'source traits' account for most of the differences between people in terms of their personalities. These source traits are intercorrelated and can be understood in terms of a smaller number of about half a dozen broader, higher-order dimensions (just as the first-order factors we identified in some of the research discussed in earlier chapters, e.g. Chapter 13, could be analysed in terms of a smaller number of second-order factors). Eysenck (e.g. 1970) has suggested that three of these higher-order dimensions—'extraversion', 'neuroticism' and 'psychoticism'—are especially important in understanding personality and, indeed, have greater validity than the 'source traits' identified by Cattell. The source traits, however, have been replicated in a number of independent studies and of course provide a much more detailed analysis of personality than a smaller number of higher-order factors. It is for these reasons we shall focus our attention on the source traits in looking for qualities that the manager of tomorrow will need. The description of the source traits will be based on the information provided by Cattell, Eber, and Tatsuoka, (1970) in their *Handbook for the Sixteen Personality Factor*

Questionnaire (*16PF*)—a questionnaire developed as a convenient, reliable and valid method of measuring the main source traits.

Given the complexity of the office environment and the differences between managers in the particular kinds of situations with which they have to deal, it would be too gross a simplification to assume that any one pattern of personality traits is *the* desirable pattern and that any deviations from that pattern are to be avoided. Some variety in personalities is itself desirable. Furthermore, it is more a matter of the way traits are combined in a person than a person's standing on particular traits taken in isolation, so the comments which follow concerning particular traits should be regarded only as general 'rules of thumb'. What is needed in practice is expert judgement by a professional psychologist or a specialist with adequate training in psychometrics.

Given these cautions, we can say that as a general rule the following source traits will be among the more desirable for the manager of tomorrow.

Affectothymia (*A+*). Affectothymic individuals prefer occupations dealing with people, and we have seen that the manager of tomorrow will be called upon to deal with people even more than the manager of yesterday. They can form groups readily, are generous in personal relationships, and not overly afraid of criticism. They can adapt flexibly to compromises with human failings and accept having to deal with a continuous stream of 'people problems' that are rarely entirely soluble and that, in the words of Cattell, Eber, and Tatsuoka, 'might drive the exact logician or the careful scientist mad!' We might note in passing that the opposite kind of person—sizothymic (*A−*)—likes things, machines, logic and words, working alone and tends to reject compromises. These qualities would be very useful, for example, in an operator or supervisor of a word-processing system.

High ego strength (*C+*). Ego strength is an especially interesting trait in the present context. High ego strength is often a characteristic of leaders, and in groups it contributes to high group morale. For both of these reasons it would seem to be a desirable characteristic for the manager of tomorrow. By contrast, the person low on ego strength (*C−*) is easily annoyed, is dissatisfied with his or her own circumstances, with the world, with his or her health, and feels unable to cope well with life. Low ego strength is associated with most psychological disorders, probably sometimes as cause and sometimes as effect. It is interesting that business executives vary widely in ego strength, and this may reflect the accumulated effects of occupational stress. This is discussed in more detail below, where we consider how the manager of tomorrow can train himself or herself to cope with stress more effectively and maintain a healthy level of ego strength.

Parmia (*H+*). According to Cattell, Eber, and Tatsuoka, evidence indicates this to be one of the two or three most highly inherited of personality traits. The H− (threctic) person appears to have a very responsive sympathetic nervous system which makes him or her especially susceptible to threat.

Such people are intensely shy, report themselves tormented by a sense of inferiority, are often slow and impeded in expressing themselves, dislike too many personal contacts or large groups, and find it difficult to keep in touch with all that is going on around. In situations of prolonged stress, there is some tendency toward schizoid disorders, tuberculosis, or ulcers. The H+ (parmic) person by contrast is less susceptible to threat, and this can generate a certain boldness in social, sexual, emotional, and physically dangerous situations. Parmic individuals feel free to participate in group situations. Their resistance to threat helps them cope with occupations demanding an ability to face wear and tear in dealing with people and gruelling emotional situations. Executives, not surprisingly, tend to be parmic rather than threctic, and this would seem to be a desirable characteristic for the manager of tomorrow. It is unfortunate that there is some assosication between parmia and heart attacks.

Shrewdness (*N+*). The N+ person is ingenious, flexible in viewpoint, can quickly get to the root of a problem, and is inclined to 'study the angles'. (S)he is alert to manners, social obligations and the social reactions of others. In groups, such people tend to lead in analytical, goal-oriented discussion, and in providing constructive group solutions. Whilst this may be a desirable trait in moderation it is possible to have too much of a good thing, and Cattell, Eber, and Tatsuoka suggest there may be too much efficiency and survival ethos in N+ for people very high on this trait to be tolerant of most people and their failings. This would mitigate against success in the manager of tomorrow, so we should conclude perhaps that the successful manager of tomorrow will be towards N+, but not too far.

High strength of self-sentiment (*Q3+*). This has been called the 'gyroscopic' factor in personality. It represents the strength of a person's concern with his or her self-concept and social image. A person with strong self-sentiment shows socially approved character responses such as self-control, persistence, foresight, considerateness of others, conscientiousness, and regard for etiquette and social reputation. These behaviours contribute to success in school. Such people are often chosen as leaders in groups and even more often are routinely effective in groups. They make more comments than others, especially in relation to raising problems and offering solutions. Amongst other things, the trait is associated with success in organizational activities.

Openness to experimentation (*Q1+*). Called 'radicalism' by Cattell, Eber, and Tatsuoki, this trait is better described in the present context by the term we have chosen. The Q1+ person tends to be well informed, inclined to experiment with problem solutions, less inclined to moralize, and less unquestioning about views generally. Such people contribute more to group discussions, and the trait is associated with leadership more generally. Not surprisingly, executives tend to be Q1+, and this would seem to be even more desirable in the manager of tomorrow. With the office environment changing so rapidly under the impact of the new technology, the successful manager surely will be the one who is willing and keen to experiment with new possibilities rather than stick 'safely' to the 'well-tried' (even if somewhat inefficient) methods of yesterday.

It must be emphasized that the trait descriptions presented above do little more than give a flavour of what is involved. In some cases, one might be concerned about other traits not mentioned above, such as unduly high guilt proneness (O+) or protension (L+, discussed below in connection with stress). Also, it is the general pattern of traits, the way they combine that is most important. There is not the space here to consider all the many different possible patterns. What is needed is good judgement by a qualified psychologist at the time these principles are being applied—whether it is in relation to recruitment, promotion, selection for special training programmes, counselling, or whatever.

The 'Psychological Mirror'

The role of this kind of personality analysis in counselling bears elaboration. We have seen that there is no single personality pattern that is 'right' to the exclusion of all others. Some variety is itself desirable. Managers can capitalize on this if they take the trouble to look at themselves carefully, as they might look at themselves in a mirror to adjust their hair, or check their clothing. Properly validated measures of temperament (and motivation, discussed below) provide a 'psychological mirror'.

A good example of the usefulness of the psychological mirror is provided by the case of a person—Mr X—who came to the author for assistance in self-knowledge. With the aid of validated psychological measures, Mr X discovered he was extremely 'threctic' (susceptible to real or imagined threats in the environment). This discovery helped him to understand some of the difficulties he had been having in his working relationships and to adjust his behaviour. A typical incident will serve to illustrate his basic problem: his boss came into his office and casually asked 'What are you doing?' Mr X immediately felt this was a challenge—an implication that he was not spending his time productively. In other words, this person habitually tended to interpret events as threatening even when there was no real reason to do so. This made life difficult for himself and for the people around him (who learned they had to be especially careful about what they said to him, so as not to alarm him). Once he realized he was much more 'threctic' than most people, he was able to learn to deal with this—for example, by making a point of consciously asking himself under apparently threatening circumstances if there was really good reason to believe a threat existed or whether another interpretation of the event might be possible. Before seeing himself in the 'psychological mirror' he had had no reason to question the validity of the threats he perceived.

Need for Adequate Measurement

Another point worth emphasizing is that measurement of psychological traits requires adequate measurement instruments. We should avoid the argument that properly validated instruments should be avoided 'because' they impose too much rigidity and take away the element of human judgement. Such an argument is spurious. There is nothing to prevent the counsellor, or manager selecting people for training programmes, using criteria other than the kinds of source traits discussed above, and making full use of whatever intuitive skills (s)he feels that (s)he has. The point is, if personality needs to be considered it is sensible to base one's decisions on precise measurements. If we go to a tailor, we expect him or her to make precise measurements, not just look and with a skilled eye say 'quite large' or 'about average'. Such a tailor would not be doing us any service by his or her freedom from rigid measuring instruments. Also, the use of precise measurement techniques does not preclude elements of human judgement; indeed, we have seen above that skilled judgement is very important in the use of psychological measurement techniques. It would be most unwise to use the techniques mechanically. The tailor also uses judgement, often in consultation with the client—about how tight a fit is needed, where to leave a little extra room, and so on—but these judgements come after and are based on precise measurements. There is an even greater need for this skilled combination of good judgement based on precise measurement in the case of human personality, where we are dealing with something much more complex than a new suit.

Thanks to the careful research over many years of Cattell, Eysenck, and other psychologists, instruments are available today which allow personality traits to be measured with a high degree of reliability and validity and very conveniently. Of special note are:

- The Sixteen Personality Factor Questionnaire (16PF) (Cattell, Eber, and Tatsuoka, 1970), for the measurement of source traits and higher stratum factors; and various instruments developed by Eysenck and his colleagues, including:
- The Eysenck Personality Questionnaire (EPQ) (Eysenck and Eysenck, 1975), for the more rapid assessment of two of the main second-stratum personality factors (also covered by the 16PF) and a third dimension of particular significance in clinical rather than occupational applications.

Existing data on executives and other occupations, a detailed review of the main personality factors, how questionnaire data relate to objective behavioural measures, and a detailed discussion of methods for handling and interpreting information about personality traits, as well as general background information about the 16PF, are presented by Cattell, Eber, and Tatsuoka, (1970).

MOTIVATIONAL STRUCTURE

What 'drives' a person (motivational structure) is as important as his or her general 'style' of behaviour (personality). The same general principles apply to the measurement of elements in the motivational structure as to the measurement of personality, especially: no service is done to anyone by relying on impressions gained by talking to a person or in other ways when more precise measures are available, but the precise measurements need to be interpreted by a suitably qualified person and used in conjunction with other criteria. In this section we shall consider two types of elements measured by the motivation analysis test (MAT):

- ergs—roughly, biological drives such as sex and hunger (although the hunger drive is not one of those covered by the MAT because it is not usually of practical importance in contexts where the MAT is used); and
- sentiments—as important as ergs for most practical purposes but learned, e.g. sentiment toward a career, toward a spouse, and so forth.

The concepts of 'ergs' and 'sentiments' were introduced in Chapter 6 in connection with the 'information sphere'.

The MAT has been developed by Cattell and his colleagues as an objective measure of a person's current motivational structure (which will vary to some extent from time to time as some needs become temporarily satisfied whilst others become frustrated). It is 'objective' because it does not rely on a person's introspections about himself or herself but makes use of other sorts of behaviour such as associations given to words, amount of information known about particular topics, and so on. It is also 'objective' in the sense that the basic measurements made do not depend on the test scorer's subjective judgements—although subsequent interpretation of the pattern of scores requires, as we have already noted, the good judgement of a skilled specialist.

The MAT measures ten of the more important 'dynamic elements' (ergs and sentiments) and provides three measures for each:

- total motivation—an overall assessment of levels of drive in the area concerned;
- unintegrated motivation—roughly, generalized interest in the area concerned, perhaps somewhat unrealistic, perhaps not fully conscious, often not fully expressed in terms of suitable outlets;
- integrated motivation—roughly, an indication of the degree of satisfaction achieved through realistic, usually conscious expression through suitable outlets.

The differences between unintegrated and integrated levels of motivation provide indications of areas of conflict that are likely to influence a person's behaviour. There are various other measures provided by the MAT as well. Clearly, the assessment of a person's motivational structure is complex—perhaps even more complex than that of temperament—and so what follows can only be a very general indication of some of the characteristics that might be of especial interest to the manager of tomorrow in terms of understanding both himself or herself and others. The comments are based on descriptions given by Sweney (1969).

Career sentiment. A high unintegrated score in this area normally suggests high aspirations toward being successful in a suitable occupation. If coupled with a low integrated score it can indicate frustration and a source of conflict. The level of integrated motivation seems to reflect the amount of experience the person has had and the degree to which (s)he is interested in his or her current occupation. Low scores suggest feelings of failure (whether 'realistic' or 'unrealistic') or unwillingness to accept responsibility, but equally they can indicate an intellectual idealism that places self-actualization above success in a career.

The relative level of unintegrated motivation in this area compared with, say, the mating or narcism areas gives an indication of what we sometimes call 'motivation' in common parlance when referring to career, i.e. the degree to which the person is intrinsically interested in his or her career.

Self-sentiment. The unintegrated component of this represents the person's concern for his or her future, and willingness to invest effort and time in it. Too high or too low a level in this area can both be difficult for the person concerned, e.g. too high a level may indicate unrealistic goals. A high conflict score in this area can be part of the 'loser's syndrome', with a fear of looking at oneself realistically. Alternatively, high conflict can indicate a search to 'find oneself'. People who have achieved a degree of self-actualization generally show relatively little conflict in this area. Low integrated scores, indicating frustration or repression, can sometimes develop from frustrations in other areas, especially a frustrated search for status, repressed hostility, or repressed fear or anxiety.

Assertion. Called 'assertion', this area reflects a striving for status and the material manifestations of status. The level of unintegrated motivation indicates the level of generalized desire for a 'good' standard of living (however the person concerned defines that). It could be considered 'healthy', or 'useful' in moderation but if too high it can result in frustration and discontent. If higher than the level of motivation in the career area it can indicate a source of job dissatisfaction. Such a situation can sometimes be inadvertently encouraged by unrealistic aspirations induced by colleagues or friends.

Pugnacity. A high unintegrated level of motivation in this area indicates unreleased hostility. The person concerned is often unaware of this. Sweney (1969) suggests it can be either healthy or unhealthy depending on other characteristics of the person concerned, but is very important in the person's interpersonal relationships, and this is the chief reason for considering it in relation to the manager of tomorrow, for whom interpersonal relationships will be more important than ever.

A high level of integrated motivation indicates the person can express his or her hostility directly and comfortably. This is important in dealings with people and can be one of the more important contributors to popularity with one's peers. It is as if the clear and natural expression of the hostility and competitiveness that is met and needed in everyday life actually makes the person concerned appear less 'hostile' in the common usage of that word. It is more likely to be the indirect expression of hostility, e.g. through hostile humour and cynicism, that can lead to difficulties. In general it would seem that high expressed hostility coupled with low unintegrated tension is desirable in occupations where contacts with people play an important role, as for the manager of tomorrow.

As explained above, these comments can do no more than give a flavour of what is involved. Motivation is a complex area and one must tread cautiously, especially when dealing with individual people. This is why it is so important to be able to call upon the aid of reliable, valid and convenient aids such as the MAT which in the hands of a specialist can provide insights simply not attainable with the same level of confidence from informal methods (such as discussion) alone.

ABILITY TO COPE WITH STRESS

We have seen above in considering the skills needed by the successful manager of tomorrow that direct contacts with people—Type A communication—will play a much more dominant role in the successful manager's activities. Such contacts, especially when important issues are involved and many gruelling hours of face-to-face contact are involved, can be stressful. The manager of tomorrow will also be under stress from at least two other sources:

- The rate of change in the office environment, having to cope effectively with new technology, new procedures, staff with different skills and interests, and so forth; and
- the rate at which events will happen in the office of tomorrow as the new electronic technology speeds up the rate at which information comes in, is processed, and new items are produced and distributed.

The manager of tomorrow will need to be able to cope effectively with more stress, and even today stress is a killer. As Blythe (1973) has said, 'certain stress-diseases are lethal, and can kill just as successfully as a well-aimed bullet'. He goes on to cite a 1964 report of the World Health Organization listing coronary heart disease, diabetes mellitus and bronchial asthma among the diseases 'generally acknowledged' to have psychosomatic components.

A quotation from a recent article by Cooper (1980) in the *Bulletin of the British Psychological Society* indicates the enormity of the problem well:

'Stress-related illnesses such as coronary heart disease have been on a steady upward trend over the past couple of decades in the UK. In England and Wales, for example, the death rate in men between 35 and 44 nearly doubled between 1950 and 1973, and has increased much more rapidly than that of older age ranges (e.g. 45–54). By 1973, 41 per cent of all deaths in the age groups 35–44 were due to cardiovascular disease, with nearly 30 per cent due to cardiac heart disease. In fact, in 1976 the American Heart Association estimated the cost of cardiovascular disease in the US at $26.7 billions a year. In addition to the more extreme forms of stress-related illnesses, there has been an increase in other possible stress manifestations such as alcoholism, where admissions to alcoholism units in hospitals increased from roughly under 6000 in 1966 to over 8000 in 1974, and industrial accidents and short-term illness (through certified and uncertified sick leaves), with an estimated 300 million working days lost at a cost of £55 million in national insurance and supplementary benefits payments alone. The total cost to industry of all forms of stress-related illness and other manifestations, a large slice of which can be attributed directly or indirectly to the working environment, must be enormous, beyond the scope of most cost accountants to begin to calculate. Some Americans estimate that it may represent in the order of 1–3 per cent of GNP in the United States'. (Cooper, 1980, p. 49).

Cooper goes on to show that stress affects people at *all* levels of the organization, not just managers. Clearly, if we could reduce the effects of stress it would benefit everyone, including:

- the person concerned and his or her family by
  - reducing the probability of an early death;
  - reducing the probability of early retirement through incapacity;
  - fostering a healthy atmosphere with fewer strains on marital harmony;
- the organization by
  - reducing the amount of salary and other costs associated with people who were absent from work;
  - reducing accidents;
  - reducing errors and loss of efficiency caused by people under stress not functioning at their normal levels;
  - fostering a healthy atmosphere with less dissatisfaction and less cause for some industrial disputes;
  - improving productivity;
- the country by
  - improving productivity;
  - reducing the costs associated with accidents, illnesses and early retirements;
  - fostering conditions in which people can enjoy life more.

258

The Nature of Stress

It is not the place here for us to go into a detailed discussion concerning all that is involved in stress. Several useful accounts are available, e.g. Cooper and Payne (1978), and Murrell (1978). It is sufficient for our present purposes to adopt a simple model so that we do not get lost in the trees and fail to see the wood.

Figure 16.2 shows that we need to distinguish two main aspects of the problem:

- the stress potential of the environment;
- the psychophysiological response of the person concerned, moderated by his or her ability to cope with stress potential.

The diagram shows a large and small circle drawn with solid lines. The large circle represents the environment. It can be divided up in any way that seems sensible. In the illustration, it is divided into four regions which are labelled. The smaller circle represents the person. The person is 'under attack' from the environment. The specific sources of stress potential are indicated by arrows. They are not labelled but in the sector concerned with new systems for Type B communication they might represent, for example, 'human' systems (such as a word processing system where the person deals with the system through a human, sympathetic intermediary) and 'mechanical' systems (such as a videotex terminal sitting on the person's desk). The

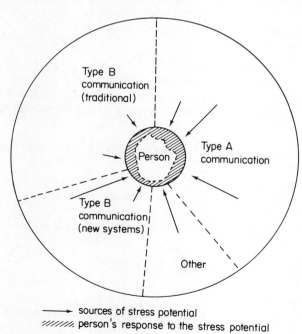

Figure 16.2.   A simple model of occupational stress.

length of the arrows can represent their relative potentials for stress. The broken line within the smaller, 'person' circle represents the impacts of the environment. The amount of 'deformation' under stress depends upon the person's ability to cope with stress in particular areas and on the degree of stress potential, which is why the deformation is irregular in shape. The size of the shaded area represents the total amount of actual stress response which the person shows.

The response of the person is said to be psychophysiological because it involves both behavioural and physiological responses. Behavioural responses under stress may interfere with relations with other people, either in the office environment itself or in the person's personal life ('taking problems home'), or with the execution of various activities (possibly even absenteeism or, in the extreme, suicide). Physiological responses can include headaches, backaches, muscular aches, nausea, asthma, some skin problems, cardiovascular disease, and so forth.

The effects of stress can accumulate over long periods of time, and this is recognized in the USA in the legal concept of 'cumulative trauma'. People in the USA have successfully made claims against companies under this concept by claiming that relatively small stresses over the years have had accumulating effects such that the person concerned has now suffered some disease. The amount of money which insurance companies have paid out on this type of claim has been rising in a positively accelerated fashion.

We have noted above that the stresses put on the office worker will increase as we move into the 1980s and beyond and unless we are willing to tolerate stress-related diseases on an even larger scale than today—and we could reasonably argue that the costs for all involved are already far too high—we must ensure that:

- every effort is made to keep the stress potential of the environment as low as possible; and
- managers and others are trained to cope with stress more effectively.

We have discussed some of the steps that can be taken to minimize the stress potential of the environment in previous chapters, especially Chapter 15. Now we shall turn our attention to what can be done to train people to handle stress better.

Need For Training in Personal Stress Management

People vary in how well they deal with stress. Some people can handle more stress than others, and any particular person is better at handling stress on some days or in some situations than on other days or in other situations. Some correlates of susceptibility to stress can be identified which have a wide degree of generality. For example, we noted above that high levels of protension (which seems to involve the habitual use of projection to deal with inner tensions) are associated with coronary attacks, especially when the person concerned is also very 'self-sufficient' (Q2+) (Cattell, Eber, and Tatsuoka, 1970) (measurements made before, not after the attacks). We also noted that low ego strength is an important correlate of stress, both as a response to high stress potential and in the sense that low ego strength means the person concerned is less able to cope with further pressure from the environment.

Since some people at some times can cope with stress relatively well, and since people do vary from time to time, it seems reasonable to suppose that people can be trained to handle stress more and more effectively, e.g. by reducing protension, building up ego strength, and in other ways learning how to cope effectively with situations involving high stress potential.

Various psychological techniques are available which can help people to learn how to deal with stress more effectively. Ellis discusses one approach, 'rational-emotive therapy' (RET) in some detail in the book by Cooper and Payne (1978), and in the same volume Beech reviews some others. It is likely that a well-designed training programme would incorporate several methods in appropriate combinations. It is not our purpose to review the various methods here as other reviews are readily available and our interest in the psychological aspects of information systems is more general than methods of dealing with the stress resulting from changes in the information environment. However, there is some value in considering one of the more specialist and—the author believes—more effective methods which is not covered well in some reviews and in which there is a resurgence of interest: hypnosis.

Hypnosis as Part of a Training Programme

The term 'hypnosis' may be an unfortunate one to use as it has a variety of misleading connotations in the minds of many people, but psychologists have not found it easy to find a more suitable term.*

Hypnosis has undergone something of a metamorphosis in the UK in recent years, especially since the setting up of the British Society of Experimental and Clinical Hypnosis in 1978. This is a professional society dedicated to a serious attitude toward hypnosis, and its membership—comprising psychologists, medical practitioners and dentists—is actively involved in the practical use of hypnosis as well as basic research on hypnotic phenomena. In addition to the setting up of this society, there is also evidence that the lay hypnotherapists are making serious efforts to put their own house in order and establish a generally recognized framework for training and practice in ethical hypnotherapy. The establishment of the Association of Hypnotists and Psychotherapists is an example of this.

* Psychologists do not have a monopoly on hypnosis. The British Society of Experimental and Clinical Hypnosis admits medical practitioners and dentists to its membership as well as psychologists. In addition to these professional groups there are the lay hypnotherapists, many of whom are highly competent within the limits of their rather restricted training. It is probably true to say, however, that occupational, educational, clinical and research psychologists have the broadest expertise in this area as hypnosis is first and foremost a psychological phenomenon.

The professional use of hypnosis has rather little to do with 'hypnotism' as seen on the stage or in some films, where the emphasis—for obvious reasons—is on drama, entertainment and mystery. The entertainer is concerned with promoting fun and spins a web of illusion in which (s)he appears somehow to 'take control' of the 'hypnotized' person, often apparently 'against the person's will'. That is fun (although it can rapidly become tedious), but the professional practitioner is concerned with the serious business of helping people to learn how to become *more* in control of themselves, not less.* By learning how to become more in control of ourselves we can become more effective, for example in coping with stress.

The professional practitioner is not under the time pressures of the entertainment world and can take time—often many sessions—to proceed carefully through a properly structured training programme, often using hypnosis in conjunction with other methods designed to help the client achieve as much as possible.

Deciding on an adequate definition of what exactly hypnosis is seems to be an endless source of interesting debate. Perhaps there is no simple answer. Certainly people differ in how they experience the state. For some it is very much like an ordinary conversation, for others it is something quite different. It depends partly on expectations and perhaps on one's ability to notice differences in the quality of awareness of one's inner state. For our purposes, we can propose the following definition which will serve to guide our discussion.

Definition: Hypnosis is a particular method of response attentiveness and structured verbal sequences by which a person can use psycho-imaginal processes to gain control over some areas of behaviour and psychophysiological responses previously outside his or her area of voluntary control.

'Response attentiveness'. Milton E. Erickson is regarded by many as having done more than any other single person in developing the art and science of hypnosis. The term 'response attentiveness' is taken from Erickson and Rossi (1979) who use it to refer to 'that state of extreme attentiveness in responding to the nuances of communication presented by the therapist' or other professional which marks the beginning of a period during which people can 'break out of their limited frameworks and belief systems so they can experience other patterns of functioning within themselves'. (Erickson and Rossi, 1979, p. 2.)

'Structured verbal sequences'. The client is helped to achieve a state of response attentiveness and guided through subsequent stages in the hypnotic episode by the psychologist (or other practitioner) who relies mainly on the spoken word to achieve this. What the psychologist says is very carefully structured to open up possibilities which the client is then able to explore in his or her own way. The way ideas are

* There is no intention here to imply that stage 'hypnotism' is necessarily anything less than genuine, but the context is markedly different from the clinical or research laboratory and it is almost certain that the behavioural factors involved are also rather different.

phrased and the sequence in which they are presented are very important aspects of the structure. Non-verbal communication, especially intonation, pauses, and other elements of speech, but sometimes involving visual or other cues, is used to support the verbal structure.

'Person can use'. Professional practitioners of hypnosis are fond of saying they never hypnotize anyone—the only people who do any hypnosis are their clients, that all hypnosis is 'self-hypnosis'. This is simplistic, of course, since it would imply that the psychologist need not be present at all, which (at least at the start of training) is not true. But it does make the point that all the psychologist can do is provide a structure which the client, according to his or her own needs and personality, can choose to ignore entirely or explore in his or her own way and at his or her own pace. The psychologist can provide an opportunity to learn, but it is up to the client to choose whether or not to accept that opportunity and how to use it.

'Psycho-imaginal processes'. An important aspect of the exploratory work that the client does involves the use by the client of his or her 'psycho-imaginal processes'. This term is deliberately obscure to help the reader avoid any temptation to interpret it too simply or pin it on to an erroneous concept. It refers to processes which anyone who has explored hypnosis 'from the inside', as it were, will be able to recognize. It relates to the constructive, deliberate use of imagination—often but not always involving definite (perhaps visual) images. But the ability to visualize things, to see things 'in the mind's eye'—although perhaps desirable—is by no means essential. It relates also to the kind of 'imaginative involvement' that allows some actors and actresses to 'lose themselves' in the roles they are playing—to 'live the part', to 'feel the part', to 'become the part'.

'To gain control'. The purpose of the series of hypnotic episodes is for the client to break free of limiting belief systems and modes of functioning, to explore new possibilities, to learn more about himself or herself, and to gain control over himself or herself in order to realize potentialities which were always there but which the client ignored, did not recognize, or did not understand. Hypnosis, used professionally in this way, is from the client's point of view the exact opposite of losing control.

'Some areas'. We can see that hypnosis is not magic. It involves quite normal psychological processes that operate in all of us every day in talking, reading an interesting book, sleeping, listening to pleasant music, day-dreaming, thinking about the shopping we need to do, dreaming, and so on. It follows that hypnosis cannot go beyond the capacity of the person to respond—it cannot 'make pigs fly' (although it can help an 'eagle' realize its potentialities in this direction). As one might expect, people find it easier to use their hypnotic episodes to gain greater control over what they in any case regard as being almost within reach of their normal voluntary

control; as clients learn more, of course, their understanding of what for them is 'voluntary' expands.

'Behaviour and psychophysiological responses'. Many of us will have had the experience of finding ourselves yawning as we watch someone else nodding off and lazily yawning, perhaps as the warm sun streams in on a hot sleepy day in a railway carriage, when we are very relaxed and sleepy ourselves, and quite likely to yawn ourselves, anyway. Just thinking about drowsiness, hot days, hot streaming sun in a sleepy railway carriage, people yawning widely, can sometimes make us feel how nice it would be to open our mouths, put our head back in a huge yawn and take in a wonderful, yawning breath of air.

Some of us may be able to cause ourselves to blush simply by thinking of an embarrassing incident from the past—perhaps when we were in school, a long time ago, or very recently. An embarrassing incident—now just a thought—something we might not wish to talk about without a good reason, causes us to blush. Conversely, we may be able to 'switch off' a blush by recalling an incident when we felt especially proud of something we had achieved. Something that makes us feel proud, feel good. Some of us, when we are feeling a little drowsy, may be able to establish a feeling of alertness, of being mentally and physically refreshed, by remembering what it feels like to take a plunge into the cold sea, or to take an invigorating cold shower—how we gasp and come out tingling, refreshed, and alert.

In instances such as this, we take something (e.g. feeling alert) from one situation (e.g. a plunge into cold water) and apply it in a different situation (e.g. sitting reading). This can be useful in relation to handling stress. For example a person who finds committee meetings very stressful may be able to use hypnosis to take enjoyable feelings from a non-stressful situation (perhaps dinner parties or informal social conversations with groups of friends) and apply them in the committee situation, thereby handling that kind of situation more effectively. In this and other ways, hypnosis can help us to gain more control over our psychophysiological processes, and reduce the effects of stressful situations.

As we learn to take psychological responses from some situations and use them in others, as we learn to gain greater control over our psychophysiological responses, so we become freer to explore new kinds of behaviour, to exercise more choice in what we do—perhaps, for example, to seek out new responsibilities that involve meetings, presentations and committees instead of avoiding such situations because of the unpleasant reactions we used to experience.

'Previously outside his or her area of voluntary control'. The person who feels nauseous or tense when boarding a plane, or suffers headaches before important meetings, suffers backache on particularly gruelling days, has difficulty sleeping well, or often feels 'under the weather'—such a person experiences these things as 'outside voluntary control'. Less obviously, the person who smokes, over-eats, habitually 'feels like a drink' when getting home from the office, often gets into

arguments at home or in the office, or engages in any of many other 'voluntary' behaviours may actually find it rather difficult to change simply by an act of 'will'. The smoker, for example, may not consider himself or herself an addict and may regard the behaviour as under voluntary control—yet how many people can give up smoking once and for all, completely, simply by deciding to do so (an act of 'will')? Some do, of course, but most relapse. How many people can control their 'nerves' in stressful situations simply by telling themselves to be calm? Not many. Such feelings, such behaviours, are normally outside voluntary control. But they are amenable to a programme of training based on hypnosis.

Hypnosis can help in these and other ways to expand the area of behaviour and psychophysiological responses under our control, helping us to achieve more with less stress and to live healthier and more effective lives.

CONCLUSIONS

The manager of tomorrow will be able to off-load much of his or her more routine work to automated systems, and concentrate on dealing directly with people. These extra contacts will put more demands on the manager of tomorrow and (s)he will need more formal training in and greater understanding of interpersonal skills, group processes, personality, motivational structure, and related topics. The manager of tomorrow will also need a better understanding of his or her own personality and motivational characteristics in order to work effectively in the new environment created by the impacts of new technology. Above all, the manager of tomorrow will need training in how to cope effectively with the greater stresses that will be characteristic of the new environment, to survive and enjoy life in the 1980s and beyond.

PART 6
Conclusions

Chapter 17

Conclusions

We are standing at the threshold of a new era in the evolution of human society. We do not know precisely what the future holds for us but we know we have some influence over it. We are like babes about to take our first steps. Some of us will be more successful than others. A long journey lies ahead. We shall see many new developments. We shall learn what it really means to be able to handle information. We shall achieve new depths of knowledge, new levels of understanding. And we shall gain a new freedom: The freedom to move at will through the world of information.

Every journey must begin with a single step. To help us with our first steps we have one of the principal fruits of our 'industrial society': a primitive information technology, including systems such as:

- videotex—perhaps the most significant element, promising to bring electronic information into homes and offices around the world, linking everyone into a vast electronic network;
- word-processing systems—speeding up the creation of new items of information manyfold;
- scientific and technical information systems—handling vast amounts of information produced and used by scientists and engineers in many different contexts;
- computer conferencing systems—allowing for communication in the form of 'electronic meetings' between people who may be dispersed all around the world and yet be able to work together effectively as a team;
- personal computers—bringing electronic intelligence to the individual at home or in the office;
- integrated office systems—combining elements from the above with other systems;
- as well as a variety of related systems for the production, storage, retrieval, processing and communication of information.

This technology is primitive compared with what will be available by the close of the 1980s, but it will help us take that first important step into our future.

We do not know exactly what to expect. As Sarre and Blowers (1974) have said, the future does not exist and cannot be the object of observation, only of conjecture. But we can see indications of some likely impacts. There will be impacts on the office and some of these are likely to involve some dispersal of office functions. Some of the elements contributing to this may include the following.

Working from home. Electronic information systems will facilitate working from home, but most managers will still have to spend a significant proportion of their time away from home. This need not all be in a traditional office, however, but could be in a neighbourhood work centre or elsewhere.

Neighbourhood work centres. These might be operated as independent businesses, offering their services to whichever companies wish to use them. The centres would be somewhat similar to those companies today that offer a business address, an answering service, offices to rent on an hourly or daily basis, and various secretarial services.

They would be larger, however, and offer a wider range of services, with greater emphasis on electronic information and communications systems. Many of the routine, day to day meetings involving people in the same section or division of a company could be held in such centres, with the people involved having shorter commuting journeys than into the central city. Some travel between various centres would still be needed but computer-controlled communications networks could ensure that electronic memoranda, letters, reports, and other items would be switched automatically to the work unit currently being used by the person concerned to minimize unnecessary travel.

Community communications centres. A more speculative concept, these might evolve initially as a way for individual work centres to share particularly expensive facilities that are used relatively infrequently by individual people or their companies. These might include video telephone booths for individual tele-conversations requiring a visual channel, and perhaps a video conferencing studio for larger electronic meetings. Such centres would contain other kinds of units, as well, such as restaurants, collection points for remote shopping, and perhaps other facilities.

Developments along these lines, and the use of electronic information systems more generally, might be expected to facilitate a more flexible approach to the work day. There could be significant benefits for those who need or want to work only part time, e.g. to allow time to spend with children. There would be less strain on dual career families because of the reduction in commuting, and greater possibilities for job-sharing. And as the dispersal of office functions reduces commuting pressure, we can envisage an evolution of the central city towards a place where the emphasis is on culture, high-level meetings in business and government, scientific conferences, and other activities where face-to-face contacts, often involving relative strangers, are especially important.

Other impacts of electronic information systems are likely to include improvements in:

- the democratic process, by allowing and encouraging a greater participation in politics;
- education, especially in promoting the development of high-level information handling and problem-solving skills;
- health care, especially by freeing medical practitioners of some of their time-consuming administrative chores, and providing improved informational support to those who have to deal with emergencies;
- international communications, by promoting the sharing of information in such areas as agriculture and energy conservation.

Many of these possibilities are speculative but they illustrate how electronic systems can be expected to have impacts in all areas of our lives and at all levels—society, individual organizations, and individual people. The pattern that actually emerges will depend upon the roles the systems are allowed to play. Government will have a part to play in this, for example, by promoting the use of certain kinds of technology.

We can all point to high-rise apartment buildings, cars, and other examples where greater understanding and more careful analysis might have helped us to achieve something better. What must we be careful of in relation to information systems? Invasion of privacy? unemployment? violence on the streets? occupational stress? We have not given specific, detailed consideration to these questions, or others that might be raised. They would need a book just to themselves. We have focussed instead on the fundamental principles involved in the use of information systems by individuals and organizations—the psychology of information systems, which is essential if plans in the information area are to be based firmly on adequate knowledge and understanding.

BASIC CONCEPTS

The psychologist often uses the term 'information' without feeling any need to describe the type of information involved in much if any detail. It is necessary, however, to describe the variety of information when considering information systems. In this context, the qualitative differences between different items of information are often as important as the amounts of information involved. We have been concerned to describe the variety of information at a 'macro' level, i.e. at a level of generality corresponding roughly to the definition of items of information as individual documents, pages of text, paragraphs, books, floppy discs, and so forth. Relatively little research has been done on the empirical structure of information at this conceptual level and we have found it necessary to take a pragmatic approach, describing items of information in terms of their values on salient dimensions. We have identified four dimensions which seem likely to be especially important in most contexts. These are:

- relation to behaviour, both
  - general (relating to 'purpose')

- specific (relating to the psychological mechanisms involved);
- organizational penetration, especially in regard to
  - 'material' or 'input' information
  - 'system' or 'intra-unit' information
  - 'product' or 'output' information;
- item content, in particular
  - 'data'
  - 'basic information', and
  - 'meta-information'; and
- technological fit, where important distinctions include
  - numerical information
  - text
  - images, and
  - voice.

Description of items in terms of these and other salient dimensions can serve as a basis for assessing the value of the items in multidimensional terms.

The multidimensionality of value in regard to information is suggested by the variety of concepts that relate directly or indirectly to value in this context. These include:

- 'bits'
- relevance
- usefulness
- informativeness
- 'utility'
- 'bcu's' (binary choice units).

They all have something in their favour, and this supports the notion that 'value' is a multidimensional concept, i.e. items of information can be valuable in different ways. This multidimensionality can be related to the description of items in terms of their salient dimensions, and provides a practical basis for developing an 'information audit'. Such an audit has two main aspects: the value of information, assessed multidimensionally, in relation to its costs, and its value in relation to needs. Both of these aspects need to be considered in developing plans, perhaps involving the use of electronic systems, to improve the effectiveness of information management in an organization.

The electronic systems that in varying degrees are likely to contribute to effective information management in organizations during and beyond the 1980s include the following.

Videotex. This is a family of electronic systems for storing large quantities of information in 'page' form in computers to be displayed on television screens, with communication being 'interactive' (the user communicating with the computer) by means of telephone lines.

Prestel is the best-known example, being a British Telecom service based on the British viewdata system. France, Japan, Canada and other countries are developing systems of this general type. Videotex is likely to grow rapidly during the 1980s to provide more information to more people more quickly and more conveniently than ever before in the history of the human species. If it is marketed successfully, we can reasonably expect its impact both in the home and the office to be as great as that of the printing press or, more recently, radio and television.

Traditional STI systems. Computers containing large quantities of information, especially scientific and technical information (STI), have been around for many years. Traditional STI systems are more flexible than videotex but require more training to use and are more suited for use by specialists. Information is not usually displayed in 'page' form but in other forms such as long lists (e.g. of bibliographic references, or abstracts from journal articles). STI systems are often linked into international networks. Euronet is a prime example in Europe.

Microform. Some organizations are using automated systems based on microfiche or microfilm. A complete journal article can be held on a microfiche just a quarter of the size of an A4 sheet. In some systems, the microfiches can be produced directly by computer and accessed using computerized search procedures typical of STI systems.

Word processing. Word processing (sometimes called text processing) in its simplest forms can be thought of as computerized typewriting. The 'power typing' features of these systems (e.g. automatic closing of spaces following deletion of parts of the text) has led to their being used often for highly repetitive typing, such as standard letters that need to be personalized. Advanced word-processing systems are beginning to appear and will become more common during the 1980s, especially in medium and large organizations. The key difference between these systems and the simpler systems is the much greater intelligence in the advanced systems. The emphasis in these systems is very much on electronic information, and the distribution and on-line storage of information is at least as important in these systems as the 'power typing' facilities.

Computer conferencing. Computer conferencing seems likely to have less impact than some of the other types of systems but is interesting as a bridge between 'information' and 'communication'. These systems allow groups of people to join in on-line 'conferences' by typing what they want to say into the computer. The computer stores these messages in an organized form capable of being printed out as a record of what has been said to date, at the convenience of the user. Various special features are available, such as private messages to selected participants, use of questionnaires, and others.

Personal computers. These are microcomputers in the home or in one's own office that provide 'local intelligence'. For example, Prestel pages can be taken off the public service, stored in one's personal computer and manipulated at will. Personal computers can be used for many other applications, such as word processing or being used in networks to provide computer conferencing.

As these types of systems become more widespread, so it is likely that flexible links between them will emerge. More information will become more readily available, and more of it will be electronic. The question arises as to how the performance of systems in a network such as might evolve can be properly evaluated.

One approach to system evaluation is to relate performance to the main stages of the 'information cycle': The production, storage, retrieval, use (processing) and communication of information. A variety of specific indices of performance have been proposed that relate to one or other of these stages of the cycle, and it is clear that different types of systems vary in terms of these—simple word processors, for example, are strong on 'power typing' (production of information) whereas computer conferencing systems are stronger on communication.

It is not sufficient to consider the performance of systems taken in isolation. It is also necessary to understand the part they play in the functioning of an organization. In this regard, we can see that electronic systems will have impacts on the information taken in by an organization, on information outputs, and on all the stages in between.

An organization can be viewed as a complex network of 'sources', 'stores', 'sinks' and 'channels of communication', where these roles are played by different system components at different times and the network as a whole is in a constant state of flux. This, however, is very much a surface view of organizations. The psychologist, and the successful manager of tomorrow, needs to take account of what is going on at various levels below the surface. Seven main levels can be discerned, as follows:

- specific items of information: The outermost layer, comprising the main 'stimuli' and 'responses' of behaviour in organizations;
- information systems: The electronic or manual systems used in the production, storage, retrieval, use (processing) and communication of items of information;
- specific attitudes: attitudes toward specific objects or acts, e.g. using communicating word processors rather than the mail to send reports from one place to another;
- general attitudes: attitudes having a more general bearing on behaviour, e.g. attitudes toward automation, toward management, toward the unions, toward human factors, and so forth;
- personality: relatively stable differences between the people involved in terms of their style of behaviour in relation to dimensions which are measurable using suitable psychological techniques such as the 16PF self-report questionnaire;
- sentiments and ergs: relatively stable differences between the people involved

in terms of broad areas of 'needs' or 'drives' which are measurable using suitable psychological techniques such as the motivation analysis test (MAT).

Recognizing that these various levels are involved, we can see that different people or different parts of an organization can be in relative conflict or harmony at any or all levels.

For example, different parts of an organization may use similar systems but have different attitudes toward them (reflecting the personalities and needs of those involved as well as other factors) and use them in ways that are mutually incompatible. Or a sophisticated word-processing system may be installed throughout an organization but attitudes are such that individual managers are not given or do not accept personal computers or other suitable terminals so everything has to be printed out—thus losing one of the most significant potential benefits of such a system.

In terms of this model, there is a great variety at the surface (in relation to particular items of information) but the deeper one goes (e.g. towards personality dimensions, sentiments and ergs) the more similar the people involved become.

BEHAVIOUR

The use of electronic or manual systems involving a 'store' of information of some sort can be called 'Type B communication', to distinguish it from 'Type A' (direct person-to-person or group-to-group communication as in a telephone conversation or a meeting). The theoretical significance of Type B communication in organizations is reflected in the amount of time spent on it. There is considerable variability between different organizations and the difficulty in attaching precise figures is further complicated by the different category systems which have been used in the various studies conducted, and an apparent tendency for questionnaire respondents to overestimate the amount of time spent on Type B communication relative to Type A. In broad terms, managers seem to spend something of the order of 30–40 per cent of their time on Type B communication and some other office workers, including secretaries, may spend more than twice that amount. Type B communication therefore is a significant aspect of behaviour in the office environment.

If we look below the 'surface structure' of office activities—the division of time into convenient, non-overlapping categories (e.g. telephone calls, meetings, dealing with correspondence, etc.), we can see a more complex 'deep structure'. We can see the way in which specific office activities are related to one another in the normal course of events, i.e. which activities 'go with' which others. This general notion of a 'deep structure' to office activities assumes that specific, observable office activities derive their psychological meaning from more basic needs or processes. A telephone call, for example, may reflect a need to communicate. But how many psychologically-distinguishable communication needs do we have to take account of to 'explain' the wide variety of specific behaviour we can observe in the office environment—behaviour such as persuading, giving advice, writing memoranda, filing personal notes, using a library, and so forth?

Relatively little work has been done on the 'deep structure' of office activities. In a study conducted in the offices of the Commission of the European Communities in Brussels, the 'deep structure' of officials' office activities could be described in terms of ten main dimensions, as follows:

- dealing directly with people;
- providing information;
- clerical activities;
- teleconferencing;
- reading and evaluation;
- filling in forms;
- using document centres;
- using information (local);
- using information (remote);
- other activities.

These dimensions suggest there is no clear distinction between Type A and Type B communication at this level, but the dimensions do differ in their emphasis on these two types of communication. Some (eg. teleconferencing) emphasize Type A, others (eg. filling in forms) emphasize Type B, and others (eg. providing information) are clearly a mixture.

The dimensions above reflect the structure of the officials' responses to a wide range of questionnaire items. Many of the items may not be appropriate in other organizations but the broad structure indicated above may well generalize to other organizations to some extent. This is especially true of the second-order factors derived from the study, representing even broader dimensions. Two of these stand out especially as warranting attention in future research:

- 'person-oriented activities', where the emphasis is on Type A communication; and
- 'use of information', where the emphasis is on Type B communication.

The 'use of information' dimension is particularly interesting in relation to the work we have discussed on the use and origination of information in different circumstances (e.g. when on the telephone, at a meeting, and so on). This work suggests that people in the office environment may differ quite consistently in regard to their use and origination of information. Whilst individual patterns can be described the consistencies are sufficiently high as to suggest the possibility of a first law of information behaviour, analogous to the first laws of intelligence and attitude. This law would be:

'If any two items are selected from the universe of information behaviour items, and if the population observed is not selected artificially, then the population regressions between these two items will be monotone and with positive or zero sign.'

In relation to this hypothesis,

> 'An item belongs to the universe of information behaviour items if and only if its domain asks about the frequency of reference to or origination of items of information in relation to face-to-face communication, telephone communication, written communication, other communication, or other behaviour, and its range is ordered from very infrequent to very frequent.'

It is for fellow researchers to test the generalizability of this hypothesis and to establish more clearly the conditions under which it holds.

The close association between the use and origination of items of information supports the view that people are not passive in regard to information. The human in an information system can be regarded as a 'sink' into which information flows, but the sink is active in many ways, especially in:

- selecting sources;
- coding inputs;
- evaluating information (as coded);
- selecting overt behavioural responses (and so the amount of information transmitted).

The responses selected can be thought of as mapping out a route through a 'behaviour tree', the route being dependent upon the information received and the way it is processed.

In moving through his or her behaviour tree a person has five main classes of options available:

- to wait;
- to act;
- to generate information;
- to seek information;
- to opt out of the situation.

In some situations, especially command and control, these options can be reduced to just two main options:

- to seek further information;
- to take terminal action.

Information seeking is important in a variety of contexts and the particular form it takes depends on the interactions between many different factors. The studies we have reviewed illustrate the range of methods that have been used to map out some of the complexity involved. They show that this type of behaviour can be studied systematically. Much further analysis is needed and it is to be hoped that researchers will take up the challenge. As we move into the 'information society' of the 1980s and beyond, this surely must be an area where psychologists could contribute a great deal to the scientific description and understanding of human behaviour in an information-oriented environment.

ATTITUDES

Attitudes are of vital importance in shaping the influence of new technology. In view of this it is surprising that relatively little scientific research has been done on attitudes toward the electronic technology that promises to have such an impact on our lives. What research has been done suggests that two factors in particular need special attention in considering managers' attitudes toward the general concept of the 'office of tomorrow'. These are:

- general evaluation;
- social presence.

The 'general evaluation' factor is self-explanatory, representing a general attitude 'for or against' the office of tomorrow in terms of how generally 'good' or 'bad' it is seen to be. This evaluation is dependent on a number of factors of which the 'social presence' factor seems to be especially important. Social presence is also useful as a functionally independent index of attitude in this context. Some managers, for example, may hold a fairly positive view of the office of tomorrow (perhaps because they value the 'efficiency' it promises) despite seeing it as low on social presence.

Social presence is conceived of as a single dimension representing a cognitive synthesis of a variety of more specific factors as they are perceived by the person concerned to be present in the situation.

The capacity to transmit information about facial expression, direction of looking, posture, dress and non-verbal cues, all contribute to the social presence of a communications medium, and related factors probably contribute to judgements of the 'social presence' of the 'office of tomorrow', e.g. how 'personal' or 'impersonal', and how 'warm' or 'cold' it is felt to be. How the various factors involved are weighted is determined by the person concerned, because social presence is an attitudinal dimension of the person, a 'mental set' towards the situation.

The manager of tomorrow will need to consider ways of creating an 'office of tomorrow' that is high on social presence, i.e. 'warm' and with that 'personal' touch, whilst retaining the efficiency and related benefits of advanced electronic systems.

General evaluation and social presence are also among the factors that need to be considered in assessing attitudes toward particular information systems. Others include:

- flexibility;
- maintenance;
- comprehensiveness;
- spaciousness;
- humanness;
- speed of response;
- aesthetic appeal;
- simplicity;
- security.

Of these factors the 'humanness' factor—conceptually related to 'social presence' but distinguishable empirically—seems to be especially important in predicting the extent to which a system will be used.

Analysis of the main dimensions along which attitudes vary needs to be complemented by an experimental approach concerned with assessing the relative importance of various design features, e.g. colour compared with monochrome displays, in influencing attitudes toward systems.

The various elements needed to describe attitudes toward information systems, and their relationship to behaviour, can be brought together in a hierarchical model of attitude that encompasses the key concepts in expectancy-value theory. According to this model, specific system features (e.g. colour display) affect global factors (such as 'aesthetic appeal', 'social presence', and so on) which in turn influence a person's general evaluation of the system concerned. This combined with other factors influences attitude toward a particular behaviour (e.g. using the system in a particular context). It is this element, together with 'normative belief' about the act in question, that determines the person's 'behavioural intention', which is as near as the model can get to actual behaviour. It is clear that specific design features, whilst important, are only one element in a long chain influencing behaviour in regard to a system.

MANAGING CHANGE

Many factors need to be taken into account in order to forecast the rate and extent of change so that appropriate inputs can be made to planning processes at the organizational and national levels. We need to distinguish between the 'substitution' and 'generation' effects of new systems, and their effects on 'specific' and 'diversive' activity. The distinction between acquisition and use is also important because systems will only be used if they are acquired, although acquisition does not guarantee use. The 'behaviour tree' and the 'demand and supply matrix' are helpful in understanding the factors involved in patterns of acquisition. This kind of analysis is only 'one side of the coin', however, aimed at identifying the factors we need to consider to forecast what is likely if we act as passive observers. We also need to consider what we can do actively to support and promote change in an effective way.

Most of the literature on organizational change that is significantly relevant to the introduction of new technology or to information systems in particular can be classified very roughly into three groups, concerned with:

- documentation of significant events and processes in particular instances where technology has been introduced ('case studies').
- techniques of 'organizational development';
- the effects of new technology;

All of these are of some value but they all have limitations. The studies of effects are of interest to organizational theorists and may also have some value to organizations in helping them to evaluate likely impacts of new systems without actually having to implement them to find out. What this approach does not do very well is help the manager concerned with introducing new technology to go about doing so in the most effective way possible, or provide much guidance to the researcher concerned with the factors involved in the successful implementation of new systems. The strength of the 'organizational development' ('OD') approach lies in the way it translates general principles of organizational psychology into specific techniques that provide the manager with useful tools in regard to organizational-change programmes. However, OD seems to be more often used in relation to general shifts in the style of organizational communication than with the introduction of new systems. The generality of the approach means that it needs to be complemented by the more specific kind of information provided by studies of effects and by case studies. Case studies specifically concerned with the introduction of new information systems are a valuable source of hypotheses, 'rules of thumb', and 'things to watch out for'. These need to be interpreted within a framework of general theoretical principles, especially relating to:

- sources of resistance to change;
- a socio-technical approach to fitting the technical aspects of systems to the needs and abilities of the people involved;
- expectancy-value theory, which helps to identify specific areas where differences in attitude and behaviour can arise;
- the conflict-harmony model (derived from the 'information sphere'), which goes beyond expectancy-value theory to provide a very general framework for understanding the various sorts of conflicts that can arise in an organization, as when setting up a new information system.

Key guidelines which can be drawn from the empirical studies and theoretical context include the following:

- ensure commitment at the highest level in the organization at the very start;
- ensure adequate financial and administrative support;
- involve all key parties at the earliest possible stage;
- maximize awareness;
- monitor and evaluate the system's impacts;
- attend to 'global' system factors;
- attend to specific system features;
- attend to the needs of different user groups.

These 'organizational' factors are only half the story; it is also necessary to consider more personal factors, especially relating to:

- skills;
- personality;
- motivational structure;

- ability to cope with stress.

The extra time made available by electronic systems taking the burden of routine information handling of all sorts will mean the manager of tomorrow will be able to spend more time with people and less with pieces of paper or their electronic equivalents. The successful manager of tomorrow will need to have better and more formal training in how to work effectively with people, including such areas as:

- interpersonal skills;
- group processes;
- personality;
- motivational structure;
- and many related topics.

As well as appropriate skills in dealing effectively with people, the manager of tomorrow will need some personality traits that may not have been so important before, and a better understanding of himself or herself so as to be able to use his or her own personality characteristics to full advantage. No single pattern of traits should be regarded as 'correct' or 'ideal' but, as a general picture, we can say the successful manager of tomorrow will tend to be:

- somewhat 'affectothymic' (being more oriented toward people than things);
- high on 'ego strength' (being able to accommodate to the realities of the world and withstand everyday stresses);
- 'parmic' rather than 'threctic' (being relatively bold, feeling free to participate, and being able to face threatening situations coolly);
- shrewd (being able to 'study the angles' and get to the root of a problem quickly);
- high on 'self-sentiment' (being concerned with self-control, persistence and some other qualities often associated with success in organizational activities);
- open to experimentation (being well-informed and willing to experiment with new possibilities).

Complementing a pattern of temperament traits fitting the manager well to the demands of the office of tomorrow, (s)he will also have a motivational structure reflecting the new environment, and insight about what this is. This is a complex area and there is no single pattern that is 'right' to the exclusion of all others, but the successful manager of tomorrow will show a balance in regard to 'career sentiment', 'self sentiment', 'assertion', 'pugnacity', and other 'dynamic factors'.

Above all, the manager of tomorrow will need training in how to cope effectively with the stresses of the new environment. Such training will benefit all concerned, including:

- the individual, e.g. by reducing the probability of illness or an early death;
- The organization, e.g. by improving productivity;
- the country, e.g. by improving productivity and fostering conditions in which people can enjoy life more.

Various psychological techniques are available which can help people to learn how to deal with stress more effectively. These need to be complemented by a programme designed to reduce the sources of stress as much as possible consistent with achieving agreed personal, organizational and national goals.

A psychological technique in which there is a resurgence of professional interest is hypnosis. The establishment of the professional British Society of Experimental and Clinical Hypnosis as well as efforts by lay hypnotherapists to get their own house in order are evidence of a scientific, professional, serious approach to the subject. It seems likely that this technique will have much to offer the manager of tomorrow in aiding in the control of personal stress, enhancing personal effectiveness and helping the successful manager to survive and enjoy life in the 1980s and beyond.

REFERENCES

Abrams, M.E. (1975)
Problems of computing in general practice. In J. Rose and H.J. Mitchell (eds). *Advances in Medical Computing*. London: Churchill Livingstone.

Aiken, M. and Hage, J. (1971)
The organic organization and innovation. *Sociology*, **5**, 63–82.

Alderfer, C.P. (1976)
Change processes in organizations. In M.D. Dunette (ed.) *Handbook of Industrial and Organizational Psychology*. Chicago: Rand McNally.

Allen, T.J. and Cohen, S. (1969)
Information flow in research and development laboratories. *Administrative Science Quarterly*, **14**, 12–19.

Allport, G.W., and Odbert, H.S. (1936)
Trait-names: a psycho-lexical study. *Psychological Monographs*, **47**, 171.

Anderla, G. (1973)
The future of information: a challenge for governments and society. *The OECD Observer*, No. 63, 27–32.

Anon (1976)
Business Equipment and Systems Global Market Survey. U.S. Department of Commerce.

Anon (1978)
Seminar on Viewdata Classification and Information Accessing. Cambridge, 11 January, 1978. British telecom unpublished manuscript.

Argyle, M., and Dean, J. (1965)
Eye Contact, Distance and Affiliation. *Sociometry*, **28**, 289–304.

Arms, W.Y., and Arms, C.R. (1978)
Cluster analysis used on social science journal citations. *Journal of Documentation*, **34**(1), 1–11.

Ashby, W.R. (1956)
Introduction to Cybernetics. London: Methuen.

Baird, J.E., Jr. (1977)
The Dynamics of Organizational Communication. London: Harper and Row.

Baker, J.D. (1970)
Quantitative modelling of human performance in information systems. *Ergonomics*, **13**(b), 645–664.

Barnlund, D.C. 1968)
Introduction. In D.C. Barnlund (ed.) *Interpersonal Communication: Survey and Studies*. New York: Houghton Mifflin, pp. 3–14.

Barron, I., and Curnow, R.C. (1978)
The Future of Information Technology. Report CSE(78)3, Department of Industry (computers, Systems and Electronics Requirements Board).

Bass, A.Z. (1969)
Refining the 'gatekeeper' concept: a UN radio case study. *Journalism Quarterly*, **46**, 69–72.

Becker, G.M. (1958)
Sequential decision-making: Wald's model and estimates of parameters. *Journal of Experimental Psychology*, **55**, 628–639.

281

282

Belkin, N.J. (1977)
A Concept of Information for Information Science. Ph.D. Thesis, University of London.
Belkin, N.J. (1978)
Information concepts for information science. *Journal of Documentation,* **34**(1), 55–58.
Belkin, N.J. and Robertson, S.E. (1976)
Information science and the phenomenon of information. *Journal of the ASIS,* **27,** 197–204.
Bell, D. (1973)
The Coming of Post-industrial Society: A Venture in Social Forecasting. New York: Basic Books.
Berlyne, D.E. (1960)
Conflict, Arousal and Curiosity. New York: McGraw-Hill.
Bertalanffy, L.V. (1968)
General Systems Theory. New York: George Braziller.
Bettman, J.R. and Jacoby, J. (1975)
Patterns of Processing in Consumer Information Acquisition. Paper No. 31, Working Papers Series, Center for Marketing Studies, University of California, Los Angeles.
Blau, P.M. and Scott, W.R. (1963)
Paul.
Blum, M.L. and Naylor, J.C. (1968)
Industrial Psychology: Theoretical and Social Foundations. London: Harper and Row.
Blythe, P. (1973)
Stress Disease: The Growing Plague. London: Arthur Barker.
Bonini, C.P. (1964)
Simulation or Organizational Behaviour. In C. Bonini, R. Jaedicke, and H. Wagner (eds.) *Management Controls; New Directions in Basic Research.* New York: McGraw-Hill, 1964.
Borden, G.A. and Nelson W. (1969)
Toward a viable classification scheme: some theoretical considerations. *American Documentation,* **20**(4).
Borman, L. and Mittman, B. (1972)
Interactive search of bibliographic data bases in an academic environment. *Journal of the American Society for Information Science,* May–June, 164–171.
Brookes, B.C. (1968)
The measures of information retrieval effectiveness proposed by Swets. *Journal of Documentation,* **24,** 41–54.
Bucklin, L.P. (1966)
Testing Propensities to Shop. *Journal of Marketing,* **30,** 22–27.
Burns, T. (1957)
Management in Action. *Operational Research Quarterly,* **8**(2), 45–61.
Burns, T. and Stalker, G. (1961)
The Management of Innovation. London: Tavistock.
Bush, G. (1977)
Viewdata: Design of Structure of Post Office Routing Pages. Interim Report. Unpublished British Telecom report, TSS6.2.
Bush, G. and Williams, E. (1978)
Viewdata: The Systematic Development and Testing of Post Office Routing Trees. Unpublished manuscript, February 28, 1978: British Telecom.

Campbell, J.P., Bownas, D.E., Peterson, J.G., and Dunnette, M.D. (eds) (1974)
The Measurement of Organisational Effectiveness: A Review of Relevant Research and Opinion. San Diego: Navy Personnel Research and Development Center.

Carlson, S. (1951)
Executive Behaviour. London: Stromberg.

Cattell, R.B. (1965)
The Scientific Analysis of Personality. Harmondsworth, Middlesex: Penguin.

Cattell, R.B., Eber, H.W., and Tatsuoka, M.M. (1970)
Handbook for the Sixteen Personality Factor Questionnaire (16PF). Champaign, Illinois: Institute for Personality and Ability Testing.

Cawkell, A.E. (1978)
The paperless revolution—2. *Wireless World*, August, 69–74.

Champness, B.G. (1973)
The Assessment of User Reactions to Confravision: II Analysis and Conclusions. Unpublished Communications Studies Group paper No. E/73250/CH. British Telecom, 88 Hills Road, Cambridge, England.

Chapanis, A. (1971)
26(11), 949–961.

Chapanis, A. (1976)
Engineering Psychology. In: M.D. Dunnette (ed.) *Handbook of Industrial and Organizational Psychology.* Chicago: Rand McNally, pp. 697–744.

Cherry, C. (1978)
World Communications: Threat or Promise? A Socio-technical Approach. London: John Wiley.

Christie, B. (1979)
Face to File Communication: Psychological aspects of electronic information systems. Report for the Departments of Environment and Transport (File Reference DGR 489/10).

Christie, B., Delafield, G., Lucas, B., Winwood, M., and Gale, A. (1972)
Stimulus complexity and the EEG: differential effects of the number and the variety of display elements. *Canadian Journal of Psychology*, **26**(2), 155–170.

Christie, B. and Elton, M. (1979)
Research on the differences between face-to-face communications and telecommunication, Chapter 3 in R. Smith (ed.). *Impacts of Telecommunications on Planning and Transport.* London: Department of The Environment and Department of Transport, Research Report No. 24, 1979, pp. 55–84.

Christie, B. and Kingan, S. (1977)
pational Psychology, **50**, 265–273.

Conway, D. *et al.* (1974)
Information generation. In A. Debons (ed.) *Information Science: Search for Identity.* New York: Marcel Dekker, pp. 385–397.

Cook, K.H. (1970)
An experimental on-line system for psychological abstracts. P Vol. *33rd Annual Meeting of American Society for Information Science*, **7**, 111–114.

Cooper, C.L. (1980)
Work stress in white- and blue-collar jobs. *Bulletin of the British Psychological Society*, **33**, 49–51.

Cooper, C.L., and Payne, R. (eds.) (1978)
Stress at Work. Chichester: John Wiley.

Copeman, G., Liujk, H., and Hanika, F. de P. (1963)
How the Executive Spends his Time. London: London Business Publications.

Corcoran, D.W.J. (1971)
   Pattern Recognition. Harmondsworth, Middlesex: Penguin.
Cox, D.F. (ed.) (1967)
   Risk Taking and Information Handling in Consumer Behaviour. Boston: Div. Research, Graduate School Business Administration, Harvard University.
Cunningham, B. (1976)
   Action research: toward a procedural model. *Human Relations*, **29**(3), 215–238.
Dance, F.E.X. (1970)
   The 'concept' of communication. *Journal of Communication*, **20**, 201–210.
Dashiell, J. F. (1935)
   Experimental studies of the influence of social situations on the behaviour of individual human adults. In C. Murchison (ed.) *Handbook of Social Psychology*, Worcester, Massachusetts: Clark University Press.
Debons, A. and Montgomery, K.L. (1974)
   Design and evaluation of information systems. *Annual Review of Information Science and Technology*, **9**, 25–55.
Dirlam, D.K. (1972)
   Most efficient chunk sizes. *Cognitive Psychology*, **3**, 355–359.
Donington, J. (In preparation)
   The Automated Office. London: John Wiley.
Dordick, H.S. and Goldman, R.J. (1978)
   Social services and telecommunications: innovation in human services delivery. *Telecommunications Policy*, **2**(2), 137–145.
Dorfman, D.D. and McKenna, H. (1966)
   Pattern preference as a function of pattern uncertainty. *Canadian Journal of Psychology*, **20**, 143–153.
Douglas, A. (1957)
   The peaceful settlement of industrial and intergroup disputes. *Journal of Conflict Resolution*, **1**, 69–81.
Drucker, P.F. (1973)
   Rise of the knowledge worker. *Britannica Book of the Year*. Encyclopedia Britannica: Chicago, pp. 15–29.
Eason, K.D. (1976)
   Understanding the naive computer user. *The Computer Journal*, **19**(1), 3–7.
Edwards, E. and Lees, F. P. (1972)
   Man and Computer in Process Control. London: The Institution of Chemical Engineers.
Edwards, G.C. (1978)
   Organizational impacts of office automation. *Telecommunications Policy*, **2**(2), 128–136.
Edwards, W. and Slovic, P. (1965)
   Seeking information to reduce the risk of decisions. *American Journal of Psychology*, **78**, 188–197.
Ekehammer, B. and Magnusson, D. (1973)
   Decision time as a function of subjective confidence and amount of information. *Perceptual and Motor Skills*, **36**, 329–330.
Engel, G.H., Groppuso, J., Lowenstein, R.A., and Traub, W.G. (1979)
   An office communications system. *IBM System Journal*, *18*(3), 402–431.
Erickson, M.H., and Rossi, E.L. (1979)
   Hypnotherapy: An Exploratory Casebook. New York: Irvington Publishers, Inc. (John Wiley.)
Etzioni, A. (1972)
   Minerva: an electronic town hall. *Policy Sciences*, **3**, 457–474.

Eysenck, H.J. (1970)
The Structure of Human Personality. London: Metheun.
Eysenck, H.J. and Eysenck, S.B.G. (1975)
Manual of The Eysenck Personality Questionnaire. Sevenoaks, Kent: Hodder and Stoughton Educational.
Farrace, R.V., Monge, P.R., and Russell, H.M. (1977)
Communicating and Organizing. London: Addison-Wesley.
Farradane, J. (1976)
Towards a true information science. *Information Scientist*, **10**, 91–101.
Ference, T.P. (1970)
Organisational communication systems and the decision process. *Management Science*, **17**, 83–96.
Fishbein, M. and Ajzen, I. (1975)
Belief, Attitude, Intention and Behaviour: An Introduction to Theory and Research. Reading, Mass.: Addison-Wesley.
Fordyce, J.K. and Weil, R. (1979)
Managing with People: A Manager's Handbook of Organization Development Methods (2nd edn). Reading, Mass.: Addison-Wesley.
Fried, L.S. and Peterson, C.R. (1969)
Information seeking: optional versus fixed stopping. *Journal of Experimental Psychology*, **80**, 525–529.
Friedlander, F. and Pickle, H. (1968)
Components of effectiveness in small organisations. *Administrative Science Quarterly*, **13**, 289–304.
Frierson, E. and Atherton P. (1971)
Survey of attitudes towards SUPARS. Section IV-B-6 of final report on *Large Scale Information Processing Systems*. Syracuse University: School of Library Science, pp. 105–116.
Frost, P.A. and Whitley, R.D. (1971)
Communication Patterns in a Research Laboratory. *Journal of R&D Management*, **1**, 71–79.
Gale, A., Bramley, P., Lucas, B., and Christie, B. (1972)
Differential effect of visual and auditory complexity on the EEG: Negative hedonic value as a crucial variable? *Psychonomic Science*, **17**(1), 21–24.
Gale, A., Christie, B., and Penfold, V. (1971)
Stimulus Complexity and the Occipital EEG. *British Journal of Psychology*, **62**(4), 527–531.
Galer, I.A.R. (1976)
Projector Slides—Preparation, Construction and Use. *Applied Ergonomics*, **7**(4), 190–196.
Gibson, J.J. (1960)
The concept of the stimulus in psychology. *The American Psychologist*, **15**, 694–703.
Glover, J. (1974)
Long range social forecasts: working from home. *Long Range Intelligence Bulletin 2*. The Post Office.
Glover, J., Bush, G., Cleevely, D., and Young, I. (1975)
Long range social forecasts: attitudes to work. *Long Range Intelligence Bulletin 8*. The Post Office.
Goddard, J. and Pye, R. (1979)
Telecommunication and office location. In R. Smith (Ed.) *Impacts of Telecommunications on Planning and Transport*. London: Departments of The Environment and Transport, Research Report No. 24, 1979, pp. 169–226.

286

Gode, A. (1959)
    What is communication? *Journal of Communication*, **9**, 5.
Goldmark, P.C. (1973)
    The New Rural Society: Report from the Department of Communication Arts, Cornell University, Ithaca, New York. (Reference: Papers on Communication, No. 5.)
Gordon, F.E. (undated)
    Telecommunications: Implications for Women. Impact Paper 24, Graduate School of Business, Stanford University, Stanford, California.
Graney, M.J. (1975)
    Communication uses and the social activity constant. *Communication Research*, **2**(4), 347–366.
Green, M. (1967)
    Biology and the problem of levels of reality. *New Scholasticism*, **41**, 427–449.
Hardman, Sir H. (1973)
    The Dispersal of Government Work from London. London: Her Majesty's Stationery Office.
Harkness, R.C. (1978)
    Office information systems: an overview and agenda for public policy research. *Telecommunications Policy*, **2**, 91–105.
Harmon, G. (1970)
    Information need transformation during inquiry: a re-interpretation of user relevance. *Proceedings of the 33rd Annual Meeting of ASIS*, **7**, 41–43.
Harrary, F. and Schwenk, A.J. (1974)
    Efficiency of dissemination of information in one-way and two-way communication networks. *Behavioural Science*, **19**, 133–135.
Harrigan, J.E. (1974)
    Human factors information taxonomy: fundamental human factors applications for architectural programs. *Human Factors*, **16**(4), 432–440.
Harwood, B.T. (1973)
    Expressed preferences for information-seeking behaviours and their relationship to birth orders. *Journal of Genetic Psychology*, **123**(1), 123–131.
Heilbronn, M. and Libby, W.L. (1972)
    Comparative Effects of Technological and Social Immediacy upon Performance and Perceptions during a Two-person Game. Paper read at the Annual Convention of the American Psychological Association, Montreal.
Hilgard, E.R. and Bower, G.H. (1966)
    Theories of learning. New York: Appleton-Century-Crofts.
Hillman, D.J. (1973)
    Customized user services via interactions with LEADERMART. *Information Storage and Retrieval*, **9**, 587–596.
Hiltz, S.R. and Turoff, M. (1978)
    The Network Nation: Human Communication via Computer. London: Addison-Wesley.
Hoben, J.B. (1954)
    English communication at Colgate re-examined. *Journal of Communication*, **4**, 76–86.
Holland, W.E. (1972)
    Information potential: a concept of the importance of information sources in a research and development environment. *The Journal of Communication*, **22**, 159–173.
Howe, M.J.A. and Godfrey, J. (1977)
    Student Note Taking as an Aid to Learning. Exeter: Exeter University Teaching Services Centre. (ISBN 0 905314 02 6.)

Howell, W.C. (1966)
Task characteristics in sequential decision behaviour. *Journal of Experimental Psychology*, **71**, 124–131.
Hutchinson, T.P. (1978)
An extension of the signal detection model of information retrieval. *Journal of Documentation*, **34**(1), 51–54.
Irwin, F.W. and Smith, W.A.S. (1957)
Value, cost and information as determiners of decisions. *Journal of Experimental Psychology*, **54**, 229–232.
Janis, I.L. and Mann, L. (1977)
Decision Making: A Psychological Analysis of Conflict, Choice, and Commitment. London: Collier Macmillan.
Jarnecke, R.W. and Rudestam, K.E. (1976)
Effects of amounts of units of information on judgmental process. *Perceptual and Motor Skills*, **43**, 823–829.
Johansen, R., DeGrasse, R. Jr., and Wilson, T. (1978)
Group Communication Through Computers. Final report on grant APR 76-00412 from The National Science Foundation. Menlo Park, California: Institute for The Future (2470 Sand Hill Road).
Johansen, R., Vallee, J. and Spangler, K. (1979)
Electronic Meetings: Technical Alternatives and Social Choices. London: Addison-Wesley.
Kalthoff, R.J. (1976)
Document vs. data based information systems. *The Journal of Micrographics*, **19**(2), 79–88.
Katz, D. and Kahn, R.L. (1978)
The Social Psychology of Organisations (2nd edn). London: John Wiley.
Katzer, J. (1972)
The development of a semantic differential to assess users' attitudes towards an on-line interactive reference retrieval system. *Journal of The American Society for Information Science*, March/April, 122–127.
Kegan, D.L. (1970)
Measures of the usefulness of written technical information to chemical researchers. *Journal of The American Society for Information Science*, **21**(3), 179–186.
Kent, A. (1974)
Unsolvable problems. In A. Debons (ed.) *Information Science: Search for Identity.* New York: Marcel Dekker, pp. 299–311.
Klemmer, E.T. and Snyder, F.W. (1972)
Measurement of time spent communicating. *The Journal of Communication*, **22**, 142–158.
Lambert, Z.V. and Durand, R.M. (1977)
Purchase information acquisition and cognitive style. *The Journal of Psychology*, **97**, 3–13.
Lamond, F. (In preparation)
The Last Rush Hour. London: John Wiley.
Levine, J.M. (1973)
Information seeking with conflicting and irrelevant inputs. *Journal of Applied Psychology*, **57**(1), 74–80.
Levine, J.M. and Eldredge, D. (1972)
Effects of ancillary information upon photo-interpreter performance. *Human Factors*, **14**(6), 549–560.
Levine, J.M. and Samet, M.G. (1973)
Information seeking with multiple sources of conflicting and unreliable information. *Human Factors* **15**(4), 407–419.

Levine, J.M., Samet, M.G., and Brahlek, R.E. (1975)
Information seeking with limitations on available information and resources. *Human Factors*, **17**(5), 502–513.

Louviėre, J.J. and Norman, K.L. (1977)
Applications of information processing theory to the analysis of urban travel demand. *Environment and Behaviour*, **9**(1), 91–106.

Lowe, E.A. and Tinker, A.M. (1976)
The architecture of requisite variety: an empirical application of managerial cybernetics to the organization of socio-economic enterprises and their information for control systems (Part 2). *Kybernetes*, **5,** 197–207.

Lumsden, D.L. (1977)
An experimental study of source-message interaction in a personality impression Tast. *Communication Monographs*, **44,** 121–129.

McCormick, E.J. (1976)
Human Factors in Engineering and Design. New York: McGraw-Hill.

Machlup, F. (1972)
The production and distribution of knowledge in the united states. Princeton, New Jersey: Princeton University Press.

Mackay, D.M. (1960)
What makes a question? *The Listener*, **63,** 789–790.

McKendry, J.M., Enderwick, T.P. and Harrison, P.C. (1971)
A subjective value approach to information utility. *Human Factors*, **13**(6), 503–509.

March, J. and Simon, H. (1958)
Organizations. New York: Wiley.

Martyn, J. (1974)
Information needs and uses. In C.A. Cuadra, A.W. Luke, and J.L. Harris (eds.) *Annual Review of Information Science and Technology*, **9,** 3–23.

Mayes, J.T. (1977)
Information and memory. *The Information Scientist*, **11**(2), 65–73.

Mead, M. (1965)
The city as a point of confrontation. In *Transactions of the Bartlett Society, Vol. 3., 1964–65.* Bartlett School of Architecture, University College London, pp. 9–22.

Meadow, C.T. (1970)
Man-Machine Communication. New York: John Wiley.

Miller, G.A., Galanter, E., and Pribram, K. (1960)
Plans and the Structure of Behaviour. New York: Holt, Rinehart and Winston, 15–19.

Miller, R.B. (1969)
Archetype in Man-computer Problem Solving, IBM Systems Development Division, Poughkeepsie, New York.

Miller, S.J. and Zikmund, W.G. (1975)
A multivariate analysis of purchase deliveration and External search behaviour. In *Advances in Consumer Research*, **2.** Urbana, Illinois: Association for Consumer Research, 187–196.

Miron, M.S. (1969)
What is it that is being differentiated by the semantic differential? *Journal of Personality and Social Psychology*, **12,** 189–93.

Mitroff, I.I., Williams, J. and Rathswohl, E. (1972)
Dialectical inquiring systems: a new methodology for information science. *Journal of the American Society for Information Science*, Nov–Dec., 365–378.

Morley, I.E. and Stephenson, G.M. (1969)
Interpersonal and interparty exchange: a laboratory simulation of an industrial nego-
tiation at the plant level. *British Journal of Psychology*, **60**, 543–5.
Morley, I.E. and Stephenson, G.M. (1970)
Formality in experimental negotiations: a validation study. *British Journal of Psy-
chology*, **61**, 383.
Mumford, E. (1965a)
How the computer changes management. *New Society*, 23rd September.
Mumford, E. (1965b)
Clerks and computers: a study of the introduction of technical change. *The Journal
of Management Studies*, May, 138–152.
Murrell, H. (1978)
Work Stress and Mental Strain: A Review of Some of the Literature. Work Research
Unit Occasional Paper No. 6. London: Department of Employment.
Neisser, U. (1963)
Decision time without reaction time: experiments in visual scanning. *American Journal
of Psychology*, **76**, 376–385.
Neisser, U. (1967)
Cognitive Psychology. New York: Appleton-Century-Crofts.
Newell, A. and Simon, H.A. (1963)
GPS: A program that simulates human thought. In Feigenbaum and Feldman (eds.)
Computers and Thought. New York: McGraw-Hill, pp. 279–293.
Newman, J.W. and Staelin, R. (1972)
Prepurchase information seeking for new cars and major household appliances. *Journal
of Marketing Research*, **9**, 249–257.
Norman, K.L. (1977)
Attributes in bus transportation: importance depends on trip purpose. *Journal of Ap-
plied Psychology*, **62**(2), 164–170.
Noton, D. and Simon, H.A. (1970)
A theory of visual pattern perception. *IEEE Transactions on SSC*, **6**(4), 349–357.
Nystedt, L. (1974)
Consensus among judges as a function of amount of information. *Educational and
Psychological Measurement*, **34**, 91–101.
O'Keefe, R.D., Kernaghan, J.A., and Rubenstein, A.H. (1975)
Group cohesiveness: a factor in the adoption of innovations among scientific work
groups. *Small Group Behaviour*, **6**(3), 282–292.
Olsen, E.E. (1977)
Organizational factors affecting information flow in industry.
Aslib Proceedings, **29**(1), 2–11.
Osgood, C.E., Suci, G.J., and Tannenbaum, P.H. (1957)
The Measurement of Meaning. Urbana, Illinois: University of Illinois Press.
Otten, K.W. (1974)
Basis for a science of information. In A. Debons (ed.) *Information Science: Search
for Identity.* New York: Marcel Dekker, pp. 91–106.
Otten, K.W. (1975)
Information and communication: a conceptual model as framework for development
of theories of information. In A. Debons and W.J. Cameron (eds.) *Perspectives in In-
formation Science.* Leyden: Noordhof, pp. 127–148.
Palmer, A.W. and Beishon, R.J. (1970)
How the day goes. *Personnel Management*, 36–40.
Parker, E.G. (1976)
Social implications of computer/telecoms systems. *Telecommunications Policy*, **1**(1),
3–20.

Payne, J.W. (1976)
Task complexity and contingent processing in decision making: an information search and protocol analysis. *Organizational Behaviour and Human Performance*, **16**, 366–387.

Peace, D.M.S. and Easterby, R.S. (1973)
The evaluation of user interaction with computer-based management information systems. *Human Factors*, **15**(2), 163–177.

Pearson, A.W. (1973)
Fundamental problems of information transfer. *Aslib Proceedings*, **25**(11), 415–423.

Pelz, D. and Andrews, F.M. (1966)
Scientists in Organizations. New York: John Wiley.

Pitz, G.F. (1968)
Information seeking when available information is limited.
Journal of Experimental Psychology, **76**, 34–75.

Pitz, G.F. (1969)
Use of response times to evaluate information seeking. *Journal of Experimental Psychology*, **80**, 553–557.

Pitz, G.F. and Reinhold, H. (1968)
Payoff effects in sequential decision making. *Journal of Experimental Psychology*, **77**, 249–259.

Pratt, A.D. (1977)
The information of the image. *Libri*, **27**, 204–220.

Pye, R. (1976)
Effect of telecommunications on the location of office employment. *OMEGA, The Journal of Management Science*, **4**(3), 289–300.

Rapoport, A. and Tversky, A. (1966)
Cost and accessibility of offers as determinants of optional stopping. *Psychonanic Science*, **4**, 145–146.

Ravensborg, M.R. (1970)
Empirical validation of automated nursing notes: informational utility. *Psychological Reports*, **26**, 279–282.

Reid, A.A.L. (1971)
The Telecommunications Impact Model. Communications Studies Group Paper No. P/71161/RD. British Telecom, 88 Hills Road, Cambridge, England.

Roberts, I.H., O'Reilly, C.A. III, Bretton, G.E., and Porter, L.W. (1974)
Organizational theory and organizational communication: a communication failure? *Human Relations*, **27**(5), 501–524.

Roberts, N. (1977)
Then what is information science? Is it really a science? Critique of the criteria. *Library Association Record* **79**(10), 556–557.

Robertson, A. (1975)
The effects on an organization of communication with the outside world: The relationship between free flow of information and an organization's effectiveness. *Aslib Proceedings*, **27**(8), 339–345.

Robertson, S.E. (1975)
A Theoretical Model of the Retrieval Characteristics of Information Retrieval Systems. Ph.D. Thesis, University of London.

Robertson, S.E. (1977)
Theories and models in information retrieval. *Journal of Documentation*, **33**(2), 126–148.

Rosenberg, V. (1967)
Factors affecting the preferences of industrial personnel for information gathering methods. *Information Storage and Retrieval*, **3**(3), 119–127.
Rowe, R.G. (1975)
Hospital activity analysis—the health service information base-line. In J. Rose and J.H. Mitchell (eds). *Advances in Medical Computing*. London: Churchill Livingstone, 1975, pp. 158–172.
Salton, G. (1969)
A comparison between manual and automatic indexing methods. *American Documentation*, **20**(1), 61–71.
Salton, G. (unpublished)
Mathematics and information retrieval. Unpublished paper referred to in N.J. Belkin (1978) information concepts for information science. *Journal of Documentation*, **34**(1), 55–85.
Sarre, P. and Blowers, A. (1974)
General Introduction In A. Blowers, C. Hamnett, and P. Sarre (eds), *The Future of Cities*. London: Hutchinson, pp. 1–5.
Sashkin, M., Morris, W.C., and Horst, L. (1973)
A comparison of social and organizational change models: information flow and data use processes. *Psychological Review*, **80**(b), 510–526.
Schreider, Iu.A. (1965)
On the semantic characteristics of information. *Information Storage and Retrieval*, **3**, 221–233.
Schreider, Iu.A. (1969)
Semantic aspects of information theory. In *Theoretical Problems of Informatics*. (FID 435). Moscow: VINITI, 143–164.
Seashore, S.E., Inoik, B.P., and Georgopoulos, G.S. (1960)
Relationships among criteria of job performance. *Journal of Applied Psychology*, **44**, 195–202.
Shannon, C.E. (1948)
A mathematical theory of communication. *Bell System Technical Journal*, **27**, 379–423, 623, 656.
Short, J., Williams, E., and Christie B. (1976)
The Social Psychology of Telecommunications. London: John Wiley.
Shye, S. (1978)
On the search of laws in the behavioural sciences. In S. Shye (ed). *Theory Construction and Data Analysis in the Behavioural Sciences*. London: Jossey-Bass, pp. 2–24.
Sime, M.E., Arblaster, A.T., and Green, T.R.G. (1977)
Structuring the programmer's task. *Journal of Occupational Psychology*, **50**, 205–216.
Singleton, W.T. (1974)
Man-Machine Systems. London: Penguin.
Sletten, I.W. and Ulett, G.A. (1972)
The Present Status of Automation in a State Psychiatric System. *Psychiatric Annals*, **2**(12), 42–57.
Smith, E.I. (1973)
The employment and functioning of the homebound disabled in information technology. *The American Journal of Occupational Therapy*, **27**(5) 232–238.
Smith, P.C. (1976)
Behaviours, results, and organizational effectiveness: the problem of criteria. In M.D. Dunnette (ed.) *Handbook of Industrial and Organizational Psychology*. Chicago: Rand McNally, pp. 745–775.

Smith, R. (1979)
    Telecommunications technology: current trends. Chapter 1 in R. Smith (ed). *Impacts of Telecommunications on Planning and Transport*. Department of the Environment and Department of Transport, 1979.
Stamper, R. (1973)
    Information in Business and Administrative Systems. London: Batsford.
Steers, R.M. (1975)
    Problems in the management of organisational effectiveness. *Administrative Science Quarterly*, **20**, 546–558.
Stewart, R. (1976)
    To understand the manager's job: consider demands, constraints, choices. *Organisational Dynamics*, **4**(4), 22–32.
Streufert, S.C. (1973)
    Effects of information relevance on decision making in complex environments. *Memory and Cognition*, **1**(3), 224–228.
Swanson, R.W. (1975)
    Design and Evaluation of Information Systems. In C.A. Cuadra, A.W. Lunk, J.L. Harris (eds.) *Annual Review of Information Science and Technology*, Vol. 10, Chapter 2, pp. 43–104.
Sweney, A.B. (1969)
    A Preliminary Descriptive Manual for Individual Assessment with the motivation Analysis Test. Champaign, Illinois: Institute for Personality and Ability Testing.
Swets, J.A. (1963)
    Information retrieval systems. *Science*, **141**, 245–250.
Swets, J.A., Tanner, W.P. Jr., and Birdsall, T.G. (1961)
    Decision Processes in perception. Psychological Review, **68**(5), 301–320.
Taylor, J.C. (1971)
    Some effects of technology in organisational change. *Human Relations*, **24**(2), 105–123.
Teplitz, A. (1970)
    The design of microfiche systems. *Human Factors*, **12**(2), 225–233.
Thompson, D.A. (1971)
    Interface design for an interactive information retrieval system: a literature survey and a research system description. *Journal of the American Society for Information Science*, **22**, 361–373.
Thorngren, B. (1972)
    Studier: Lokalisering. Ekonomiska Forsknings-institutet, Stockholm.
Tomita, T. (1975)
    The volume of information flow and the quantum evaluation of media. *Telecommunication Journal*, **42**(6), 339–349.
Udell, J.G. (1966)
    Prepurchase behaviour of buyers of small electrical appliances. *Journal of Marketing*, **30**, 50–52.
Uhlig, R.P. (1977)
    Human factors in computer message systems. *Datamation*, **23**(5), 120–126.
Ulett, G.A. (1974)
    Automation in a state mental health system. *Hospital and Community Psychiatry*, **25**(2), 77–80.
Vickery, B.C. (1973)
    Information Systems. London: Butterworth.
Weaver, W. (1949)
    Recent contributions to the mathematical theory of communication. In C.F. Shannon and W. Weaver, *The Mathematical Theory of Communication*. Chicago: University of Illinois Press, pp. 1–28.

293

Weick, K. (1969)
The Social Psychology of Organizing. Menlo Park, California: Addison-Wesley.
Weyl, H. (1949)
Chemical valence and the hierarchy of structures. In *Philosophy of Mathematical and Natural Science*. New Jersey: Princeton University Press.
White, W.J. (1970)
An index for determining the relative importance of information sources. *Public Opinion Quarterly*, **33**(4), 607–610.
Whitley, R. and Frost, P.A. (1973)
The measurement of performance in research. *Human Relations*, **24**(2), 161–178.
Whitley, R. and Frost, P.A. (1974)
Task type and information transfer in a government research laboratory. *Human Relations*, **25**(4), 537–550.
Whittemore, B.J. and Yovits, M.C. (1973)
A generalized conceptual development for the analysis and flow of information. *Journal of the American Society for Information Science* **24**(3), 221–231.
Wiener, M. and Mehrabian, A. (1968)
Language Within Language: Immediacy, a channel in verbal communication. New York: Appleton-Century-Crofts.
Wolek, F.W. (1972)
Preparation for interpersonal communication. *Journal of the American Society for Information Science*, Jan–Feb., 3–10.
Wright, P. (1977)
Presenting technical information: a survey of research findings. *Instructional Science*, **6**, 93–134.
Wright, P.L. (1974)
The harassed decision-maker: time pressures, distractions, and the use of evidence. *Journal of Applied Psychology*, **59**, 555–561.
Yovits, M.C. (1975)
A theoretical framework for the development of information science. In *Problems of Information Science* (FID 530) Moscow: VINITI, pp. 90–114.
Yovits, M.C. and Abilock, J.G. (1974)
A semiotic framework for information science leading to the development of a quantitative measure of information. *Proceedings of the 37th Annual Meeting of ASIS*, **11**, 163–168.
Yuchtman, E. and Seashore, S. (1967)
A system resource approach to organisational effectiveness. *American Sociological Review*, **32**, 891–903.

Author index

Page numbers set in bold type refer to the list of references.

Subject index

300

General resistance to change 229
Generalized reaction against change 229
Generation 213, 216
Generation effects 277
Global system factors 240, 277, 278
Goals 101, 229–31
Government 5, 162, 164, 269
Government extension personnel 161, 162
Government pamphlets 162
Granularity 230
Graphics 62
Group goals 229, 231
Group processes 248, 279
Groups 97
Growth 88
Guidelines for introduction of new systems
    237, 278
Guilt proneness (G+) 252

Handwriting 220
Harmony 100, 231, 273
Headaches 259
Headquarters city 21, 26
Health care 8, 269
Hierarchical model of attitude 205
Home of tomorrow 21
Homebound persons 25
Human communication 3
Humanness 190, 192, 276
Hypnosis 260, 261, 280

IBM 106
Ideal system 76
Image information 46, 72
Immediacy 173
Impacts 211, 268, 272
    of electronic systems 90
    of new technology 27
    on democracy 27
    on education 28
    on health care 28
Incentives 14
Individual differences 141
Individual goals 229, 231
Industrial democracy 16
Industrial society 3, 88, 267
Industry 162, 164
Informal networks 97, 160
Information
    data 44, 46
    external 161

internal 161
    relation to behaviour 40
Information access and use 8
Information amount 50, 53, 62, 81, 152,
    162
Information audit 56
Information behaviour 136, 148
    definition of 136
    first law of 131, 137, 274
Information categories 37
Information channels 3, 91
Information classification 41
Information communication 267, 272
Information concept 34
Information cycle 77, 83, 272
Information exchange 160
Information exposure 160
Information input 42, 90
Information items 272
Information load 81
Information management 57, 86, 87, 88
Information modes 150
Information needs 57, 135, 141
Information origination 131, 137
Information output 90
Information potential 160
Information preferences 149
Information processing 149, 267, 272
    cost of 90
Information production 79, 267, 272
    cost of 86
Information providers 64, 214
Information provision 117, 127, 128, 274
Information purchasing 153
Information resources 152
Information retrieval 62, 70, 77, 93, 156,
    164, 272
Information role 86
Information seeking 117, 148, 155, 213,
    275
    home 164
Information service providers 214
Information society 3, 11, 30, 88, 275
Information sources 152, 161
    everyday 155
    usage 195, 215, 272, 275
Information sphere 97, 100, 148
Information storage 70, 267, 272
Information structure 269
Information systems 5, 59, 272
    attitudes towards 185

Muscular aches 259

Naive user 242
National goals 280
National projects 66
Nausea 259
Negotiating 117
Neighbourhood work centres 12, 14, 21, 23–5, 223, 268
Neighbours 162, 164
Network model 95
Network Nation: Human Communication via Computer 10
Networked information systems 8, 163
Networks 95, 97, 99, 160, 223, 272
New facilities 14
New Rural Society 24
New tasks 220
New technology effects 277
Newspapers 161, 162, 165
NLS system 220
Non-verbal cues 172
Normative belief (*NB*) 41, 205, 231, 234, 277
Norms 214, 230
Notes 116, 135, 145, 155

Observation 156, 157
Office activity 105, 113, 134
Office dispersal 12
Office environment rate of change 256
Office functions dispersal 21, 268
Office information system 71
Office location 6, 211
Office of tomorrow 17, 171, 177, 214, 220, 276
Office portability 221
Office relocation 12
Office roles 14
Openness to experimentation (Q1+) 251, 279
Operant-conditioning theory 93
Optical character readers (OCR) 20, 71, 72, 80
Optimization 223
Optional stopping 153
Options 233, 275
Oracle 60, 67
Organizational boundary 42
Organizational change 219, 277
Organizational development (OD) 223, 277

Organizational goals 88, 229, 231, 280
Organizational penetration 42, 270
Organizational performance 75, 86
Organizations 14
Orientation activities 40, 245
Outcome evaluation 233
Output information 42

PACTEL 105, 115, 133, 164, 175, 185, 196
Pages 62, 269
Paired-comparisons technique 161
Paperless office 71
Papers 116, 134, 135
Paragraphs 269
Parmia (H+) 250, 279
Part-time employment 25, 26
Patient-integrated medical record 225
Payoff 153
People 14
Performance 75, 97
Performance evaluation 272
Performance indices 77
Person-oriented activities 129, 172, 274
Personal approach 196
Personal assistant functions 16
Personal computers 9, 18, 21, 62, 74, 243, 267, 272
Personal files 186
Personal goals 280
Personal matters 173
Personality 36, 99, 248, 272, 278, 279
Personality factor questionnaire 249–50, 253
Persuading 117
Petroleum refinery 219
Photocopiers 116, 135
Physical arrangements 20
Physically disabled persons 25
Picture telephones 7, 20, 171, 173, 174
Piggybacking 159
Planning activities 40, 245
Policy-makers, interest to 5, 6
Portability of office 221
Post-industrial society 88
Post offices 12, 164
Potency 191
Potential value 54
Power typing 70, 171
Precision 50, 79
Presentations 117